Public Servant, Private Woman

At 19 Cliveden Place soon after my marriage to Francis.
The décor is by Marion Dorn

Public Servant, Private Woman

AN AUTOBIOGRAPHY

DAME ALIX MEYNELL

LONDON
VICTOR GOLLANCZ LTD
1988

First published in Great Britain 1988
by Victor Gollancz Ltd,
14 Henrietta Street, London WC2E 8QJ

British Library Cataloguing in Publication Data
Meynell, Alix
    Public servant, private woman.
    1. Meynell, Alix   2. Great Britain —
    Officials and employees — Biography
    I. Title
    354.41006'092'4   CT788.M5/

ISBN 0–575–04086–6

Typeset at The Spartan Press Ltd,
Lymington, Hants
and printed in Great Britain by
St Edmundsbury Press Ltd, Bury St Edmunds, Suffolk
Illustrations originated and printed by
Thomas Campone Ltd, Southampton

To Max Reinhardt whose idea it was that I should write this book, to granddaughter Kate and John Verney but for whose encouragement in its early and later stages I doubt if it would have been continued or ever in course of years completed, and to step-son Benedict who has supported and advised me throughout and who, because he also was a civil servant, has been able to keep me straight on matters official.

Contents

List of Illustrations

Foreword

My only justification for writing about my life is the fact that I was a pioneer woman among the male 'mandarins' of the Civil Service, and so I have brought my story to an end when I retired in November 1955.

I thought at first that it would be enough to write about *what I did* – about the facts and incidents of my office life – but I found that to make a believable life story, it must also be about *what I was*. In trying to tell this with truth and balance, I found myself making an intimate journey through the first fifty-two years of my life. It has been a kind of self-analysis in the course of which I have discovered things about myself and my life that I had not realised before – not least that my memory is selective and suppresses things I would rather not remember.

This journey would have been much shorter had I not been an inveterate diary writer and recorder of thoughts as well as events. I have also been able to refer to my mother's diaries for two important years in my childhood to my grandfather's early history of the family and to my grandmother's daily diaries that she kept from her marriage in 1864 to her death in 1927 and that were continued by my aunt until her death in 1936. As well as these, I have a multitude of letters from family and friends and a number of my own letters too have survived. All these have helped to stimulate memory and sometimes to correct it and, where they seemed important as contemporary evidence, I have given verbatim quotations.

In the Civil Service I was always Alix Kilroy and A.K. amongst my colleagues, even after I married.

ALIX MEYNELL

Acknowledgements

I begin with a special thankyou to my editor, Elfreda Powell, for her stalwart, highly professional and always cheerful help in the difficult late stages of my book, to David Burnett who had enough faith in my manuscript to think it worth publishing, and to Jenny Hughes (goddaughter of my friend the late Evelyn Sharp) but for whose interest I should never have approached David. Special thankyous are due also to Maggie Hobson, Clare Middleton and Moira Wilson who have so often housed and fed me while I wrote in comfortable peace, and to my secretary Anne Springall for her patient repeated typing and re-typing and for her inspired suggestion for my title.

In the course of writing this book I have had to consult very many people, friends, relatives, former colleagues as well as official sources. I am immensely grateful to them all, both for their careful advice and for giving it to me in every case so speedily: Stuart Abbott, the late William Batting, Dr R. J. Bingle (India Office Library and Records), Maggie Bishop, Nigel Bruce, Sir Alec Cairncross, Dr Nicholas Cox (Public Record Office), Waldo Dowson, Marguerite Dupree, Stewart Edwards, Anthony M. Goodenough (Foreign & Commonwealth Office), Susan and Reg Hicklin, Jean Hix, the late Laura Z. Hobson, William Hughes (formerly Monopolies Commission), Professor the Lord Kahn, Joan Kelly (H.M. Treasury), Guy Kilroy R.N. (retd.), William H. Knighton (Department of Trade & Industry), Stanley I. Levene (Department of Trade & Industry), Sir Henry and Lady Lintott, James MacGibbon, Sir Ronald McIntosh, Helen Mercer, Alice Meynell, Benedict Meynell, Kate Meynell, Capt George Middleton R.N., John Greg Murray, Frances Partridge, Eric Phillips (formerly Monopolies Commission), Julian Potter, Professor Brian Reddaway, Max Reinhardt, Jack Rendle, The Librarian (Somerville College), Sir John Verney,

Gordon and Kitty Waterfield, Frieda Young (formerly Diplomatic Service), Martin Zander, the Fawcett Library.

Finally, I am grateful to Basil and Christopher Streat for permission to quote from the diaries of their father, Sir Raymond Streat, and Kate Cornford for allowing me to quote from my uncle's letters to her, and I acknowledge the following sources of material quoted in the book: Stephen Potter, *Gamesmanship*, Rupert Hart-Davis, 1947; Cecil Weir, *Civilian Assignment*, Methuen, 1953; Morris West, *Harlequin*, Collins, 1947; The Schuster Committee, PRO (FO 366/928); Claire Tomalin, *The Life and Death of Mary Wollstonecraft*, Weidenfeld & Nicolson, 1974.

A.M.

I

Golden Wedding

'I, one, am many men
By their births multiplied'

from *Inheritance*, Francis Meynell

It was early morning on 9th September 1913, and we five children were climbing a ladder on to a balcony outside our grandparents' room at Upper Broughton near Nottingham. Our aunt Maud played a small harmonium (smuggled up to the balcony the night before), while we serenaded our grandparents on their Golden Wedding morning. 'Awake, Awake, and greet the happy morn,' we sang. Our grandparents were sitting up, side by side, in their four-poster bed holding out welcoming arms. Grandpa was unashamedly wiping away a tear. He was seventy-seven and had a patriarchal white beard and friendly pink cheeks; he was tall. Granny, though only sixty-nine on this day, seemed ageless to her grandchildren. She was small, with grey hair plaited in a circle on top of her head like a crown and her face was seamed all over with smile wrinkles: she was comfortably tubby or at least appeared so, for she wore many petticoats. This was revealed to us once when we were on Bolt Head at Salcombe, where the gorse bushes had been blown into solid lumps by the wind: Granny said they made marvellous chairs and demonstrated by sitting firmly down on one, protected by her petticoats!

My eldest sister was eleven and named Maud (after our mother's only sister, the aunt playing the harmonium) Greg (my grandmother's family name) Winifrede – but she was always called Bimbi. Next came I aged ten. I was named Alix after my Grandmother Alice and Hester after my mother, but always called Bay which was the name my mother believed her much-admired Mrs Patrick Campbell called her son. My brother, aged nine, came next. His name was Robert Alexander, but he was called Robin by everyone except me: I called him Berto. Then came Angela Bernadine aged seven, known as Toto, and lastly Mona Gabriel aged six.

The grandparents in the four-poster bed were Dowsons, my mother's parents, the only grandparents we knew. My father, Lancelot Kilroy, was a doctor in the Navy and estranged from his parents so we never knew our Kilroy grandparents.

We also knew and saw very little of our father while we were children. He was almost always away at sea and on his rare appearances in our home, he seemed almost a visitor, an intimate stranger to whom, as a child of seven, I didn't hesitate to bar my mother's door when she had her so frequent three-day sick headaches, because it was I who nursed her through them.

It was natural to us to have only one set of grandparents and it was also natural to us that their house, Broughton, should be more like home than anywhere else for we moved from place to place in childhood living where we could be most cheaply housed and never calling anywhere 'home' but simply by its place-name.

We were surrounded and fondly cherished through all our young lives by the large Dowson family – my mother was one of ten, eight brothers and one sister – and it was as Dowsons much more than as Kilroys that we grew up. Their attitude to life, their liberal convictions and their support of Women's Suffrage were to be a very powerful influence. They made me what I am.

All the Dowson family are in the photograph taken that day on the tennis lawn, the only absentee being my father who had to return to his ship, and the only extra person being Emily, nurse to the younger of Granny's children and by then a permanent member of the family. So all the people who most influenced me in my early life were there: my grandmother and my mother, my aunt – always called just 'Maudy' – the twin uncles, 'Axie' and 'Chin', who were more like second parents to us, and uncle Will and his wife Nellie against whom I was to measure myself and the men I met as I grew up.

The twin uncles were both small and lively and had red hair. Axie was director of a cotton spinning mill in Manchester, Chin a solicitor in Nottingham, but their weekends were spent at Broughton which remained their home to the end of their lives,

Golden Wedding of Alice and Benjamin Dowson, my maternal grandparents. *Back row standing:* Will (eldest uncle), Nellie (his wife), uncle Robin, Felix (youngest uncle), Maud, Gerard and Hilda (his wife); *middle row sitting or kneeling:* Bimbi (standing) beside Mum (kneeling), Granny and Grandpa, Toto (standing), Tom, Lena (Hubert's wife), Emily and on her knee Susanna (then the youngest grandchild); *front row:* Hubert sitting on chair, Robin, Ina (Robin's wife), Chin, self, Ben (eldest grandson), Molly, Axie and Mona

LEFT: My grandmother at 70.
BELOW RIGHT: Surgeon Colonel P.W.F. Kilroy RAMC, my paternal grandfather
OPPOSITE TOP: Parent's wedding in Malta, 5th December 1900. *Left to right standing*: best man, great aunt Isabel, my father; *sitting:* aunt Maud, Granny, my mother, Grandpa, great aunt Katie.
OPPOSITE BOTTOM: Uncle Will with aunt Nellie in the first car to be registered in Nottingham (AUI) on the lawn at Broughton. With Bimbi, aged 2, and Granny with parasol; *background*: aunt Maud with self or Robin in pram. The number AUI is now owned by my cousin Waldo Dowson

ABOVE: My family at Salcombe, Summer 1910. *Left to right*: Robin, self, Bimbi, Toto, Mona
BELOW: The whole family at Bective Road, Kirkby Lonsdale, during the First World War. *Left to right back*: Robin, Mum and me; *front*: Dad, Toto, Mona, Bimbi and our dog Gyp – a cross between a black retriever and a sheepdog

where they never gave up their shared boyhood bedroom. Neither ever married, though each contemplated it at one time. Like the Cheerible brothers in *Nicholas Nickleby*, they were full of kind and cheerful charity and carried through life an almost childlike innocence. Axie had a crooked mouth which seemed always to be smiling, though he was the family's kind disciplinarian who saw to it that the children helped with domestic tasks like washing-up and rolling the tennis lawn. Chin (whose real name was Bernard) was more solemn and serious-minded; he was also more easy-going with us.

The clothes worn for this grand occasion were typical of Dowson unconventionality. With the exception of Uncle Hubert the men were in grey flannel suits and I and my sisters all had short hair and bare legs.

Our grandparents gave each of their children and grandchildren a commemorative card and letter. The card was printed in gold with poems and their motto: 'Experience worketh hope'. The letter was from Grandpa, written in his own hand and duplicated in purple ink, I have mine still in its small matching envelope, addressed to 'Alix'. It ends:

> Times have enormously changed in the last hundred years. In both the families from which you have descended, there are notable men and women whose blood runs also in your veins; keeping alive in your hearts those who have gone before should be a real assistance in the difficulties and duties of life.

– Victorian sentiments which accompanied a real belief in progress.

In spite of the specialness of the day, there were some routines that were maintained. There was breakfast for all in the dining-room, a room almost entirely filled by a long Victorian dining table and stalwart matching chairs with padded leather seats. The Georgian sash windows were open on to the gravel drive and the front lawn with its orderly beds of red geraniums in full flower. Grandpa sat at one end of the long table and Granny presided at the other. I can almost smell the bacon and eggs and the porridge and kedgeree that was served from the hotplate on the sideboard on to the table with its crisp white cloth. Tea (never coffee) was poured from a large silver teapot and a silver hot-water kettle heated by an oil lamp. I looked forward to Broughton lunches, especially to the puddings. We were allowed two helpings on Sundays and three on birthdays and other important days. There was normally trifle made with ginger wine (which Granny thought was non-alcoholic) and syllabubs in small glasses with handles.

When we children asked if we might 'get down', Granny would give her invariable answer: 'Yes, if you go out of the room'. Probably we followed our usual custom of climbing the huge copper beech in front of the house. It amused us to frighten our relatives from this tree as it dominated the lawn on which, by custom, the grown-ups walked after lunch talking, walking round and round the tree with linked arms in long lines like the spokes of a wheel.

After lunch on this special day the grown-ups gave a concert – Maud played the piano and uncle Will the 'cello – and we children performed 'the Mad Hatter's tea-party' from *Alice-in-Wonderland*. And Bimbi had organised us into a scout play in the garden.

I do not remember how we finished this special day, but I am sure that Granny made time to show us her Bible pictures which she often brought out and told stories about on Sundays. They were large and beautifully coloured individual pictures and even now I can remember in detail the picture of the finding of Moses in the bulrushes. As Catholics (my mother was a convert from the Unitarianism of her family) we were not taught the Old Testament, so these few pictures and Granny's stories about them were all our scattered knowledge of that body of history. Just before bed too Granny would have played a hymn, sitting at the grand piano in the drawing-room.

Before supper, as always, the large hand-bell on the table in the hall was rung twice. It would not occur to the men of the family to change into dinner jackets, though Axie did put on his brown velvet smoking jacket. Nor were drinks served, either before the meal or at it. The supper consisted of soup and a cold fowl looking delicious with its white sauce jacket: but I am sure my uncle Axie would have said that he felt certain no one wanted any chicken after such a large lunch and tea – and to the disappointment but not surprise of the children, the chicken would have gone out to the kitchen uncarved.

And so to bed, with good-night chocolates brought to us by the twin uncles and a chapter read aloud to us by Maudy.

So, or very much so, the day must have ended, as ended many and many days that I and my family spent at Broughton.

The year 1913, the year of the Golden Wedding, seems to me and my generation to have been the last period of quiet, of *non*-change, before the storm of two World Wars and of the incredible scientific advance and violence of the twentieth century. But perhaps this pre-war lull was not such a peaceful time as one imagines, for my grandmother's diary records some horrifying public event for each year: 1900 'the awful Peking massacre' and the assassination of the King of Italy; 1901 murder of the American President . . . 1903 the assassination of the King and Queen of Serbia . . . 1905 Revolution in Russia and massacre of Jews . . . 1907 Congo atrocities . . . 1909 Revolution in Turkey; 1910 Revolution in Portugal . . . 1912 war between the Balkan states and Turkey.

Into this world I had been born – on 2nd February 1903 – in my grandparents' house in Nottingham.

On the afternoon of my birth, my mother went on a carriage drive with my grandmother in the hope, she said, of speeding things up. And sure enough she was back only just in time for me to be born in bed. 'A nice plump little thing' Granny Dowson recorded 'with dark hair, weighing 8½ lbs'.

I am told that Grandpa Dowson's comment on his first sight of me was: 'Well, at least she has a big mouth and that's a good sign'. My big mouth did a good deal of early crying.

My father was away on his ship when I arrived and daily telegrams were sent to him. He first set eyes on me when I was already four months old. Granny had taken great pains to give him a good welcome but I spoilt the effect by having a long crying fit.

Sadly, my father never really fitted into my mother's family, though Granny took at all times the greatest pains to make him welcome. He accepted the gentleness, the unworldliness and the radical in my mother and in the women of her family; but he never understood it in my uncles. He would have preferred his children to be influenced by men he would have regarded as more 'manly'.

The Kilroys were protestant, military, conservative, stemming from Southern Ireland but fiercely British. Both grandfather and great-grandfather Kilroy were doctors in the British forces and great-grandfather served twice on convict ships to Australia.

The Dowsons, my mother's family, on the other hand, stemmed from the English Midlands and East Anglia and were non-military, Unitarian, gentle, liberal, even radical. Physically too it was a marriage of opposites. The Dowson men were country-loving, usually red-haired and rather spare in figure – and they were fond of all games but not the 'gentlemanly' sports of hunting, shooting and fishing. My father was a keen fisherman, and had a figure tending to corpulence. His attitude to gardens was that the ground would be much better paved over. He was completely bald except for a fringe of hair round the base of his skull which he kept closely shaved 'to avoid the bother and cost of going to the barber', he said. I had almost no other information about my father until I was going through family papers before I began writing this book. There was an old cardboard box in which my burrowing hand came across a large envelope addressed in Grandpa's unmistakable writing:

Letters etc. re Hester's Marriage
1914 & 1915. Arrangements re Lancelot
away at war etc.

Two of the letters it contained were by my father and were written one to each of my grandparents after my father had proposed to my mother but before she had accepted him. They show his determination and her hesitation. He has undertaken, he says, not to urge or worry Hester on the subject for six months, after which she has promised an answer. 'In any case,' he writes, 'I shall never marry anyone else'.

There was a second problem about my parents' marriage which I discovered from that packet of letters in the box. The following letter was from my Kilroy grandfather in the Isle of Wight.

Dear Sir,

As the time is I believe rapidly approaching when my son Lancelot purposes marrying your daughter, I believe with your consent, I think it right to send you my views on the matter and firstly I hope you will accept my remarks as without offence to yourself, your daughter or your family. My great objection is of course that the family of Kilroy who for generations have been protestants shall by the violent intervention of the Priests be made to become Catholic. In my opinion no worse degradation could possibly happen than this. My son being a protestant born and bred is called upon by the priests as the price of their permission to the union to first filch or steal from his unborn son his birthright of a free Englishman and then present it to them, making his position infamous and degrading beyond all compare. I cannot think how your daughter can possibly entertain the idea of marrying a man who would be guilty of such an utterly dishonest action. I write strongly as I feel; perhaps you will not understand me, you see your daughter's children will be Kilroys, not Dowsons. Your family is not degraded. He is my eldest son. The practical point that I wish to put to you is this. My son is not in a position to maintain a wife and family as he has absolutely nothing to look to but his pay. He went into debt directly he entered the service. He is in debt now and is never likely to be out of debt. I don't say he is dishonest but he is utterly feckless. This being the case I leave you to judge what your daughter's chances of happiness are likely to be. From me he will have nothing to get as in the event of the marriage taking place, he will never put his foot inside my house till I am dead.

> I am dear sir
> Yours truly
> P. W. F. Kilroy.

My grandfather Dowson's splendidly terse reply was as follows:

Dear Sir,

I have your letter. I am sending it to your son. Whether I shall have any further occasion to write to you will depend on what I hear from your son.

> Yours truly

In the correspondence which followed between Kilroy father and son, my father wrote:

> Among [my] privileges, I count the right to choose my own wife. You seem disposed to deny me that right. I must respectfully tell you that I insist on it.

If my father hoped that his father would withdraw his accusations and objections to the marriage he was disappointed. There were no Kilroy relatives at the wedding and so far as I know my father never saw his father again.

The wedding took place in Malta on 5th December 1900. Unfortunately the voyage out was so rough that all the family party except Grandpa were seasick for most of the time, Hester especially so. There was a reception for some thirty-five naval officers and their wives and on the evening of the next day the family party sailed for England, leaving Hester – inevitably – collapsed with one of her sick headaches.

The early days of their marriage were dogged by my mother's illnesses. She became so ill in Malta during her first pregnancy that Granny was sent for and had to stay until my mother was well enough to be brought back to England where Bimbi was born. So my parents' first year of marriage was a year of separation as well as of sickness. And this was to set a pattern for the future.

Both my mother's parents came from a long line of large Victorian families. Grandpa's father came from East Anglia where the family business was corn-merchanting; his mother from the Nottingham area. Granny's father was Samuel Greg of the Lancashire cotton firm at Quarry Bank, now preserved by the National Trust as an example of enlightened industrial management in the nineteenth century. My grandparents' first child was a son, William, born in 1864. Granny later confided to me with obvious shame that the pain of giving birth had been such that she never wanted to have another child. Yet she went on to bear ten children, all in the first fifteen years of marriage.

Although she had help from nurses and governesses, she always concerned herself closely and personally with the upbringing of her family. She kept a 'commonplace book' in which, at the end of each year, she examined her children's characters one by one; if they had faults it was her responsibility.

It might have been thought that with such a large family to rear and educate, Granny and Grandpa would have little time for public affairs. But not so. Both were Liberals and fervent supporters of Mr Gladstone and in May 1877 they went together to a great Liberal meeting in Birmingham addressed by Mr Gladstone at which an estimated 30,000 people were present.

Granny was also an active member of the Women's Liberal Association and threw herself into battles for the oppressed both at home and abroad: amongst her causes were campaigns for district nursing and for chairs to be provided for shop assistants, and for humane killers in butchery. She also spoke against vivisection; and, in a hunting county, the hounds were never allowed on Broughton land. I note a letter from her published in the *Manchester Guardian* in 1911 protesting about cruelties carried out by Italy, and at the refusal of the British Government to take any line about it which would be 'likely to be offensive to a friendly power'. 'Where', she asks, 'is the spirit that prevailed when we had a Gladstone with us in the days of the Bulgarian atrocities?' Inevitably, she was among the many in Britain who opposed the Boer War.

Granny's life was as crowded as any modern's, despite a considerable amount of illness – usually undiagnosed and undoctored. When her children grew up, she still kept her finger on the family pulse and she had innumerable guests to stay each year as well as doing much general entertaining. When they moved to Broughton she also took on all the village visiting that was expected of the chief lady of the village in those days – her 1912 diary lists eighteen families to be visited.

On Christmas Day she would go round the village after breakfast taking parcels of tea and sugar to those she judged most in need; and when I was old enough I went with her. And there would be a party for all the village children. There was great poverty in the countryside at that time. 'At 4.o'clock,' Granny wrote in her diary for 1907, 'came the 55 children of the village. Felix had been to town for the buns etc. He and Alex had the big boys to tea in motor house, big girls we had in parlour and little ones in nursery and games in drawing-room. The christmas tree was in drawing-room, where they finished up – all had presents, toys and sweets and it went off capitally so Maud felt her trouble was well spent. It cost we thought about £7 or £8.'

But alongside this strong sense of public duty there undoubtedly went an unquestioned sense of class. I find the following entry in Granny's diary for November 1887 when Grandpa had lost his seat on Nottingham Council: 'he is beaten (alas) by a most inferior man. In some wards publicans and low sporting people have been elected and the tone of the town seems very low. I am so glad Ben would not canvass or stoop in any way.'

In due course Grandpa set up his own law firm and was joined by two of his sons – Hubert and Bernard (my uncle Chin) and it was here that, from the age of seven, I was to picture myself at work sitting behind my own office desk when I should be grown up. The office was in a small square called 'Weekday Cross'. There was an attractive odour of old documents and furniture polish and an atmosphere of solidity and learning which I found romantic.

By far the most important of Granny's causes was Women's Suffrage. As early as 1880 she had seconded a resolution about it at a public meeting in Nottingham. 'She did it very nicely,' wrote Grandpa, 'her clear voice being heard distinctly in all parts of the hall'.

It is now often taken for granted that the *suffragettes* (the militants) alone won votes for women. But the *suffragists* (the constitutionalists) also contributed much to change the climate of opinion and many of them believed indeed that the militants did more harm than good. As well as my grandmother, Maudy and my uncles' wives – Nellie, Lena and Hilda – were all devoted workers.

Granny's diaries for these years are full of references to 'the Movement' and they show that often besides my aunts, one or other of the uncles joined the meetings and marches, though there were occasions when, as Granny writes, 'None of the he's cared to go.' Granny was in London to join the march in 1911. I am proud of this but I am quite as proud of the fact that my father – who I am sure was out of sympathy with the cause and even more, no doubt, with this public expression of it – insisted nevertheless on marching along beside his mother-in-law as his code of behaviour would have required.

Both suffragists and suffragettes joined these big marches, and they made a great impression as is shown from newspaper cuttings that Granny tucked between the pages of her diary.

For example, *The Times* for 18th June 1911 says that 'the procession of 40,000 persons stretched for 5 miles' and that 'the women suffragists, constitutional and militant, made high festival in London for their cause. . . . The surprise was the unexpected strength of the constitutionalists. . . . Women of every class of society seemed to be united in the demonstration.' (Mrs Pankhurst, Christabel Pankhurst and Mrs Pethwick Lawrence were all there).

Neither meetings nor marches were always free from violence even for the constitutionalists. At one open-air meeting in Nottingham market place, organised by my aunt Nellie in July 1909, the police did not arrive on the scene (though warned in advance) until a hooligan element had had time to try to break it up, hustling and striking the women. It is a special horror to me that my kind and gentle aunt Maud was one of those on the platform, having nerved herself to speak, and that she was struck on the breast. The marchers too had to accept abuse and aggressive protest in some places but aunt Nellie told me that they could always be sure of courtesy in the mining villages.

However, as a child, I knew nothing of my grandparents' and aunts' involvement in public affairs. My grandmother appeared to us simply as the ever-loving Granny who always had time and thought for us and we loved her dearly in return. I have been happy to find between the pages of her diary for 1907 this letter for her birthday from Bimbi, then aged five – printed carefully in capitals on a tiny piece of paper: DEAR GRANNY I LOVE YOU. SO DOES BAY. BIMBI.

I find that one's earliest memories take the form of unconnected pictures, like the stills of a film. Mine are of a tall narrow house in Nottingham near the arboretum where we were taken for walks. In the first I am sitting in a four-wheeler cab beside my mother who has a baby in long clothes on her knee. I know somehow that the baby is Mona and that we are going for her christening, so I was then within two months of my fourth birthday. In the second picture, my uncle Chin is bringing me a white teddy bear as large as I am – it still survives. And in yet a third picture, I am following Bimbi along the passage to our bathroom and I see that it has been made strange by a table in the middle covered with a sheet. I know without fear that it has been turned into an operating theatre and that Bimbi and I are both having our adenoids taken out there.

Amongst my earliest memories of Broughton are Christmas parties for the village children but Christmas also meant being taken by the uncles to the pantomime, sitting in a row on the red plush seats of the old Theatre Royal in Nottingham. I have never understood why pantomimes are supposed to be so suitable for children; one made a great impression on me because Maudy was so upset by what she thought the vulgarity of a man dressed as a woman that she walked out: I have always disliked that kind of joke ever since. In any case we much preferred the patriotic children's play, *Where the Rainbow Ends*, in which a band of children do brave deeds 'for St George and England'.

We were not encouraged to believe seriously in Father Christmas. Indeed we could not have done so for long since, perhaps by careful design, one of the pictures pasted on the screen in the Broughton drawing-room was of a mother and father creeping into their children's room to fill their stockings with toys.

At Broughton there was a pianola on which I could imagine myself playing works like Beethoven's 7th Symphony, for it had levers with which you controlled speed and sound. Bimbi played the violin from an early age, and I the 'cello and we were encouraged to play trios with Maudy at the piano. But what we liked best, was to hear Maudy sing 'The Arab Love Song', accompanying herself on the piano; with what drama did the song gather speed and how we sympathised as the horse's owner realised that he could not part with his friend for money and galloped away, declaring 'I fling them back their gold'!

Maudy was always the centre of those visits to Broughton but the uncles also showered us with loving attention and we would sometimes go to stay with our married uncles, especially uncle Will and aunt Nellie: 'Bay is always in such roaring spirits there and Will and Nellie both spoil her,' wrote Mum on such a visit when I was four. Wherever we went we were made to feel wholly welcome, indeed that it was a privilege for our uncles and aunts to have us to stay; and conversely a deprivation for the Broughton relatives to part with us. We took this so much for granted that it never surprised us.

The twin uncles were really good at games: Chin had played hockey and tennis for the county and both were serious about chess yet they made us believe that they preferred to play with us. At chess each would take a child as partner playing alternate moves, the rule being that advice could be given only three times during the game. And we were never left long on the sidelines of the tennis court. 'I want to have this next set with Bay,' Chin would say, 'and I with Bimbi' from Axie. Sunday mornings were a problem for Granny did not really like us to play tennis during the church service, but it was the best time for playing because it was usually only on Sunday that our uncles were there to play with us. 'All right,' she relented. 'You can play as soon as the Church bells stop ringing. People will be in Church then and won't be able to hear the thud of the balls.'

Our grandparents' house at Upper Broughton, drawn by Colin Milne

2

Two Mothers: A Feminist Childhood

My grandparents owned a yacht and one day sailed into Salcombe harbour and saw above the little town, standing alone amongst the yellow gorse on the top of the hill, a white house with three arches over a long verandah. They fell for it at once and in September 1906 they took a five-year lease for £26 a year.

The house was 'La Tourelle' which was to play a vastly important part in my childhood. We quite often spent family holidays there but we lived there fully from January 1910 until the end of 1911: two years only but so much our childhood seems to have been enclosed in those two years.

We children were very close in age: the eldest, Bimbi, was born in November 1901 and the youngest, Mona, in December 1906. Belonging to the last pre-Freud generation, my mother and aunt Maud knew nothing of the jealousies that are now supposed to exist between the children of one family: we were expected to love each other dearly – and this we did and I have no recollection of resenting the arrival of my brother and younger sisters. Indeed, so devoted were the five of us that we were a largely self-sufficient group who made in consequence few friends of our own age; and we remained through life each other's best friends. We were, however, a disappointment to our mother in the matter of naughtiness. 'You stupid things,' she would say. 'Can't you think of anything naughty to do?' She herself had been very much of a rebel in her childhood and it was a great disappointment to her that we were all quite boringly good. She tried to stir us up by instituting what she called a 'mobbing day' when we were to be as naughty as we liked but still we disappointed her. However we managed quite imaginative games together. We spent happy hours with a ladder set up between two chairs to make a ship, of which inevitably Robin was captain and Mona cabin boy and we acted interminable plays with tiny dolls under the seat of a dining-room chair. Outdoors, we established gorse houses and secret passages in which we could crawl unseen all the way from one road to another. And we bowled our hoops down the Salcombe roads faster and faster until, inevitably, we fell and barked our so frequently bandaged knees, and howled.

My mother was not one to stop us doing things like climbing trees for fear that we might get hurt, and we were left unsupervised to learn the possibilities of a trapeze, on which we swung upside-down unprovided with such modern safeguards as a trampoline. She did not blench either as we ran along the precipitous Salcombe cliffs on the narrow coast-guard paths, and she let us go riding alone, only specifying that we have leather toe-holds in place of stirrups so that we couldn't get our feet caught if we fell. Most surprising of all she allowed us to go bathing alone when I (at seven) was the eldest of the group: Robin was then just within a few days of his sixth birthday and Toto was only four!

Our mother had been trained as a nurse. As children we had our fair share of illnesses which were all nursed at home as a matter of course. Bimbi had cholera in Malta whe she was only four months old, Robin and I had pneumonia (I twice) and we all had whooping cough and measles, then serious diseases. Our minor childish ailments were usually treated by Mum with homoeopathic remedies – and I am sure she slipped these in too with the prescribed medicines when we were more seriously ill, as she had done, so she told me, for her patients in hospital: a few drops of *aconite* when we were feverish or restless or of *belladonna* for colds; and *hepar sulph* was marvellously soothing for a sore throat licked from the palm of your hand. She also had some amusing 'medical' ideas of her own; binding up our chins at night so that we shouldn't develop a habit of snoring – with the result that when I snore it is with my mouth shut. But the essential for us was that she was a natural nurse so that when we were ill we got sympathy as well as professional competence; we sank into a cocoon of loving care and we have all expected (and given) sympathy as well as care in illness ever since.

My mother, Hester, and her only sister differed greatly in character. Maud was gentle, kind, unselfish to a fault, the only person I have ever met who makes Esther in *Bleak House* a believable character – indeed I once told her that she made everyone else selfish by her insistent selflessness. By contrast Hester was uncompromising, assertive, adventurous, a natural rebel: she loved mountains and her spirit was there rather than in the plains. The sisters were also quite unalike physically: Hester had red hair, bright blue eyes, a rather prominent nose and a large laughing mouth with a full under-lip; Maud, almost alone in the family, was dark-haired with soft gentle features and what are called 'speaking' dark eyes. Both were beautiful.

But different as they were in character, their love and their commitment to each other were total through life and they were both natural mothers. We were fortunate indeed in being the central object of love and care of both, a love and care that was given without either jealousy or competition between them for our affections. Maudy mothered all her nieces. My mother was later to write to me: 'She is your second mother. Maudy loves you as much as I do and often in a truer way.'

Hester could never have been satisfied with a stay-at-home life and the age of twenty-two was accepted by Shadwell Children's Hospital as one of their youngest probationers, receiving no wage during training but having, on the contrary, to pay the hospital a guinea a week. In the following eight years she held appointments at a number of different hospitals. She was never long at any one hospital either because of illness or because her mischievous and rebellious spirit made her unacceptable to the authorities. Her longest stay was at University College Hospital but she had to leave there when she wrote a letter to the *Daily Chronicle* about:

> the distressing howling and moaning of dogs coming from buildings opposite the hospital where licensed vivisection is carried on . . . sounds which disturb the patients and are terribly distressing and appalling to the feelings of the nurses.

Though signed only 'A hospital nurse' it led to her dismissal.

At one hospital she had formed a strong attachment to another nurse who died suddenly, turning Roman Catholic at the last. It was then that my mother too decided to become a Catholic.

My mother's decision to become a nurse meant in those days that Maud would almost inevitably have to remain at home to look after her parents. And that is in fact what happened; from then on she became the indispensable support of the family home as well as the sure guide and help to whom her sister never turned in vain. 'Maud as ever the mainstay and mainspring of the family' wrote Granny in 1910.

I have always felt that Maudy was an example of the sacrifice of daughters to their parents that was so common in Victorian times and so much admired in the novels of Charles Dickens and George Eliot. Maybe, between her loving care for her parents and their brothers, wives and children and especially for her sister and for my immediate family, there was little room for a man in her life. We were all the gainers. I hope she was not too much the loser.

In 1897 my mother was one of twenty-five trained nurses who volunteered to go out to nurse a serious outbreak of bubonic plague in India.

She must have known that she was embarking on a dangerous adventure into the unknown. Indeed two of the nurses caught the plague and died, one being her great friend and constant companion Nurse McDougall. The kind of absence she faced would be difficult to imagine today: 'It seems so strange,' she was to write after her friend's death, 'that all I have been living through this last week was unknown to you and that I might be dead and buried from the plague before you could know I was ill.'

She wrote many letters describing her life in India.* The nurses arrived in Bombay in early December when deaths from plague were under a hundred a week but the disease gained ground with terrifying speed. She wrote: 'The plague is getting worse and worse and the work much harder than I expected. In our hospital there are about 150 plague beds and 48 in each of two acute wards, each of which has only two English nurses in the morning and one only thereafter. Most of the acute cases would, if in England, have two special nurses each.'

The peak was in the week ending 18th March 1898, when the deaths totalled 1194, an appalling number out of a population in the city of Bombay of just over 800,000. All the real nursing had to be done by Indian ward boys who were largely untrained and difficult to discipline and who 'having become so familiar with

*They were printed privately and are now in the India Office Library.

death and disease are often far from kind to the poor suffering creatures'. The hours in the crowded wards were long and she felt the heat very much.

> The work is very hard and trying. All the people are so ill and delirious, and so difficult to feed and manage. There is such a rush to get even the larger part of one's work done. We have lunch in a tent which is like an oven. We have only time to take Doctor's orders, give medicines (which are all 2 hourly and some every half hour) take temperatures; give feeds; and see that the boys do their work. We have all sorts of castes and religions in the hospital. Some of them don't like us to touch them, and most refuse to take food at our hands. We have to try to get hold of the ward boy of the same caste before they will take it, unless they are delirious. . . . We often have as many as nine new cases in the day, and sometimes we find we have lost nearly as many during the night. Nearly every one of them is off his head, and has to be tied in bed, or they would be out of the Hospital in no time. The wards are just a long low shed, with flat four-legged bedsteads made of cane.

Language was a serious problem. She and Miss McDougall had started learning Hindustani on the voyage out and they tried to go on with this while at work, but the authorities gave no help or encouragement. So communication between doctors and nurses and their patients had to be conducted almost entirely through the ward boys. 'I fear a good many of the natives hate us,' she commented too. 'One of the nurses was stoned when she tried to catch a patient that was running away from the hospital.'

It was not long before there were riots and the nurses had to be protected by soldiers when going to and from their work. In March some Europeans (including the plague commissioner and a British officer) were killed in riots, and my mother wrote that the nurses in one hospital 'were within an ace of being beaten to death by a mob'. The riots had been sparked off by the Government's attempts to contain the disease both through house-to-house searches so as to get people treated as quickly as possible, and by compulsory examination of corpses to find out whether death had been from plague. My mother told me herself of one of the house searches where a man, already dead of the plague, had been propped up to appear to be alive and playing cards with his friends.

During the first three months there had been a happy side to her life. She and Miss McDougall shared a bungalow and became as inseparable as their hospital duties allowed. They enjoyed their life together, making their bungalow into a home. But their happiness was sadly interrupted by Hester's frequent headaches and by the mosquitoes, which caused hands and feet to swell and ache.

In spite of the gruelling work and the time necessarily given to rest and to the fun of setting up house, the two young women had time for some social life. Mostly this revolved round their army friend who appears in the letters always as 'Mr P.' but they had also met some naval officers who took them sailing, possibly including 'Dr K.' whom I assume to have been my father.

Then, in the middle of February, came the tragedy of Miss McDougall's death from the plague. Starting one day with a sore eye, it spread to her throat, and in less than a week she was dead. Hester nursed her until she became ill herself. It was believed for a time that she also had the plague. So for a second time in her young life she had lost a close woman friend and this time in a strange land away from her family.

After a period of convalescence she was offered a choice of three other hospitals where the work would be less hard, but she insisted on returning to Bombay to carry on her friend's work, an act, it seems to me, of special courage now that she had had intimate personal experience of the danger of death from the plague.

In fact it was not until February of the following year that she came home and then only because, as she said, 'her health made it necessary'.

From what my mother said or hinted to us at various times in later life, both Mona and I gained the impression that she had fallen in love in India with a married man, probably (I surmise) the Mr P. of the letters. That impression is strengthened by what, looking back into memory, I can only describe as the aura of romance in which she taught us to think of India. If there was such an attachment, it would explain the great change in her which Granny was to notice on her return. From all that is said and not said in Granny's diaries and letters I conclude sadly that my mother was very unhappy when she came back to England.

She went back to nursing in London, first in a hospital for epileptics, then in a fever hospital, and two years later 'after' writes Granny 'much hesitation and indecision' she became engaged. My mother's hesitation would have been due to the fact that she could not return my father's love in kind owing, as I have suggested, to a hopeless attachment that she had made in India; I think that she overcame it chiefly because of her longing for children; and she must have realised that time for her was slipping away since she was already thirty-three. I think too that my father prevailed in part through the very depth and vehemence of his love. 'If you were consumed by fire so that only charred bones remained, I should still love you,' he wrote to her.

I wish I had understood more about the one-sided relationship between my parents when they were alive. We could not fail to be aware as children that we and not my father were the centre of my mother's life and it was the one gap we saw in her halo. I have found a sad little letter from her to Granny written in the early years of marriage when she was in Bermuda with my father taking Bimbi and baby Robin with her and leaving me at Broughton: 'The life here is difficult and hard as you can understand but I am trying my very hardest to make it a success,' she wrote, 'but love on one side and only companionship on the other does not smooth away the everyday rubs and difficulties. . . . I sometimes feel the only two things I am capable of are loving and suffering. . . .'

Were we spoilt? We were certainly surrounded by love and approval to a quite extraordinary degree. And in return our elders could do no wrong and our anxiety when we went to school was lest any friends we made might not measure up to our relatives, not the other way about.

In spite of our all being so close in age, Mum always made a big distinction between the two eldest and the two youngest. We had different lessons and different bed-times and the elder ones were expected to look after 'the little ones'. I took it very much for granted that I should lead in this. I called them 'the babes' and I was clearly bossy with my two younger sisters. I later found out that behind my back they called me the C.O. Toto remembered my teaching her the first steps in reading and I have a picture of myself setting 'the babes' simple sums, carefully making them so easy that they couldn't go wrong; sometimes I even took on the duty of wiping their bottoms after the morning 'potting' which was the invariable routine after breakfast.

It is only now that I wonder why I not Bimbi, the eldest, became the family leader. Possibly it was because Bimbi's bent was artistic rather than active; she had perhaps less wish to lead, was less sure of herself in that sphere, was more of a loner. I find that she is a more shadowy and less insistent figure than the rest in my memories of childhood – a surprising fact since we were treated almost as twins.

My mother's attitude also contributed to my position, for it was to me that she turned most often for help when she had her terrible sick headaches. Probably I happened to be a more natural nurse for it was I at seven (and later Mona) who held her head while she was sick and bound it tight again and again with a cold wet dishcloth. Hardly a week went by without one of these 'heads' and since they lasted three days they were a very insistent part of our childhood.

Being the family boss carried duties with it: I was the one to deal with my brother's young tantrums and to comfort him when he had his bad dreams, and when Toto (aged four) was unwell and could not go on a family picnic, it was a matter of course for Mum to say that 'Bay will stay with Toto'. Inevitably too, I became the family spokesman and diplomat when any-thing was to be argued on behalf of any of us. Maybe all this explains why I have always felt that I was grown up at seven. I feel sometimes that my seven-year-old self is still there inside me, surprised to be received as an equal by 'grown-ups'.

Religion also contributed to this feeling for it was at seven that I took my First Communion and I was very serious about it. I used to sit up in bed praying after my three sisters were asleep. I fear I saw myself as a budding saint. Recently I came across a note of Granny's:

Bay – 6 yrs old, re dreams. 'Do you know, I dreamt I slept with God! Wasn't that nice? I *did* like it! I got into his bed! – I did feel happy! I felt as if I didn't want anything else! – You don't even feel as if you wanted people you're fond of on earth!'

I found confession a problem. I liked the kind voice of the hidden priest addressing me as 'my daughter' and I liked calling him 'father'. But what could I confess? The worst thing I could think of was masturbation but how could I speak of that to a man? And anyhow I did not know the word. I stammered out something about being 'dirty' and I expect he understood. I could certainly have confessed to spiritual pride, only I did not know what that was either.

Inevitably, Bimbi and I took our First Communion together. On the great day we went to Kingsbridge in the paddle-steamer, dressed in bridal white, on a lovely morning – but on an empty stomach. After mass the kind nuns plied us with a splendid feast which impressed me much more than the holy wafer I had swallowed in church.

I suspect that the strong injection of religion I got at that age helped to keep me free of it in adult life, and my mother's sceptical attitude to dogma also contributed. Her catholicism was emotional rather than rational. She taught us about the kindly Jesus and our personal 'guardian angel' and not about the uncomfortable things like hell or even purgatory except as a very 'short-stay' place. And moreover Maudy was not a catholic and was the height of goodness in our eyes, so that we knew for certain that the Church was wrong in saying that you must be a catholic to reach the best in goodness. So we were questioners from the first. I have recently found a definition of unitarianism as 'protestantism without its black insistence on guilt . . . breathing the spirit of prudent optimism in which [unitarians] were inclined to view this world and the next.' This accords well with the Dowson ethos and I find it attractive myself.

It was basic to our puritan/Victorian/Dowson upbringing that self-denial and unselfishness were prime virtues: when we came back from a party, Granny's first question might be 'Well, my dears, how did you enjoy yourselves?' but it would be followed quickly by a second, 'And what contribution did you make?' So strong was the dose of unselfishness in our moral diet that it sometimes became difficult to remember your own wishes – or even to be sure that you had any.

All this was added to my father's 'officer-and-gentleman' code, which was made easy by the fact that our mother subscribed to both. We were not often parted from her but, when we were, she wrote frequently to us with moral teachings as well as with love. I remember particularly her using Scott's death and Oates' sacrifice in their South Pole journey, to point up to us the virtues of self-sacrifice and courage.

I believe that my father was devoted to us children but sadly he did not know the way to our understanding and our hearts. His certainties, sudden angers and strong language repelled – even frightened – us all. We resented too the instant obedience of the 'theirs not to reason why' variety, that he expected, so different from my mother's form of gentle discipline that allowed for discussion, though when our childish 'why?'s became too bothersome she did sometimes retreat to the answer 'because I say so' to which we found no riposte. My father tried hard on his rare visits to adapt himself to Mum's and our way of life and there are happy accounts of him coming camping. As will happen with adults who see little of children, Dad's attempts to communicate with us took the form of teasing. Me, he teased for clumsiness and for wanting 'my bucket'. He must have been present on a very early occasion when we were all arriving at the Salcombe house by carriage. There were many packages to be unloaded and carried into the house by travel-weary parents, and small babies to be attended to and Dad maintained that I could think of nothing but my bucket and spade: my spade was on the surface but my bucket was not and I maddened everyone by bursting into tears and sobbing over and over 'I want my bucket'. This my father never let me forget, though always in a kindly, joking way.

He had a strong sense of humour and being a very good mimic he could tell stories delightfully in many dialects, particularly Somerset. And he also had a way of putting things which never failed to charm me. He usually referred to himself in the third person and then, for some reason, as 'Henry', not Lancelot. 'Henry', he would say, 'suggests that we should cancel our picnic today for the following six reasons: One, it's pouring with rain. The other five reasons don't matter.' Had we seen more of him when we were young these traits might have had time to endear him to us with well-loved anecdotes and tales.

The reality was that we all and always preferred our mother's company. I have a memory of him arriving for a short leave at Salcombe when I was seven and my brother six and he brought the news that he would take Robin back to his ship (then lying at Plymouth) for an evening in the mess. What fun for a boy of six! But he did not think of it as fun. He was merely unhappy at having to leave home for the first time and we were all unhappy for him.

Being a very down-to-earth child, experiences that could be called imaginative were few for me. All that I remember were in that Salcombe period. In one, Bimbi and I are in a rowing boat with Maudy and the uncles on a quiet night of stars and the oars make magical fiery light as they dip in and out of the water: it is the only time I have seen phosphorescence. Next, we had taken the single-line train which then ran from Kingsbridge to Loddiswell for an 'open day' at the Trappist monastery; on the way back, we played all afternoon in the brown water of the river, dappled with sun and shadow and I was consciously aware of beauty. My third memory is of a hot spring afternoon when I was alone on a hillside surrounded by bluebells, young bracken and primroses and I heard the cuckoo, and took deep breaths of inexpressible happiness.

What kind of life did we lead in those so important Salcombe days? Lessons, with a succession of governesses, took up the mornings, and walks or the many games we played together, the afternoons. But Mum did not hesitate to interrupt the routine for a specially fine day, to go for expeditions of many miles. Mum took it for granted that we should all be able to manage it though the youngest walker (Toto) was only four. She was the moving spirit in all we did, bathing with us and enjoying quite as much as we did the fire-lighting which accompanied our picnics, and she was not one to let us be disappointed of a planned expedition by rain. 'Right,' she said on one unforgettable occasion, 'You can go and bathe in the puddles.' When she found a deserted cove we were allowed to bathe naked, including Robin aged six.

Though the town of Salcombe in our childhood was surprisingly little different from what it is now, the population was a great deal smaller, and the roads were safe from traffic as the

'Tourelle' as it stood alone at the top of the hill above Salcombe before
the First World War, drawn by Colin Milne

motor car had not yet arrived. We must have been a well-known
sight with our short hair, bare legs and sandals, rushing down the
ferry steps with our beautiful red-haired mother or our twin
uncles, armed with freshly made 1d. 'bathing buns'; or walking
up and down the steep narrow roads leading to Bolt Head where,
in memory, the high banks are always covered with primroses
and bluebells and pale green 'lords and ladies' and there is a
pervading scent of wild garlic. Wherever we went there was the
sound of the sea-gull's cry, and the end of the day meant a steep
pull up for tired legs to our house on top of the hill, with the
evening call of innumerable rooks cawing round their nests in the
tall trees. As I look back, I seem always to have been tired at
Salcombe.

Inevitably, with so much opportunity, we all learned to swim
early; Bimbi and I got a shilling for swimming ten strokes within
two days of each other when she was seven and I six. But diving
was another matter. For how many minutes at a time and on how
many days have my kind uncles stood round shivering in the cold
Salcombe water, waiting to receive me as I counted 'one, two,
three – oh I thought I'd gone that time!'

Our lessons consisted of the three R's plus the elements of geography. We were taught phonetic reading (which left us all appalling spellers) and we learnt an unusual attitude to geography: most people see the world as a map, but we all saw it (and still see it) from the terrace of the house at Salcombe, looking out to sea with our feet planted firmly on the south coast of England: behind our heads are Scotland and the North Pole, Europe is to the left, Ireland and America to the right. For some reason Mum decided to take upon herself the task of teaching us French verbs. It is the only time I remember her to have got really cross with us. She even used a ruler on our hands. She simply could not understand why we were not word perfect in at least one verb after each lesson.

We absorbed without teaching that day's accepted notions of 'class'. We knew that there were three main classes – higher, middle and lower – and that we belonged to the middle, which meant that we were 'ladies' and could hold up our heads in any company, including that of the 'highers'. In my mother's diary for August 1910 there is the following, revealing entry about her interview with a possible governess for us: 'Very nice, but no lady, so off.'

Before bed there was musical drill with 'Indian clubs', singing and reading aloud – reading to ourselves was thought to be a little anti-social and I have felt it to be so when in company ever since. What did we read? Amongst fairy stories, I was fascinated by *The Little Mermaid* who, for love of the Prince, abandoned her tail in exchange for legs, and felt as if she was walking on swords. *The Wind in the Willows* and *The Secret Garden* were great favourites and Kingsley's *Water Babies* and of course Jules Verne. And we were regular readers of the weekly boys' papers *The Scout* and *Chums*. We despised what we thought of as 'girls' books.

We each had our special songs and poems. My poem was 'How Horatius Kept the Bridge' from Macaulay's *Lays of Ancient Rome* and Robin's was 'The Eagle'.

> Boy, may the eagle's flight ever be thine;
> Onward and upward and true to the line!

Can words learned in childhood affect character? My brother became a fearless pilot in the Fleet Air Arm.

He was able in a remarkable way to be differently 'special' to each of his sisters without creating rivalry, and this lasted throughout our adult lives. But he and I were perhaps the closest playmates.

I don't think we behaved badly towards our governesses but they clearly did not always have an easy life and when we were ill, they were expected to help with nursing and carrying up meals. I know this from a shaming occasion when we four sisters were all being kept in bed for some minor illness and our governess was bringing up our lunch on a tray; the pudding, inevitably, was rice pudding and, as children will, we cried with one accord: 'Not rice pudding again!' Whereupon, our governess burst into tears.

Very likely the worst we did to our governesses was to expect them to handle and enjoy the white rats that were our chief pets. Some were wholly white and some black and white, like saddleback pigs. We enjoyed nursing them and stroking their soft bodies. There was great excitement when Bimbi's rat had a litter, but there was also a horrifying occasion when mine died and was given solemn burial in a shoe-box, only to be dug up by our dog, Puck, again and again, smelling worse each time. Puck was a small whippet that I remember only with pain and shame, because of a scene in which our governess is beating it for disobedience and a passer-by threatens to call the RSPCA. We were not doing the beating, but we suddenly realised that we were supporting it by not intervening. The experience was made more painful by the fact that Puck shortly afterwards died of distemper.

We had the usual tortoise but it received *un*usual treatment being taken with us when we went to bathe and spend the day on the beach.

Like all children, we loved to be told stories and my youngest uncle (Felix) was the best at this. One story that I specially remember was about the hedgerow elves who tried in vain to stop the first *motor* buses from Kingsbridge to Salcombe by spinning gossamer ropes across the road. I used to keep 'the babes' happy with a long-running saga about a family of pygmies who lived along the Kingsbridge Road in the old 'Beacon' – a black bee-hive shaped construction about six feet tall on the side of the road. I fear that Mona and Toto were at this time mainly an audience for my stories, or minor characters in my games – live dolls to be taught and led and used in play.

When Robin went to school our games became more feminist. We had never resented the fact that, as a boy, he alone had the privilege of serving at Mass; nor had we questioned that he would be captain of our ladder-ship. But we did resent the fact that he could join the Navy and we could not. So we decided to start our own 'Girls' Navy'. Members were expected to be able to row, swim, do some first aid and cooking and to harness and ride a horse and even to drive a car. As to the last requirement, aunt Nellie allowed me to drive her Zedal when I was ten years old, there being in those days no driving licence requirements.

The four of us were obvious founder members of our Girls' Navy but being sufficient hitherto to ourselves in our games and taught by a governess instead of going to school, we had few local friends: so we set out to find members by calling at houses along the roads round-about. I don't think that we had any success.

My father returned to England from a three-year appointment abroad in January 1911 and my mother went to meet him at Plymouth though (as usual, alas for my poor parents) with one of her bad heads.

There followed two years at Plymouth where we lived in a large Georgian house just outside the gates of the Devonport Naval Hospital to which Dad was next appointed – the first time in our childhood that my father had a home appointment and could live with his family. It is possible that foreign postings meant more money, in which case Dad would have felt it his duty to apply for them in view of our financial circumstances.

It is clear that there was absolutely no provision in our budget for extras or emergencies of any kind and that my parents had to borrow from my grandfather (paying back the loans at the rate of £1 a month) for everything not specifically provided for such as dentists, and even train fare for my mother to join my father on his few days' leave. This was the only period when we lived as a family with two parents.

Unfortunately, we were all ill most of the time at Plymouth. I had double pneumonia, we all had acute measles and Mum herself was very ill for some months right up to the day when

Dad's appointment ended and the house had to be vacated. So even during these two years we saw little of Dad and my only clear memory of him there is that when we were recovering from measles he insisted that we swallow a whole tablespoon of undiluted cod-liver oil every day; no following of sweets could get rid of that yellow oiliness.

3

Growing Up

On 4th August 1914 we were at Broughton and so it was there that we saw the newspaper placards with the one word WAR. We heard people say that it would be over by Christmas but uncle Will said: 'Before it is over we may all be living in caves'. Neither statement had any reality for us for the character of our happy lives didn't change. Our special uncles were not of an age to be called up to fight and it was no change to have our father absent. He was in the Battle of Jutland under Jellicoe but he spent most of the war on H.M.S. *Ajax* with the Grand Fleet at Scapa Flow and I find him making the surprising comment in a letter to Grandpa that 'time passes quickly owing to its excessive monotony'.

After Plymouth, we lived for a time in Nottingham, all four sisters going to school at 'Miss Churley's Academy for Young Ladies'. It was the first time we had been without a governess, so that Mum had no help at home with her young family. We soon got another lesson in the physical frailty of the adult world. It was like the time our governess burst into tears over bringing us rice pudding in bed. This time our aunt Nellie had been to tea and had asked if one or two of us would like to go back for the night with her, as she thought Mum looked tired. We all refused and were mystified when, as soon as she had gone, Mum burst into tears: 'None of you think of me,' she said. We stood round her in a sad little circle; it had not occurred to us before that we could possibly be other than a comfort and help to her.

Our next house was in Tavistock in Devon, and was called 'Brookfield'. A stream ran through the garden and beyond it was a railway cutting where we watched for the trains. Mum used to go to Plymouth on some days to help in a hospital.

We four sisters went to school at St Michael's just along the road and Robin was now at Uncle Felix's preparatory school, 'Cressbrook' that he had opened in 1913 with eight boys, including his two nephews, Ben and Robin. When he left there at thirteen Robin would go to Osborne as a Naval Cadet.

It was at St Michael's that I made my first friend outside the family. She was Betty Clotworthy, a dark-haired cheerful girl a year or two older than I, who was admitted to what, looking back, I fear we saw as the 'privilege' of our family life. She joined in our games, became a member of the Girl's Navy and came with us on our bicycling trips. There was one when Mum got us up at four a.m. and we cycled all the way from Tavistock to Salcombe. Sometimes we went camping which was such a rare thing in those days that established camping-sites were unknown. We used to set up our tent wherever we fancied. But there was one shocking occasion when an enraged land owner objected to our having lit a fire close to *his* wood. I can see him now, red-faced and kicking out our fire, just before the kettle had boiled for Mum's tea.

Three other important things happened to me at Tavistock: I learned to dive off the top board in the local swimming pool and off the side of the bath with my hands held by my side; I was given a 'cello of my own in an important-looking black wooden case; and I started to menstruate. Mum made us feel that menstruation was a matter for pride as the entry to womanhood though it was to be a woman's secret, not shameful in itself but shameful for men to know about, even our brother or father.

My mother had let us all know quite naturally and matter-of-factly how children were born, by telling us about her experiences as a midwife in London. I cannot have been more than seven when she described to us how she would hurry through the London streets at night to a poor family usually all living in one room, often all in one bed and of the contrast between these conditions and the beautiful new baby coming out of the mother's body. But information about the act of sex was another matter. Mum, the rebel, was surprisingly Victorian in her lack of teaching about physical sex. She bought us a book called *From Girlhood to Womanhood* and left it at that. I think we were all curiously incurious about sex. I was seventeen before I was first kissed and I was uncertain then as to whether or not a baby might result! Driven to ask my mother for information, the most that she could bring herself to say was: 'There is a place in your body where the man can get in.'

Very soon we were on the move again. After less than two years at St Michael's it was decided, to our excited delight, that Bimbi and I would go to boarding school while the family home was moved to Kirkby Lonsdale, where my Uncle Felix's school was, so that Toto and Mona could go as day pupils to 'Cressbrook', the only girls in a boy's school: an arrangement no doubt accepted by Uncle Felix only because our finances could not possibly run to boarding school for all four girls, even had it been thought right to send the younger ones away. Those two thoroughly enjoyed themselves at 'Cressbrook' and they received there a much better grounding in Latin than girls commonly get, as well as such boys' knowledge as how to throw a cricket ball. I greatly envied them that. They played football too and joined in all the sports on an equal footing with the boys but when Mona won the annual cross-country run, she was not allowed to take the prize because she was a girl. She did not resent this for she held the view all through her life that boys were more important than girls. It was not, I think, so much that she felt women were inferior as that she resented more than any of us the inequality of women's opportunity at that time to have the full life open to men.

Mum had hoped that, by moving to Kirkby Lonsdale, the family finances would work out more easily than at Tavistock. At this time my father's salary was £402 a year. He calculated that, out of this and my mother's marriage settlement money of £90 per annum she should have £200 to run the household after paying rent and her share of school fees, and that this would leave him a bare minimum of £12 a month. Our household was a modest one for I know that though we had two maids as well as a governess while we lived in the family house at Salcombe (when presumably we paid no rent), my mother did much of the washing, ironing and cooking herself which was unusual for a middle-class family in those days, but she found it very hard to keep the family on £200. There are pathetic letters from her to her parents at this time, asking for small loans:

> I did not know how to get through last month. £3 out of the £4 Papa sent me went towards coal, which is frantically expensive, 42/– a ton. I am afraid I must borrow some money from you.

And again:

Is there any surplus anywhere that the children's extras can come out of? Otherwise I shall have to borrow again.

During the First World War Dad even saved up his butter ration to send us, but since he sent two pounds at a time it went bad before it reached us. Sadly we were more aware of the unwisdom of expecting butter to keep that long than his genuine unselfishness. By the time we were all being educated, my grandparents were subsidising us by contributions to the cost of education to the tune of half the expenses of the household and during the war Grandpa looked after our finances at Dad's request.

In the atmosphere of feminism in which we had been brought up it was a matter of course that both sexes would earn their own living, it was also a matter of course that education should be considered as important for the girls of the family as for the boys. When the time came to choose a boarding school for us, one of the standard questions to the headmistresses interviewed was, 'What do the girls mostly do when they leave?' The answer 'Our girls mostly marry' was very definitely the wrong one.

The boarding school chosen for Bimbi and me was Malvern Girls' College. I like to think now that it was deliberately chosen rather than Cheltenham *Ladies* College as being more under the influence of Miss Buss than Miss Beale and so more democratic, but probably the reason was chiefly financial; we were taken at a reduced fee (because there were two of us) of £160 a year for two. Also, Mum and Maudy took an instant liking for Miss Poulton and Miss Greenslade, the owners, who however retired from active management of the school the year we arrived.

I enjoyed the prospect of boarding school until there came the moment of buying our school uniform and packing. Were we really going to have to wear a horrible all-over woollen undergarment called 'combinations'? And a large hard-brimmed straw hat? AND long black woollen stockings? The navy-blue gym tunics must be of a length to touch the ground all round when you were kneeling: we learnt only later that it was the done thing to drop your shoulders during fitting so that the tunic should be as short as possible. The worst moment was unpacking at school. Desperate with homesickness, I felt that everything to do with my mother was almost 'sacred'. And so it was a kind of sacrilege for my school trunk so carefully packed by my mother to be unpacked by the profane hands of the school matron. I never got over this homesickness and the twelve weeks of each new term, in which there were no weekend or half-term breaks, seemed to stretch before me like an unending prison sentence. I remember even at fifteen years old being overcome on Nottingham station by loud uncontrollable sobs – all five foot seven inches of me. 'You must try to be braver,' Mum had implored desperately. 'Think of the poor soldiers who have to go back to the front.' I didn't find that the soldiers' greater pain in any way reduced mine.

Mum tried to get us to look forward with excitement to our first term: 'What fun you will have with midnight feasts in the dormitory,' she urged. We were not very enthusiastic about doing anything so naughty but it never entered our heads to go home after that first term without having had one. So we dutifully collected provisions and enlisted the unwilling co-operation of the other two girls in our room. The last night came and we all managed to keep awake until midnight. Alas! our room was close to that of Miss Dawson our headmistress, and we were discovered red-handed wickedly eating chocolate biscuits and drinking lemonade. Worse, Miss Dawson had left her bedroom candle alight by her bed, the wind blew and the bed curtain caught fire!

That was the end of our stay at the Junior School. Next term we found ourselves at the Middle School where we were much happier. With our short hair and odd attitude to discipline, we had been misfits in the Junior School and we found the bigger girls much more tolerant of our unusualness.

Our day at the Middle School started with a hymn and Roll Call; so far as Bimbi and I could make out, the answer you gave on your name being called, was 'Exum Extra'. So that was what we said. It was sometime before we learnt that we were supposed to be saying 'Adsum Magistra'. The routine was lessons in the morning, games (of course) in the afternoon, 'prep' in the evening before bed at nine p.m., this much resented by us who were accustomed to eleven o'clock bed. On Saturday evenings, we became young ladies in white dresses and those of us who played an instrument were subjected to a special torture when we had to walk across a seemingly unending shiny floor, and perform a much practised 'piece' before the whole school sitting on chairs round the hall. This happened once a term, twice in my case since I was learning both the piano and the 'cello. I did no more than suffer my piano lessons but I enjoyed everything to do with the 'cello except those solo performances, and playing in the school orchestra is even now a great remembered delight. At Granny's expense, I had lessons in elocution. I found that I enjoyed these and I never had difficulty in memorising a poem – if I read it three times, I remembered it. But it was an astonishment to all and not least to me when, on being asked to recite Walter de la Mare's poem 'The Listeners', at a school function, I produced a quite new voice which carried easily to the back of the large hall.

Games were more a penance than a pleasure; I was a poor performer and I was afraid of the hockey ball after I had received one full on the forehead. So I looked forward to the regular interruptions for menstruation when you were entitled to one day 'in' comfortably reading and two on 'short' or 'long' walks before games again became compulsory. But I was a keen girl guide: my arm well covered with badges, I was a very bossy patrol leader, insisting on a pitch of perfection in 'stretcher drill' worthy of a sergeant-major.

I kept a diary for some months when I was fourteen. The language of course is 'period schoolgirl'. Everything was 'ripping' or 'topping' and people were 'rippers' or 'beasts' but I see that I already had a respect for facts and precision, and a dislike of exaggeration: 'I did not enjoy myself a bit on this day – at least except sometimes,' I wrote and, 'I had a ripping – at least nice – 'cello lesson'. I recognise here the budding civil servant.

We were fortunate in our teachers; our botany mistress took us on walks on the Malvern Hills to find rare flowers; French was taught by a charming young French woman; our history mistress was an enthusiast called Miss Dixon who gave me individual coaching. I was good at exams and took 'Junior Oxford' at fourteen and 'Matric' at sixteen with comparative ease.

The school also took pains to put some culture into us at weekends – musical evenings, lectures (attended unwillingly), visits to cathedrals. And in summer there were bicycle rides and picnics for the whole school on the Malvern Hills, or tea, (and sometimes supper too) in the garden.

So why is it that I don't look back on my school years at Malvern with pleasure? One reason is that the atmosphere was too emotional. 'Crushes' are inevitable in adolescence but they were unusually numerous and highly charged at Malvern in my time. Miss Pulham (the headmistress) tried to discourage them but with little success, and one at least of the mistresses clearly enjoyed being the object of youthful worship. My diary shows that at fourteen the young Alix spent most of her thought and much of her energy on her feelings for other girls and mistresses – arranging to see them, to talk to them, to sit with them, to walk with them, or on wondering whom she loves and how she loves. She is in love with one older girl called Marjorie and manages at the same time to have a 'crush' on one of the mistresses, and these dual attachments are expected in her circle.

I put down the strength of my dislike of schoolgirl crushes to remembered shame about my over-sentimental attachment to one girl and one of the mistresses on whom we shared a crush. I even had a letter from Mum telling me that one of the mistresses had written to her about us:

> She spoke of May but I think she meant to hint at you. The mistresses used to like May but now they think she is so silly about Miss T that they do not think nearly so well of her. . . . For many reasons it is not a good thing for pupils to get very thick with mistresses. . . . So darling try not to show your liking for Miss T by running after her. . . .

Miss Pulham did not really help matters by entertaining the school on Sunday evenings with sentimental songs like 'The end of a perfect day' being 'the soul of a friend you've made'. She was full-figured with a mass of fair hair, pink cheeks and blue eyes. Her singing was preceded by unlimited sweet-eating – none was allowed on any other day – and was followed by hymn-singing, rounded off by a moral lecture.

My critical memory of school is also due to the 'honour' system that was used to enforce discipline. Encouraged by our mother to think that breaking rules at school was *fun*, we were offended to find ourselves put on our honour to keep them. And many of the rules, like no talking on the stairs or in the cloakrooms, seemed to us purposeless and unreasonable. For what were regarded as the more heinous 'crimes', the punishment was to be told that the honour of the whole school had been broken. The culprit might even be 'sent to Coventry', a particularly nasty form of school tyranny. Once the whole school was punished because four girls, including my friend Noel, went into the town alone. 'They were court-martialled and when we came out they were on the stairs howling.' Next day, however, it was decided to our great joy 'that the four need not be in Coventry any more. After evening prayers Noel apologised for the other three to the whole school for having broken our honour.' Talk about brain-washing!

The most popular form of protest at that time was for a girl to cut off her hair. I can remember almost with a shiver to this day, the hush of horror as my friend and Bimbi's friend Noel Haslam and her elder sister Joyce, came down to morning prayers one after another with short hair.

Though the impression left of Malvern is a mix of sentimental friendship, abuse of personal honour, hymn-singing, chilblains and too many chocolates, home-sickness and a painful division between home and school life, my fourteen-year-old's diary shows that this is not a fair picture. Though I wrote that I wished I 'need never go to school', I added that 'I so love the school life'.

My journey through those schooldays has made me think it was good for me to be separated by school from my home background, for that revealing diary shows that at home I was inclined to take myself a good deal too seriously as a kind of deputy mother:

> I don't know what I am going to do about Mona. She is such a pig to Toto and she spoils our games and is cross. I get out of patience. I know I oughtn't to. I am beginning to find that the difficulty now is not to spoil Toto. She *is* a ripper.

I was clearly very much of a prig and distressingly humourless, but I took on fully what might be called the responsibilities of priggishness, such as helping with the interminable mending and sock-darning for the younger ones. Also Mum's attitude tended to support and encourage my natural bossiness. She treated

Bimbi and me very much as her grown-up confidantes even when we were quite young. Again and again in her letters the phrase 'my grown-up daughters' occurs. When, as so often, there were money problems, she told us about them. When our Grandfather died she wrote of her longing that we could see the 'radiant expression of peace on his face' and of her own certainty of a glorious life after death. And when the end of the war brought her anxieties about the prospect of life shared with Dad, she wrote about that too:

> Mum is so unaccustomed to be in a home with Daddy always there. Never in fact since she married except for one unhappy year in Plymouth and one in Sheerness when you were all small babies. It must mean such a lot of fresh plan-making . . . and coming too after the shock of Grandpa's death. Sometimes it seems as if I cannot manage the strain and I long for my two dear ones so terribly. . . .

Her own diary shows that she and my father had had some happiness during his short leaves before the war, but they were so different in character and outlook and so unequal in love. On my sixteenth birthday she wrote again of this –

> Daddy has threatened to throw up his job unless I can promise to go and live wherever he is, house or no house. . . . I long for my two grown-up girls. It is the discussions that I dread. Daddy so often thinks differently to Mum.

These letters wrung my heart.

Whatever we missed in our relationship with our real father, we seem to have made up with our twin uncles, Axie and Chin, and I think their feelings for us were very much those of a father. And they provided much of the money for our education.

My father's demand for instant obedience when we were children, became as we grew up, a demand for unquestioning acceptance of any statement he made and this was an added cause for division between him and me. I knew him to be a man of the utmost rectitude and I would no more have dreamed that he would knowingly have told a lie than that the rest of us would, but he wanted me to accept as gospel what he had only heard or even his interpretation of facts. Our worst row was when he had told me of an heroic act by White Russian nurses in the Civil War which followed the Russian Revolution; that, caught in the open in a Russian winter the nurses had saved their patients by lying on top of them, themselves being found in the morning frozen to death, with their patients alive beneath them. He had been at this time with the British fleet supporting the White Russians against the Bolsheviks, while I was fired with enthusiasm for the revolution which had freed Russia from the tyranny of the Czars. I saw the story as perhaps only White Russian propaganda and in any case as being used by my father to present the whole White Russian cause as noble. Long letters followed which I read with a painful pressure at the pit of my stomach. He tried to minimise our differences by calling me his 'little Bolshevik', but I am sure our clashes were as distressing to him as to me. One of the many causes of misunderstanding between Dad and me was the fact that he saw everything, including people, in absolutes: people, if not his friends, were his enemies; and opinions as well as facts were precisely right or wrong. But he was fair within his lights, as witness this in a letter to Grandpa: 'The Germans are only just beginning to get what they need. Extermination. But they are a very gallant enemy.'

My mother was very concerned that her two elder daughters should realise what the war meant and on my fourteenth birthday, her birthday card for me at Malvern was a picture of a tired-looking, khaki-clad soldier in puttees with the caption 'A British Soldier in Flanders', and the message from her 'to put in your room to remind you of the men at the front doing their duty, and help you to do yours cheerfully and well'. She wasn't usually so austere. My fourteenth birthday, in February 1917, occurred during the lowest point of the war. But still there was nothing in our experience to give reality to her words.

My mother had no doubts about the rightness of the war and I am sure she would not have sympathised – though Maudy well might – with the conscientious objectors. Her efforts to bring home to us the meaning of the war as she saw it, and our responsibility to be worthy of the sacrifices being made, were linked and made palatable – and unusual – by the vision she set before us of the wider future and place in the world which she saw opening out for women and so for her daughters. This is from her long letter to us written just after the armistice when I was fifteen:

Yours is the future. You must see to it that England's young womanhood with its greater powers and far greater opportunities of mixing with the outside world than ever before, shall be a blessing to the human race and worthy of the willing sacrifice of the lives of brothers and fathers.

Though Miss Poulton and Miss Greenslade (the two ladies at Malvern who had so impressed my mother and Maudy) no longer took any executive part in the school, they still had some position there, and when Bimbi was moved up into the sixth form and I was not, my mother appealed to Miss Poulton over the head of Miss Pulham and, astonishingly, prevailed! I have always thought that I owe my success at subsequent examinations to this early move out of my age group, though there was the adverse side-effect that it resulted in my giving up mathematics at fourteen.

I only saw Miss Poulton twice. Stout, with a high intellectual forehead, a beaked nose and deep-set piercing blue eyes, she gave a general impression of determination. The first time she was giving a recitation to the whole school one Sunday evening. It was supposed to be humorous but no one laughed. The second occasion – in March 1917 – she read aloud to us a long letter that she had received from a friend in St Petersburg describing glowingly the first – peaceful – Russian revolution.

After I don't know what painful discussions between my parents, Dad had abandoned his plan to get a shore appointment in England or to leave the Navy and join a civilian medical practice after the war. He sailed for Malta in H.M.S. *Iron Duke* in August 1919, and since Toto was now too old to continue at a preparatory school, we moved house again. This time to London where Mona and Toto went to St Paul's Girls' School.

At first, we had rooms in an ugly, depressing terraced house in Fulham Palace Road: it was opposite a large cemetery and London's trams clanked by just outside our windows. From there we moved to Barnes and then to a down-at-heel private hotel in Earls Court Road. In the Fulham Palace Road days, when Bimbi and I were home from Malvern, my depression was added to by the fact that our landlady (who was called Miss Clutterbuck) acted as 'mother's help' and shared our meals and our sitting-room. I resented this stranger in our home, especially as she had usurped my place as my mother's deputy and even as her nurse during her headaches which had become almost a continuous illness. But I fear that my attitude was caused even more by snobbery: she was physically unattractive and 'lower class'. Worse she had the habit of wiping her finger on the lip of milk or cream jug after pouring it, to stop the drips. Ever since I have shrunk from this harmless and useful action and, as my grandchildren know, 'doing a clutterbuck' is not allowed in my house.

Fresh from a boys' preparatory school, Mona and Toto made as much of an impact for unusualness and parental intervention at St Paul's as Bimbi and I had unwittingly done at Malvern. Evelyn Sharp (who was to become a lifelong friend) was prefect there when my sisters arrived and she has told me with what a shock she, the daughter of a Parsonage, found Mona gambling for pennies with her friends on the school roof. She was also astonished when, as captain of cricket, she told young Mona how to hold her bat, to be answered back with 'Hobbs does it my way!'

My mother's next (and as it turned out final) interference with my sojourn at Malvern came in 1920 when she took Bimbi and me away from school partway through the summer term so that we might go for a holiday with her and Maudy in the French Alps. This seemed wholly reasonable to her since we had passed matric the previous year and were not intending to go to University until, at earliest, the autumn of the following year, and it had been made financially possible by a gift from a great-aunt. It was the first of many family holidays that we spent at Argentières in the lovely Chamonix valley, staying always at the Mont Blanc Hotel on the cheapest pension terms and making the money go as far as possible, never allowing ourselves extras like coffee after dinner or another pat of butter at breakfast.

Chamonix was then quite a small place, its tourism largely confined to summer climbers, and Argentières at the top of the valley was a tiny village of two or three hotels, a village shop and a church in the midst of meadows full of flowers. Everywhere there was the sound of cowbells and rushing water and the unmistakable smell of mountain air.

Our expeditions usually involved some four hours walking

and a climb of two to three thousand feet and we were surprised that Mum and Maudy were able to keep up with us. It is difficult for me to realise now that in 1920 Maudy was then fifty and Mum not yet fifty-three. But her headaches continued. I have a vivid memory of my mother sitting on a block of ice in the middle of the *mer de glace* surrounded by all five of her children; she is holding a piece of ice to her aching head and waiting for the pain to ease enough for her to climb on up from the glacier to the Montenvers Hotel and make the long walk down into the valley to join the little train back to Argentières.

In bad weather the clouds might be down on the mountains for several days blotting out all the snow mountains like a false ceiling. But there is excitement about thunder in the high Alps, rolling and repeating from mountain to mountain when the sound of the rain competes with the sound of the streams and of the river. Then we would huddle together with hot-water bottles on Maudy's bed for our reading (usually one of George Meredith's novels) and make tea in our room, on Mum's methylated stove, and we would eat wild strawberries and bilberries collected by Bimbi which we mixed together with sugar and milk.

Bimbi was due to leave school after the summer term but Mum had assumed that I would go back to Malvern in the autumn for another year. This, however, was too much for the authorities to take lying down. A letter came from the headmistress saying that 'it would be better both for Alix and for the school if she did not return'. So – I was in effect expelled. As far as I know, I had done nothing myself to deserve the stricture – 'better for the school if she did not return'. Certainly I was never made a prefect; Mum could not at all understand that! There was the silliness about my friend May and there was our support of the Haslam girls over their hair-cutting; and we had been told off for trying to proselytise our friends into being Catholics. But none of this, surely, deserved that stricture? I suspect it was my mother rather than I who was expelled. . . .

4

Green in Youth

'Bay is setting to work hard, all day and all evening too,' wrote Granny in her daily diary on 7th October 1920. Since I was not to be received back at school it had been arranged that I should work for my university entrance exam at Broughton. I was seventeen and entirely my own mistress in planning my day.

I had weekly coaching in Latin and in English essay in Nottingham but coaching in History (my chief subject) was by correspondence with Miss Graham, the history teacher at St Paul's Girls' School. She set me weekly essays for which I would browse among the shelves of the Nottingham Library collecting – like a drunkard – more books than I could possibly digest. Arriving back with my load at Upper Broughton station, I would be met by Frank (the gardener and chauffeur) in the little 'Swift' with its high back and polished brass lamps that made an unmistakable high-pitched noise with its clutch.

In the evenings, I would sometimes sit with Granny and Maudy in the drawing-room while they read aloud: Granny from a novel by Scott, or from Tennyson; Maudy from Meredith or George Eliot. Emily, the old family nurse, always came in for these evening readings and as she listened and nodded her head at passages she approved of, she would always be working with stiff arthritic fingers at some piece of sewing held close up to her only 'good' eye.

Part of my 'work' was reading newspapers, making notes and cutting out extracts about the political scene, especially about the Russian Revolution and the war between the Whites and Reds. But I was also politically aware then in other ways, strongly supported in this by Maudy; we joined the village branch of the W.E.A. together and attended evening lectures at the village school. I was all for equality and no class distinction but when I wanted to invite one of the village people we had met at the

W.E.A. lectures to tea, there were difficulties. Yes, I might invite him. But tea would be served in the Morning Room (which had become my study room) not the Drawing Room.

At weekends, the twin uncles were at home and my work routine would be pleasantly interrupted for the mandatory Sunday dog-walk, a rare game of tennis or chess and on Sundays there would be a big family gathering of uncles and aunts for tea.

In this way, I spent the autumn and spring terms of 1920/21 and was rewarded the following autumn with a minor scholarship at Somerville College, Oxford.

It was during this interlude between school and university that I came to know, as an adult, my aunt Maudy and my special uncles, the twins, uncle Will and aunt Nellie.

Maudy was my invariable and sure support in whatever I did or thought, accepting *my* judgements as necessarily right and yet always the leader herself – because of what she was, a profound influence in all my life. My standards of social behaviour were to differ widely from hers but I would never willingly fall below the ethical standards that she believed were mine.

With Chin and Axie my relationship in adult life remained like the complete trust a child has in a young and doting father, though in Axie's case not so doting that he did not make us know in the most charming way that self-indulgence (especially with food) and careless spending (especially on oneself) were reprehensible; he was that rare contrast – a cheerful puritan and a gentle stoic. These were Chin's qualities too and both were careful with money throughout their life, their only personal extravagance sea voyages to distant parts. On others, especially on our family, they spent generously.

Holidays have always held enchantment for me and the uncles had been a main part of all our childhood holidays at Salcombe. And now, in our late teens, those uncles began to take Bimbi and me with them on their strenuous walking tours in Switzerland. Walking tours have been traditional in the Dowson family starting with Grandpa and his brother, and the uncles were known to think nothing of forty miles a day. Axie was always the tour planner and sometimes he failed to take account of contours on the map which showed more valleys than he had allowed for.

It could easily happen that our day would extend over nine hours and include climbs of three to four thousand feet – and once or twice a bus or train, planned to take us part of the way, was found to start running only the following month.

Fortunately I found that after I had walked through the first tiredness I did get that second wind that one heard about, and then I could go on all day without feeling tired. Usually we carried our belongings for several days on our backs and when you took the loads off you felt as if you were walking on air. The uncles liked to start the day at a trot and, however long the expedition, Axie would say after dinner, 'Shall we go for a little stroll before bed?' and out we would drag our tired legs. There was however one point on which I could not follow their example: they liked to manage on a minimum to eat – when touring by themselves, they would subsist on chocolate and raisins carried in the pocket – but with Bimbi and me they made the concession of adding one roll and a small triangle of Swiss cheese to the chocolate and raisins. We would always stop for a splendid tea with rolls and jam and cakes but, partway through the first of these tours, there was a day when the uncles were choosey about the best place for that tea and decided to walk on to the next village, whereat I quietly fainted by the roadside! Ever afterwards they took the view that I had an unusual stomach and they were careful to see that I was fed at least every three hours.

Uncle Will was tall and handsome in a rugged fashion. He had a strong face with a prominent brow, bushy eyebrows and a full mouth, the lower lip sticking out a little to receive his cigar; he wore an oldfasioned wing collar and his trousers usually bagged at the knees. Aunty Nellie, always concerned to be fashionably dressed, must have been beautiful when she was young. In what I regarded as 'age', she was still notably good-looking with a high intellectual forehead. I would go to lunch or tea with them at 'Felixstowe', where there was an atmosphere of apparently effortless comfort and sophistication that attracted me strongly. There were always bright fires in winter, flowers in summer, polished floors, Persian rugs, shining silver and comfortable armchairs fitted with rockers. There were the books of Dostoevsky and Samuel Butler that uncle Will most admired, games of chess, music. Uncle Will was a keen botanist and a very good amateur photographer and he had a fine collection of classical records; Beethoven's *Archduke* trio and Strauss's *Til Eulenspiegel* can still transport me back to their big room where we would sit round the central hearth with its fire open on four sides and topped by a huge copper chimney. Uncle Will would smoke a cigar and tug at a strand of his still reddish hair, twisting it round and round while he decided his next move at chess. He made me see that life should be savoured in all its aspects: 'Life is so glorious,' he said. Besides running this comfortable house with the minimum of fuss, my aunt carried on what seemed a full public life, and yet always had time for visitors, including me. I promised myself that I would try to imitate her in this in later life. She was also the first person to recognise the fact that I was now of an age to be interested in young men. Since we had had no settled home as children, we had no established circle of friends of our own age. She invited young men to meet me and she gave us our first dance. She also talked to me about her public work. She had led the Women's Suffrage Movement in Nottingham before the Great War and after that victory her work was still concerned with the rights of women, whether helping to establish a hall of residence for women at the new Nottingham University or attending the police court when young girls were had up for soliciting. She had much to do with the amendment of the law which made it a crime to have sexual intercourse with a girl under sixteen.

My uncle and aunt were both Liberals in politics and, with the many others at that time, they welcomed the Russian Revolution. They also believed in reducing class distinctions. Uncle Will was the owner-manager of a small lace and embroidery factory and was known in the town as a liberal employer. He made friends of his workpeople and, on his death, left his factory in three equal shares: to his wife, to his foreman and to his works' secretary. My aunt's attempts to overcome class prejudice in her home led to an embarrassing incident for me. She had sent me to a teenage tennis party in her car, driven by 'Carrie' her liberalised parlour maid. 'When you arrive,' said my aunt, 'you must say that you have your lady chauffeur with you and would like her to come and watch the tennis.' I duly made this speech and set off with Carrie to join the group round the tennis court. My very 'county' aunt Lena, whose party it was, came hurrying. 'Is it Carrie?' she asked and when I said 'Yes' she gave poor Carrie a chair set apart from the rest of the party. For all aunt Nellie's good intentions, a serious row was to develop between the two when she demanded that Carrie, however liberalised, must sweep and polish the hall floor; Carrie was equally determined that sweeping the floor was now beneath her; sadly, it ended with Carrie leaving.

Uncle Will had owned the first motor car in Nottingham but his love of speed made him a frightening driver: he and my aunt were among the first of the motoring campers and I went with them twice to Scotland at this time; they would be in high spirits as they set out, aunt Nellie singing 'Annie Laurie' as we took the road to the north, but my pleasure would always be mixed with terror because uncle Will could not resist passing another car on a bend or on the rise of a hill.

My uncle and aunt's marriage had grown out of love at first sight and it was lifelong but they believed it right for husband and wife to part when they no longer loved and they were supportive of D. H. Lawrence and Frieda Wheatley when they scandalised Nottingham society by running away together. They had no belief in a personal God, but believed in a gradual progress through other lives to reach an impersonal Keatsian unity in love and beauty. Uncle Will could not resist poking a little fun at the received forms of religion: 'Are you going to kiss the Pope's toe?' he would ask as we went off to Mass and 'I am sorry to hear you have been confessing,' he wrote to Kate Sharp (a girl at school to whom he acted as adoptive father). 'What bally rot! Like the silly people who go to Church and call themselves miserable sinners. You are not a miserable sinner.' His letters to Kate were full of wisdom: 'Don't ever think you ought to belong to anyone, not even to a husband someday. You ought to belong to yourself for ever and ever.' And, as I see it, the most important thing that the older generation can offer to the younger: 'I am always here to fall back on. That is all.'

Truth and true dealing was a very real imperative for them both. When in 1934 uncle Will developed the cancer from which he died, aunt Nellie's code would not have let her tell him anything but the truth if he asked for it. To her relief he never did but the time came when he said, 'I am afraid, my dear, you will have to learn to live without me.' She never really did learn, though she lived another thirty years, dying on his one-hundreth birthday. With the easy certainties of my then thirty-one years, I expected her to commit suicide and, when she did not, I wrote to praise her for her courage.

I used to write to her every year on the anniversary of his death and often visited her at their house on Lake Windermere where she lived with music and poetry and her memories, making her whole widowhood a lonely memorial to him. It seemed to me sad that their joint faith gave her so little comfort.

I am sure that what I learnt from my uncles and my two aunts while I lived at Broughton was quite as important as the sum of my academic coaching. However, I was now beginning to feel that I wanted to gain experience outside the family shelter and I welcomed an opportunity to go to Paris for some weeks as 'governess' to the eleven-year-old son of Madame Bréale who was recovering from an accident. The suggestion had come from a friend of ours, Miss Bolton.

It would be my first experience alone in the big world and I pictured all sorts of experiences – romantic if possible – but it would be better, I felt, to have unpleasant, even unnamable, experiences than none at all. 'Don't worry,' said Miss Bolton to my mother. 'Frenchmen aren't likely to be attracted by Bay's very English, homely (or did she say hobbledehoy?) appearance.' I certainly had no experiences of the kind I had hoped for or that my mother had feared: I was not followed or accosted by strange men or even so much as looked at with admiration. Indeed I had no social life at all, apart from occasionally going to tea with Miss Bolton.

I saw little of Mme Bréale who was a charming cultured lady much wrapped up in left-wing politics. Though kind, she had no realisation of the depths of my unsuitability as a governess for her son who could speak better English than I could speak French, and who had been much spoiled by his mother while recovering from a broken leg. The first thing he did was to show me how to jump on to a fast-moving tram. Mercifully neither of us fell. I was told that one of our lessons must be simple physiology, and since this was not a subject taught at Malvern Girls' College, Madame Bréale gave me a book on the parts of the body to work from. Needless to say, my charge knew more on this subject than I did. Any influence I had to begin with quickly vanished and the situation became patently impossible when he barricaded me in my bedroom with piles of furniture. I was very homesick and shy and now I was humiliated too.

My employer was just then struggling with the problem of her daily woman who had been found dead drunk on methylated spirits but she realised that a crisis had arisen and I would have to go. It had always been planned that after two months in Paris, I would go to stay in Tours with Lydie Fontaine, the 'Mademoiselle' we had made friends with at Malvern. Now this plan was brought forward and I left Paris with little increase in my knowledge either of French or of the world, but with a strong respect for anyone who could succeed as a governess.

My life at Tours could not have been a greater contrast. The Fontaine family consisted of Lydie and her parents and a younger sister, Jacqueline. The family, the house, the whole set-up was extraordinarily old-fashioned, more like the France of the nineteenth than of the twentieth century.

We three girls spent our days sitting in the park with our sewing and embroidery and talking about Jacqueline's forthcoming marriage which was to be a 'mariage de convenance'. She had not yet met the man she was to marry and even when he came to call in his black coat and striped trousers, to complete the formalities with her parents, she still did not meet him; she and Lydie, and I were banished upstairs where we hung over the banisters excitedly giggling and craning our necks to catch a glimpse of the bridegroom's head. Jacqueline did not think this in any way strange and whatever Lydie thought, fresh from teaching in England, she did not say anything. Since Lydie herself did not want a marriage arranged for her, it was assumed that she would go into a convent. I accepted this monstrous diktat as a French custom. It didn't occur to me to question it.

I was not due to go up to Oxford until October 1922, and Bimbi too was waiting to go to Bedford College, London. In the meantime it was planned that we and my mother would take a house in Malta where our father's ship was stationed, and spend the winter months there being grown up young ladies.

Much thought of a non-fashionable Dowson kind was given to our wardrobe for Malta. It was all home-made except for a suit made for me by a West-End tailor in solemn grey cloth and in a style which would have been more appropriate for a dowager of sixty. For our day dresses, my father had sent home yards and yards of hand-woven blue Egyptian cotton. We each had two evening dresses. Mine were an accordion-pleated white crêpe-de-chine and a blue/green shot taffeta, made under Lydie Fontaine's guidance in Tours. Because most of the dances would be on board ship, Maudy contrived boat cloaks made of two yards of navy-blue 'face' cloth lined with brightly coloured silk and caught together at the half-way fold to make a kind of hood. With our evening dresses, we wore opaque black 'Milanese' silk stockings. When we dressed up to display our new evening dresses at Broughton, Axie said, with his charming crooked smile: 'Stand where I can see the light of the fire shine on the silk of your beautiful stockings.' Maudy said she hoped we would not take to smoking or powdering our faces. Young aunt Ina said we would want to do both before long and must not feel ashamed when we did. And Granny said: 'When you go out with gentlemen, never take wine. It's quite exciting enough without.'

Thus advised and fitted out, and supplied with 'calling cards' for Mrs and the Misses Kilroy, we set out to come out.

Dad was a Surgeon Commander, the senior medical officer on H.M.S. *Iron Duke*, which was the flag-ship of Admiral Sir John Roebuck. He had leased a little house for us in Valetta. We arrived in time for Christmas 1921 and began adjusting ourselves to a social life which must have been almost as strange to my mother as it was to us. Indeed, she made an early *faux pas* when she set out with us to pay a number of formal calls on a Sunday afternoon. It would be quite a quick business, she explained, because people would say that they were out and we should only have to leave those 'calling cards' and drive on in our hired carriage. Dad was horrified: 'It's a social convention not to call on Sunday afternoons,' he said. 'It's known that people are always at home then and can't say that they are out. Probably the Commander's wife was sitting on his knee and was in no mood for callers.' I found this suggested scene subtly exciting; I had never seen my mother sitting on my father's knee.

We had been greeted with a satisfactory-looking pile of invitations when we arrived, but they were an immediate embarrassment because they were all found to be invitations to children's parties. We had been much photographed as children and Dad had surrounded his cabin with the results. It had not occurred to anyone that the photographs might be out of date. We went to twelve formal dances in the three months we were there; most were on board ship and how well I remember the excitement of those dances beginning with the crossing of the Grand Harbour in a smart navy pinnace with a gathering sense of romance as you watched the lights of many ships reflected in the water; and arriving on the quarter deck of a battleship to find it transformed into a ballroom under an awning slung with coloured lights with the Royal Marine band already playing a dance tune, and a queue of partners waiting for you. . . . My parents were invited on all these occasions but I fear I don't remember their presence.

We were the only unmarried girls in the *Iron Duke* circle, so there was no shortage of partners or admirers though, with my straight hair, unfashionable clothes and sensible shoes, the photographs show me less than beautiful. Bimbi as the eldest and prettiest was naturally squired by the Flag Lieutenant, while a nice young Lieutenant and an airforce officer paid court to me. But it certainly never entered our heads that we might become engaged while we were in Malta; we both had our university life before us. I fear we took a general atmosphere of admiration very much for granted. As well as dances, there were lunches in the wardroom followed by a tour of the ship which included a demonstration of loading the huge 18″ guns; and there were picnics and tennis and dangerous mixed hockey on a pitch baked hard by the sun.

We also gave lunches and dinners ourselves. I find menus for these, pencilled by Mum on the back of one of our dance invitations. There were five and six courses even for lunch but the food was always very 'English': cold ham, boiled potatoes, 'queen's pudding', and jellies – though curries and risottos (Mum's specialities) creep in. We had two Maltese maids,

Giovanna and Anna, who were charming, that is until something was done wrong. And then it was 'Giovanna, she do it' and 'No, Anna, she do it'. We never challenged them on their worst sin which was to use our hair brushes, with the result that very soon after we arrived we discovered that we had nits in our hair. Every day we had to submit to the horror of a fine combing and finding tiny red creatures with wildly struggling legs caught on the prongs of the comb. Worse than this, we feared that when our partners at dances were taller than we were they might, horror of horrors, see the creatures in our hair.

The following summer Bimbi and I went to a weekend party at which there were two young naval officers who had been friends of Robin's at Dartmouth. In spite of Malta, I was still inconceivably 'younger than young' and made the *faux pas* of my life, for when I came upon Bimbi and one of these young officers kissing, I jumped to the conclusion that they must be engaged. I rushed forward, kissed them both and joyfully announced their engagement to our hostess. Neither of them had the courage to deny it. Rejoicing was short-lived for there followed with all speed a letter from the young man's father, saying that there must have been a misunderstanding; his son was quite too young to become engaged. . . .

5

Mind-Opening

'Yes, but what do YOU think?' asked Professor Macmurray.

The occasion was my first philosophy tutorial at Oxford. I had been asked to write an essay discussing Descartes' famous conclusion 'Cogito ergo sum' and had followed the method which I had developed for myself when I was working alone between school and college, taking out of the library all the books I could find that mentioned my subject and summarising the result. Macmurray's question was the most exciting I had ever been asked.

I had gone up to Oxford in October 1922 and I was studying for the then new degree of Modern Greats – philosophy, politics and economics. Macmurray's question was like a flash of light. From then on I began the adventure of digging down to the bottom of my subject, stretching my mind to its utmost. When I finished an essay, I used to feel as if I had laid an egg and I would reward myself by putting a record on my gramophone and dancing to it alone in my room; it might be 'Chicago' or 'Yes we have no bananas' or more often 'Susanna's Squeaking Shoes'.

I had come up to Somerville College with an exhibition in history. It was worth only £20 a year but when we new students lined up to receive our caps and gowns, I found that I had the right to wear a scholar's gown. Besides being rather grand, this gown was much bigger than the ordinary one and so was better for holding in front of your fire to make it draw. My pride in it was a little dampened when Miss Clarke – the history tutor – told me that she had picked me out as much for my handwriting as for what I wrote.

I had been to Somerville, once before, to sit the entrance exam and had found the experience a heady one. I had stayed up half the night talking to an undergraduate who had kindly asked me to cocoa in her room. Now that I was an undergraduate myself, I felt somehow larger than life. This was wholly different from boarding school. Now I was free to work or not and to come and go as I liked and in a place of beauty and learning, which could not, like school, be compared adversely with home. It was a thrilling adventure into adult life – and there was no unpleasant discipline and no homesickness.

Also standing in line for her cap and gown on our first morning was a short-haired, fair girl, with brilliant blue eyes, a small determined mouth and a short nose who looked as if she was rather my sort of person and might be as shy as I felt. This was Evelyn Sharp, later Baroness Sharp and one of the outstanding civil servants of her day. I had not met her before but I had known that she had been at St Paul's Girls' School where my younger sisters also were, and had been told by Miss Graham, my 'Correspondence' coach from St Paul's, that she was going to Somerville that year. So – 'Are you Miss Sharp?' I asked. 'I am Miss Kilroy and my sisters are at St Paul's'.

Evelyn was surprised to be addressed so formally but agreed that 'Yes', she was Miss Sharp, and thus began one of the most important friendships of my life. Like me, Evelyn came of a family of five and we were both born in 1903. Like me too, the assumption in Evelyn's family had always been that the girls would earn their living, though this was due in her case to a remarkable liberal father who was Rector of Ealing and not, as in my case, to a background of Women's Suffrage. Though we were friends, we did not see very much of each other at Oxford.

Evelyn was taking a different degree so that we didn't meet at lectures, and as she was good at games and less interested in dancing and generally in male company than I was in those days, our leisure was often differently spent. We made a fairly regular threesome with Agnes Headlam-Morley who, like Evelyn, was taking history and would become Oxford's first-ever woman professor. I remember her as tall, with an intelligent, friendly and slightly horse-shaped face and long untidy yellow hair.

Outside the gates of Somerville my time was spent with my school friend from Malvern, Jane Martin (later to marry Kenneth Clark*). We had both had quite enough at Malvern of a wholly

*Later Lord Clark O.M.

female society and we spent as little of our leisure time in college as we could. I had never enjoyed women's team games, so there were not even these to attract me to college life. I transferred my dislike of school to women's gatherings generally and it was a long time before I recovered from this. I regret now this isolation from the life of Somerville – especially that I saw nothing of any dons except those I had direct dealings with. Miss Bruce was then Vice Principal, Miss Darbyshire was English tutor and Miss Pope had been appointed a fellow in the year in which I went up. But their field of scholarship was remote from mine and I did not make the acquaintance of these noted early Somervillians; they were just white-haired elderly ladies of no personal interest to me.

Jane was marvellously outgoing with plenty of Irish charm and the capacity to make everyone with her feel wiser and more attractive than before. She was more interested in living than in learning, and judging from a single letter from her that has survived, she relied a good deal on my notes and comments to fill gaps in her studies for we were both working for the same degree. I in turn was wholly under her sway in all social contacts. Because she had come up a year earlier, she already knew many people and she was generous in sharing her friends with me. We must have been a fairly striking couple: she was dark and self-assured; I was fair and shy. It was much easier in those days for girls to go about in twos than separately, because the women's colleges had strict rules about socialising with male undergraduates. You were not allowed out alone with a man except (oddly enough) if carrying golf clubs – Jane took up golf; you could never go to a man's room except in couples and then only with the permission of the Principal herself; you could not go out after dinner at all without leave, and had always to be back in college by eleven o'clock; you could never ask a man to your room in college and, even when you entertained a man in one of the public rooms, you were supposed to have a member of the staff there as well. No doubt many of these rules were flouted but I know that on more than one occasion when Jane and I entertained young men to tea with bananas and cream in the small common room, a don was there as chaperone!

These were the days of the 'aesthetes' at Oxford. Jane knew several of them but she did not as a rule bring me into that circle. She probably thought, with good reason, that I should have been even more out of my depth than usual. There was however one memorable occasion when she took me with her to tea in the rooms of a noted aesthete, Aleister Crowley (later to become notorious for taking part in Black Masses in Sicily). As we came in, I saw that everyone was admiring a book which had just been published; it was the Nonesuch Press *Genesis* published in 1924 (my first remote touch with my future husband Francis whom I was not to meet for another seven years). I remember like a still-life picture: the dark panelled room, the undergraduates gathered round the dominant figure of Crowley – dark, tall, saturnine with, as it seemed to me, 'purple' powder on his face – and *Genesis* open at one of Paul Nash's marvellous black and white illustrations.

Usually Jane and I made up a foursome and went on the river in summer or for walks in the clear autumn weather that seemed to be special to Oxford, or to the cinema or theatre. There were many river picnics when we took a gramophone and played the latest records. We could both punt quite well but usually this fell to the men, if only because the clothes that Jane had designed for us were apt to be more suitable for sitting and being admired in than for wielding a punt-pole. We usually made our own clothes in a distinct, outré style which she decreed. I made myself an ankle-length coat of smooth brown cloth decorated with Chinese embroidery, and a summer dress so narrow that I had to walk with mincing steps; so absurd was I that I went to a tennis party in this dress. Amongst the male undergraduates the fashion was for 'Oxford bags', a fashion which spread rapidly beyond Oxford. I remember my father's horror when Robin – then a sub-lieutenant stationed at Greenwich – ordered a pair of them from his naval tailor! It needed quite a lot of courage on my brother's part.

Jane and I tried our hand at canoeing but that was less suitable for parties of four and we gave it up when the canoe overturned and we were both deposited in the water; we were driven back to Somerville dripping wet in one of Oxford's rare hansom cabs.

For me the most important social occasions were the dances at Eights Week and the 'Commem' balls at the end of the summer term. Here I needed no support from Jane; I knew that I was a good dancer and I never lacked for invitations. I felt in those days as if I could dance all night and on these occasions I sometimes did; in my last year I was asked (and went) to three in succession, ending up with a romantic early breakfast in a punt, with a member of our party whom I had met only that evening.

It was the practice for little notes from admirers to be deposited at the Porter's Lodge, and I had a satisfying number of these from one particular young man. He took me to several Gilbert and Sullivan operas and it was with him that I saw a first performance of Bernard Shaw's *Heartbreak House*. At the end, the author himself strode on to the stage and lambasted the audience for laughing at the wrong things: 'One day a writer will commit suicide for this kind of reception, and serve you right,' he said. Though I liked this young man I had no idea of marrying him, so when he asked me to spend a whole day with him in the country Jane had no doubt what was the right thing for me to do: 'I am sure he means to propose to you,' she said, 'and since you don't mean to accept him, you must on no account go. I will meet him and tell him that you have toothache and cannot come.'

Unfortunately we did not decide on this course until the last moment, so the poor young man was left to eat his picnic alone. On another occasion, one of our acquaintances suddenly transferred his attentions from Jane to me without explanation. Again Jane decreed our behaviour: 'We must cut him next time we meet him,' said she. I can still remember the surprise on his face when we did just that.

However, it was through Jane that I made friends with Gordon Waterfield to whom for a time she was engaged. He and I used to go for long walks during which, he says, I insisted on discussing philosophy. I always preferred what I called 'serious' talk to any other. What a bore I must often have been, but it did not prevent a friendship developing which, with his wife Kitty, was to be lifelong.

At this time, of course, University education was open (with few exceptions) only to the well-to-do who could pay the fees. The only way in which the less wealthy could get to University was to take up teaching when you could get loans from the Ministry of Education. Many of the women students, Evelyn (and probably Jane) amongst them, were supporting themselves at University in this way. Any man could get to Oxford if he could afford it, but for a woman there was a stiff competitive entrance examination because there were very many fewer women's colleges. In my year, the total number of entrants at Somerville was only forty.

I did not have to face the choice – 'Be a teacher or you can't go to college' – because the uncles and aunt Maudy paid my fees. They kept a 'parental' interest in all that I was doing and thinking at college and several times one or other of them came to visit me during term.

My weekly tutorials with John Macmurray became the most enjoyable as well as the most important hours that I spent at the University. The Macmurrays had a small house at Oxford and it was there that I went for those mind-stretching periods at which I was fortunate to be the only student. I think Macmurray sometimes enjoyed them as much as I did for often he forgot the time. So much so that once his wife set an alarm-clock which went off with a loud ringing in the middle of our discussion. We were much too earnest to see the joke.

What did we discuss with such absorption? Under the general heading of 'metaphysics' we could debate the meaning of meaning – for example, 'What is chance?' – to our hearts' content. 'Mental gymnastics' my mother called it but learning to use your mind and make it grow seems to me to be one of the proper purposes of a University education and, for that, the subject matters little. Macmurray's method and his question that had so impressed me at his first tutorial was more appropriate to philosophy than it would have been to any other discipline: each student is as free to reach a conclusion on the nature of reality as is a Descartes or a Bishop Berkeley – or an Oxford professor.

Of course we did also study the various philosophers and set books that were in my syllabus (Kant's *Critique of Pure Reason* and his *Moral Law*). But these were never Macmurray's main interest; indeed he told me that he had not read Kant himself until the summer of 1923 which was just before I became his pupil. All this may account for the fact that I remember startlingly little from these set books; from his *Moral Law* – 'Never use a man as a means only, always as an end' – and, from his *Critique of Pure Reason*, the conception that the human mind works in certain fixed categories of which cause-and-effect is one, but that there is no reason to suppose that reality has any truck with these categories. I have found this conception comforting if I begin to wonder whether, behind the 'Big Bang' there is, or can be, a real beginning – a First Cause. But nowadays I am no longer much interested in a subject which can never be more than speculation.

Macmurray had a narrow triangular-shaped face and a slightly crooked jaw (perhaps a war wound) and with his straggly brown beard, he looked a little like an El Greco version of Jesus Christ. But to me he was a mind only; my love affair was with his teaching not with him, though we remained friends after I left Oxford. At this time he was Jowett Lecturer in Philosophy at Balliol. Later he became Professor of Mind and Logic at London University and then Professor of Moral Philosophy at Edinburgh University. When he died in 1976, the long and much praising *Times* Obituary hailed him 'Distinguished Moral Philosopher'. I was indeed fortunate to be given so much of this remarkable man's individual teaching.

However my admiration for him did not prevent me from sampling other Oxford philosophers. My policy was to ask to have individual tutorials from any lecturer whom I found especially interesting. In this way I had one tutorial with Dr Lindsay who had just become Master of Balliol and who later wrote the introduction to the Everyman edition of *The Critique of Pure Reason* and several with Professor J. A. Smith; I find a letter from my Somerville tutor saying that Professor Smith 'would like to have you every week and count the alternate essayless weeks as "consultation with him as Professor".' I remember, alas, nothing of the teaching of either of these great men.

My other degree subjects were always very secondary. Evelyn Sharp has since told me that Miss Clarke, my history tutor, was a medievalist so she may have had little enthusiasm for the modern history which was my syllabus. My third subject, Economics, bored me and I have always said – and half-believed – that what I learnt of it at Oxford was almost entirely confined to Clay's *Economics for the General Reader*. I hope my beautiful and intelligent tutor, Miss Rhodes, will forgive me for this confession.

In the Christmas holidays of my last year at Oxford, Bimbi and I joined a winter sports party for our first non-family holiday. It was a momentous time for me because it was there that I met Garrow Tomlin who, next to my husband, was to be the most important man in my life. He introduced himself during dancing at the hotel, by the age-old gambit of being sure he had met me somewhere before. When I denied it, he claimed to remember my dress. I was pleased with that dress – it was made of purple and pink taffeta arranged in alternate rings, like a collapsed crinoline – so I easily swallowed his excuse. In any case, I was proud to meet him; he already had the reputation in the hotel for being a very good skier quite out of our class. He had the stocky figure of a born skier. He had fair curly hair and large eyes, a handsome, friendly face in spite of an underhung jaw.

Garrow made it clear from the first that his interest was in me and not in Bimbi which I found surprising for I had no opinion of my looks and much of hers – and I was a poor skier. Moreover, I was a very young twenty-one and he was twenty-six. He had been in the war and was socially and sexually experienced, a member (as I found later) of the Bloomsbury movement of which as yet I had never even heard. Add to this that he was an uninterested and indifferent dancer and we would appear to be a very ill-matched pair. But we both loved to argue and were happy to occupy the long hours which had to be spent in climbing uphill to the ski slopes in discussing philosophy or music and plays – or almost anything else. He usually won the argument but I felt that I gave him enough of 'a run for his money' to make it interesting and fun for him, as well as for me.

He had no hesitation in showing that he was physically attracted to me and in taking every opportunity to sit close enough to touch me or hold my hand. Of course I liked this but my puritanical code was shocked by it, and by the open pleasure he took in physical sensations of all kinds, from lying in the sun to hand-holding. Bimbi and I agreed together that he was 'a not quite respectable person'. When I got to know him a bit better I shocked him in turn by suggesting that part of the pleasure of physical contact was because it was *wrong*!

There were no ski schools in those days; you learnt and tumbled about on the practice slopes as best you might. Garrow spent many hours teaching me ski turns and would not let me 'funk it', saying it was easier to make the turns on the steep slopes. One evening, he persuaded Bimbi and me to join him in the exhilarating experience of skiing by moonlight. 'You had better follow in my tracks,' he said, 'because the moon throws little shadow so it's difficult to judge the surface.' Whereupon he disappeared from sight down an unsuspected hill and we came upon him spreadeagled against the opposite slope like a bit of putty on a wall.

Garrow's holiday came to an end before ours and we met the sleigh taking him to catch his train in Gstaad as we were coming back from a day's expedition. I felt a great blank and wept to myself all the way back to the hotel but I was comforted by finding a note of goodbye that he had left for me. Bimbi said, 'Perhaps it is the beginning of a romance for him'. I knew myself so little that, in spite of my recent tears, it didn't occur to me that it might be the beginning of a romance for me.

When I got back to Somerville I had a letter from Garrow in which he proposed to come to Oxford in February for a performance of *Peer Gynt* by the O.U.D.S., for which his brother Stephen had made the masks; he hoped to see me. It was a chatty letter telling me, amongst other things of the frustrations of his work at the Bar, and poking fun about a play he had seen that I 'would have thought coarse and called vulgar'. It was the longest letter I was ever to have from him and it ended: 'By the way, what is your christian name? I know you only as Miss Kilroy.'

I went with him to *Peer Gynt* but my memory of the occasion is not of Garrow but of the scene with the 'button-maker' and my keen identification with the discarded buttons which were put back in the melting-pot; I felt they represented the ordinary man and I hated the superior attitude of the button-maker. It was an impressive performance for a full orchestra played Grieg's music written for the play and the main part was taken by the actor R. W. Speaight, then an undergraduate at Lincoln College.

Garrow and my friend Jane did not take to each other. I think their worlds were too far apart and Garrow, with his barrister's 'uniform' of black jacket and striped city trousers a little baggy at the knees, did not fit well into Jane's clothes-conscious Oxford scene. I was mortified to have Jane and her friend Kenneth Clark say that we were 'like Beauty and the Beast' and I suspect that her opinion confirmed my own first impression of Garrow as being 'not quite respectable' and contributed to the slow development of our friendship.

Soon after we came down from Oxford, Jane and I lost touch. It was my choice not hers and I don't think it had anything to do with her attitude to Garrow. Inevitably, our paths divided: I went into the civil service; she to teach at a prestigious girls' boarding school where she said she was turning all the girls from little Conservatives into little Liberals. I was one of the very few people who went to her wedding to Kenneth Clark and soon after they settled in their first home at Wimbledon, Mona and I went to stay for a weekend. It was not a happy occasion. We felt that the circle of high art and art criticism in which Jane now moved was too knowledgeable and rarified for us; and we were almost literally chilled by the atmosphere in which it seemed that the temperature was adjusted to the pictures rather than to the humans in the house. It seemed to me that Jane was forcing herself into a mould which did not really fit the outgoing, natural person she had been and that the friend I had known was disappearing under it. I was not alone in having this feeling; Evelyn told me that she had felt the same. In my young arrogance, I decided that we no longer had enough in common for continued friendship and I wrote to tell her so.

It had always been understood that after college I would join the family law firm of Dowson and Wright, though it was not until after the Great War that the profession of solicitor was opened to women. Oxford had shown me wider horizons and I had also now had a taste of London life because our 'home' was now the residential hotel in Earls Court Road. Here Mum and Mona (who was still at St Paul's) were the permanent occupants and here was my base in the holidays. Bimbi was a resident at London University's Bedford College, studying for an honours degree in chemistry, and Toto had gone to a finishing school in Lausanne.

The theatres, concerts and cinemas of London were an attraction both to Mona and me and to Mum who, I am sure, felt at home there from her years as a nurse before her marriage. Mona and I had both been 'stage-struck' in our early teens by our first *Hamlet* – Martin Harvey was mine, Russell Thorndyke

Mona's. But we also discovered the interest of going to the public gallery of the House of Commons. The first time we went, we saw Sir Austen Chamberlain (then Foreign Secretary) stride into the Chamber wearing morning coat and top hat, remove the hat with a sweeping gesture, say something searing from the Despatch Box and sit down, disdainfully putting his feet up on the Table bearing the Mace, replacing the top hat and pushing it over his eyes. This, we felt, was high drama. We became frequent attenders and came to enjoy even the unmistakable aroma of old stone which anyone who has sat waiting in the entrance hall to go up to the gallery will recognise.

Now, my meeting with Garrow had raised in my mind the possibility that I might live in London following the more glamorous legal profession of a barrister which also contained the challenge that it had only just been opened to women. (The first woman was called to the Bar in 1922). My decision to be a barrister in London instead of a solicitor in Nottingham must have been a great sadness to my uncle Chin who, having paid my expenses at College, now found that his hope of having me working with him was dashed. Wisely he had seen it coming. 'I am afraid your office career is sinking into the dim, dim distance,' he had written to me in my birthday letter, February 1925.

I chose to join Lincoln's Inn because that was Garrow's Inn and, while I was still at Oxford, I began to 'eat my dinners' in Hall – that quaint convention which is supposed to show that one has spent a certain period of study at the Inn. Garrow came with me to eat my first dinner. The dining hall is reached by a long flight of steps and the hall is large and dark and imposing with a very high ceiling. I was the only woman there and even Garrow's presence could not prevent the occasion from being more awe-inspiring than pleasant.

John Macmurray had told me in my last spring term at Oxford that he considered it would be his fault rather than mine if I did not get a first. In the event, however, my degree was an average second in which I was told I had achieved exactly the same B+ mark in every one of my subjects. I don't think I was disappointed. I had not really expected more in spite of all that had been said but I was annoyed that I had the same mark for my despised economics as for my dear philosophy. John Macmurray's disappointment must have been great. My unconscious has buried the memory of the sad exchange of letters there must have been, for I had left Oxford by the time the results came out. But the difference between a second and a first class degree is of fading importance once you have left University. Macmurray gave me something a very great deal more important than that difference.

I would still have several terms of 'dinners' to eat and my Bar exams to pass when I left Oxford before I could be 'called to the Bar' and start to earn my living as a barrister. How was I to support myself meanwhile? I learned (I don't remember how) that the competitive examination for the Administrative Class of the Home Civil Service was being opened to women for the first time in this year 1925 and that it would be held that summer after the end of the University term. If I were to succeed in that competition I could support myself in London while preparing to become a barrister, and I should incidentally be entering for another job which was newly opened to women. Bimbi too was wondering what she should do. She had just gained a first class honours in chemistry at London University. It was decided that we would both try for the Civil Service. So it was very much by chance and not by design that I entered my life's profession.

6

Pioneer by Chance – First Years in the Civil Service

'Red letter day' reads Granny's diary for 29th September, 1925. 'News in *The Times* of Bay's great success – an appointment in the Civil Service! She is 12th in order of merit and one of only two women ever admitted, out of 200 candidates! Oh how excited we all were!'

Telegrams and congratulations poured in. For once, Mum was actually surprised by the success of one of her children; her time in India had given her a respect, amounting to awe, of the Indian Civil Service and she could hardly believe I had won a place in the examination which also recruited these splendid mortals, but Granny was more excited than anyone. She had found the announcement in *The Times* over her breakfast in bed and it was there that I read my name in print for the first time; the Nottingham papers described the examination as 'world's stiffest' and proudly claimed me as 'a native of this city'.

The odd thing is that I don't remember what I felt myself in the midst of all the excitement. All I have is a flat, wholly unemotional memory of getting the news, standing half-dressed in my home-made calico knickers in the 'barrack room' at Broughton, and of Granny in her four-poster bed sitting surrounded by newspapers and smiling all over her wrinkled face: 'None of my children has "set the Thames on fire"' she said as she kissed me, 'but now one of my granddaughters has'.

There was more rejoicing when we learnt that my sister Bimbi had missed success by only one place: 'That two sisters should not alone enter but score so highly in this most difficult of all examinations, constitutes a family record which one need not expect to see repeated', wrote the *Daily Telegraph*. In fact, Bimbi would undoubtedly have got in if she had not decided on a whim to take English Literature (about which she had absolutely no academic knowledge) as one of her extra subjects; she got only 40 out of 200 for it, yet missed overall success by a mere 6 marks. I hope Bimbi was comforted but I fear that in all the excitement I may have been too little concerned about her feelings.

To enter for this examination, you had to be over twenty-two and under twenty-four years old, so because Bimbi and I both happened to come between these ages in the summer of 1925, we both became pioneers by chance of birth. Two other women were successful and both would reach high rank in the Service; they were (Dame) Enid Russell Smith who had 14 more marks than I had and who would become deputy head of the Ministry of Health, and (Dame) Mary Smeiton who beat Bimbi to the last place and would become head of the Ministry of Labour.

The examination had been held at Burlington House, where we spent six hours each day of a very hot week in August. Our papers as well as our desks were headed only by our number so that the sex and the race of the candidate (there were a number of entrants from India and the Middle East) were not known when the papers were marked.

The examination that we took was very different from the one that is set today. There were no I.Q. tests or interviews with psychologists and you were not judged upon skills you had not studied, like answering imaginary parliamentary questions or chairing meetings. Instead, you were examined mainly on the subjects you had studied for your degree, which still seems to me a more dignified and better way to assess the potentialities of grown-up people. There was a viva worth 300 marks and five compulsory general papers worth together 500 and you could take as many other papers as you liked up to a total for the whole examination of 1900. The result of having to take so many papers was to give all-rounders as much chance of success as brilliant specialists, which was just as well in my case for I find that I won my place solely because I could achieve a good average in all my papers. In my year the difference between the top and bottom marks of successful candidates was only 347.

We went for our vivas wearing cotton dresses and sandals and with our legs bare for coolness. We must have been a consider-able shock to the Civil Service Commissioners, accustomed only to interview young men in the stereotyped outfit of that day. They are said to have remarked that it would be little use taking in women like us since we should certainly marry but they gave us both high marks nevertheless: Bimbi 255 and me 245. I have always wondered about that difference of 10.

The day after the announcement in *The Times*, a letter arrived from the Civil Service Commission summoning me to London for an interview. There (after the medical examination required before you could be taken into pensionable service) I was told which government departments had vacancies and was asked to name three in order of my preference. I am staggered at my ignorance then. For it is astonishing but true that though British Constitutional History was included in my degree at Oxford, I knew nothing at all about the British Civil Service or the nature of the work which went on behind and beside Parliament. Equally, I knew nothing, apart from what their names conveyed, of the different responsibilities of the various government departments.

Thus ill-prepared, my first choice was the Colonial Office because it seemed the next best thing to the Foreign Office which I should have liked of all things but which was not yet open to women; but the two candidates at the top of the list had chosen the Colonial Office and there were only two vacancies there. I put the Home Office second for no better reason than that I was interested in prison reform. I had been reading about the new thought in America on this subject and I had (and still have) a vivid memory of being taken by my aunt Nellie to visit Nottingham prison which, even then, was an example of old buildings and methods, with the passages of cells built storey after storey round an oval well. Again, however, I had chosen a department that others wanted; all the three vacancies at the Home Office went to men above me on the list.

So I got my third choice, the Board of Trade. Picked chiefly because a visit to W. R. Greg's Cotton Spinning Mill in Stockport before going to college had fired me with interest in manufacturing processes. My uncle Axie was executive director there and I went under his auspices. I had spent one whole morning working beside one of the mill girls and trying to master her job which was to join together the threads of cotton when they broke. I felt stupid and slow but she was kind with a

Lancashire warmth and told me that, 'You will make a mill girl yet'. That gave me a glow, for this was 1920 and I was very much under the egalitarian influence of the Russian revolution.

My uncle had shown me over the mill and explained the processes and I had found myself full of interest and questions, especially about the experiments they were making with spinning a shiny new man-made fibre called 'rayon'. Ever since that visit the clanging and intricacies of industrial processes have had a romance for me and I have thought sometimes that I should have liked to work in a factory for at least part of my life – though no doubt I should have vastly disliked the repetitiveness.

My letter of appointment from the Civil Service Commission instructed me to present myself on October 25th 1925 at the offices of the Board of Trade in Great George Street, a massive stone-faced building forming one side of Parliament Square. As I walked from Westminster Underground Station on that first Monday of my official life, pride was added to some natural trepidation in the realisation that my place of work was to be opposite the Mother of Parliaments. Each day, I would walk to work past the statues of makers of our history like Palmerston, Disraeli, Gladstone and Abraham Lincoln, who had been held up to me as great men not only at school and college but also – more importantly in a formative sense – by Granny and Maudy.

I advanced upon my unknown career with surprising confidence that I should be able to cope with whatever it turned out to be. I had butterflies in my stomach, of course, but I was not really nervous or worried. Partly this attitude stemmed from the self-reliance Macmurray's teaching had instilled in me – but I am sure it was due as much to my mother's assumption that everything should be possible to her children. In any case, I was very much aware of being the first woman in my job and I was consciously determined not to fail.

My letter of appointment had informed me that for my rank of assistant principal (the lowest grade in the administrative class), my pay would be £240 a year and my hours of work ten to five. I was to present myself at the Board of Trade at ten a.m. and to ask for a Mr Baker who was Chief Establishment Officer. If he was curious to see what the first woman administrator was like he certainly didn't show it. He was grey-haired and tight-lipped. Having given me a form to sign under the Official Secrets Act, he told me that I was to work in the Industries and Manufacturers Department and explained, as we took the lift together to the second floor, that staff might only use the lift if going *up* two floors or more, or *down* three or more. That was the sum of the instrution I had from him: new recruits were expected to learn on the job and were given no general training or instruction of any kind.

Mr Baker and I now walked along a passage quite wide enough to allow a London taxi to drive down it and quite lofty enough to have made room for a double-decker bus. The walls of the passages and indeed of all the offices too were painted what I called 'office-of-works cream', and the tall doors were dark green. Mr Baker explained that the second floor was built on a grander scale than the others because, by tradition, this floor housed the offices of 'The Great'; he showed me with suitable awe the door belonging to the outer-office of the President of the Board of Trade himself. As I quickly learned, the President was the political head of the department, the equivalent of a Secretary of State, and an automatic member of the Cabinet. I was on this floor only because I was to have a desk in the outer office of Sir Percy Ashley, the head of my department-to-be, sharing it with Miss Christie, his secretary/typist. Thus, delicately, did the Board of Trade provide chaperonage for their first woman assistant principal.

PECKING ORDER OF THE BOARD OF TRADE

Permanent Secretary

Deputy or Second Secretaries

Under-Secretaries

Principal Assistant Secretaries

Assistant Secretaries

Principals

Assistant Principals

Mr Baker took me in to meet Sir Percy Ashley, a balding, middle-aged man with a little moustache and fleshy face who talked with his eyes partly shut. I was far from presuming to make judgements about so grand a personage, but I did notice in his disfavour that he wore boots. He always treated me court- eously but, since I sat in his outer office, he had inevitably to ignore me most of the time and I rarely dealt with him direct. On that first day he did no more than welcome me to the department and ask Miss Christie to 'take Miss Kilroy to Hutchinson's office'. Mr Hutchinson was to be 'my principal', the man under whom I was to work as trainee. He was tall and had a long face with a sideways slant to it. His office was a fine high-ceilinged room on the ground floor overlooking St James's Park. He introduced me to our four 'staff officers' who then completed the number of our small department and who sat together in one room. I soon gained a great respect for these officers. At that time, their rank was rather like that of non-commissioned officers: they had entered from school not college, belonged to the executive class (one below the administrative) and tended to be specialists, staying longer in one job than did administrative officers. Their job in our department was to know about the structure and manufacturing techniques of particular industries. It was by no means unusual however for people to be promoted from staff to administrative officer and among our four was one permanent-secretary-to-be, William Palmer, then our expert on iron and steel and engineering – and any other industry that no one else claimed – later he would be Sir Will and head of the Ministry of Supply during the Second World War. There was also C. K. Hobson, (nephew to J. A. Hobson, the economist) who knew more than any man living about the restrictive practices of industry, and there was also Mr Nash our cotton expert. I ventured to refer to my visit to my uncle's mill and to say I hoped to have the opportunity to make other such visits of discovery. 'No, no,' said Mr Hutchinson, 'Everyone to their own job. You will be at your desk. You will find that these four officers can tell you everything about our industries that you or ministers, our political masters, need to know and that indus- trialists will come to us here in London to discuss the matters of policy that you and I will be dealing with.' In spite of which he gave me – unwittingly I am sure – an embarrassing moment a day or two later when he asked my opinion on the correct Customs classification for a female garment. It is the job of H. M. Customs to record for entry in the annual Trade Returns, the amount and value of goods imported into or exported from this country and, in those days, if there were problems of classification, they sought the advice of our department of the Board of Trade. It now happened that they asked about a garment called a 'chemise'.

Normally all such enquiries would have been dealt with by one or other of our staff officers but – 'Ah,' said Mr Hutchinson, 'we have now a woman on our staff. Let us ask Miss Kilroy what this garment is.' And Miss Kilroy was covered with confusion, not from modesty but from ignorance. She was still wearing a home-made undergarment that she called a bodice (very tight round the chest to give a flat effect) and she did not know how to answer this first appeal for her advice as a civil servant!

Now, at last, I had achieved my childhood ambition, my own office desk. It was a thrilling moment when I first sat down behind it, though there was nothing on it but the regulation Civil Service pen, ink-stand, pencil and rubber, two empty brown wooden trays marked, respectively, IN and OUT and (in the right-hand top drawer) a duster, a piece of office soap and a hand towel. But as to what I was to do at my desk, since as yet I could clearly do nothing useful, the department seemed at first to be at a loss. I learned later that the news of my appointment had been received with horror by the Board of Trade establishment – perhaps not surprisingly, for it forced them to become leaders in the experiment of employing women in positions of responsibility in which the State was then so very much a pioneer. There could not have been a single woman in the Board of Trade above the rank of clerk or secretary-typist at the time I joined. Moreover, industry and trade at executive level were also then normally the exclusive preserve of men, so the department could be forgiven for thinking that I should not be welcome amongst the people I should have to deal with.

It was not only because I was a woman that I was a new problem to the Board of Trade; I was also their first entrant to the grade of assistant principal since 1919, when a truncated 'Reconstruction' examination had been held for returning servicemen.

The result was that the three or four others of my rank in the Board of Trade were a great deal older than I was – the age gap must indeed have been nearer ten than five years since those entering after war service would usually have been older than the normal university entrant. One by one, they looked in to shake me by the hand but none of them was asked to talk to me about my work. In my first month, I found that I had time on my hands and I began bringing some law books with me and spending part of my time in studying for my Bar examinations.

When I got my cheque for £20 at the end of my first month, I felt ashamed that I had done so little to earn it.

Though I was very much aware all the time of being the first woman in my rank at the Board of Trade, it did not occur to me that my male colleagues would be excitedly curious about me when they came to introduce themselves. I saw them just as officers of my own rank and I wanted, above all things, to be accepted and treated simply as one of them – not as a woman; I suspect that I was trying so hard for this that in some sense I unsexed myself towards them. Certainly, though I developed a confident, easy relationship with them in the office, I kept my private and my office life in separate compartments and in the early days did not make friends among my colleagues. No doubt, too, they were shy of me outside the shared occupations in which we were 'clothed' in our respective ranks. As well as being older, they had all been in the war while I was still a schoolgirl, and most were recently married.

Felix Hooper was an exception. He was a principal in our Mercantile Marine department, handsome in a Ronald Colman way and a man of considerable charm, heightened by the fact that he had lost an arm in the war and did not let this interfere with a normal, active life; he had even taught himself to serve at tennis, throwing up the ball and hitting it in what looked like a single quick action with his one arm. He asked me out to dance and, as he was not married, my rigid code of that time allowed me to accept with a clear conscience. He became quite a fan of mine and of my sister Bimbi, making no distinction between us in his affections; he wrote a long poem to 'The two beautiful sisters'.

Bimbi and I had rented a flat together in Nevern Square, Earls Court, on the same day that I joined the Board of Trade. Mum and Maudy had helped us to furnish it and Mum had found us a pleasant cook/charwoman called Mrs Pearmain; it was not expected in those days that we would do our own cooking. We each paid 17s 6d a week to cover all running expenses including Mrs Pearmain's wages. Our ideas about food were extremely simple and inexpensive and we did not yet drink at all.

Bimbi had been told by the Civil Service Commission that it was usual for Government departments to declare vacancies as they occurred through the year and to take candidates from the waiting list. As she was top of that list, we looked forward confidently to her getting an early appointment. In the event, not a single vacancy was declared throughout that whole year. I believe that when it was seen that a woman was at the top of the list, departments decided not to declare their vacancies. This is not mere speculation; it was the course adopted by my own department, who produced the additional argument that it would not be reasonable to expect them to employ two sisters! So Bimbi lost her chance and worked instead in the research laboratories of J. Lyons and Co., at Cadby Hall until her marriage in 1927.

Having thus waited to declare a vacancy until the 1926 examinations, the Board of Trade nevertheless got another woman. To my delight she was my friend Evelyn Sharp, who was to be a maker of civil service history as the first woman to be head of a Government department. But it was only through me that she became a civil servant for I had spent a weekend convincing her to change her career from teaching: 'We deal all the time with public affairs which you would be sure to enjoy as you are so interested in history,' I told her, 'and you would work only with men. It will be much more fun than teaching in a girls' school.' Unlike me, she dressed very carefully for the viva borrowing freely from her elder sister's wardrobe. But it was, of course, her extraordinary capacity for quick and penetrating thought (which was to characterise her whole career) that got her 288 marks out of 300 and she came seventh in her year.

Unfortunately Evelyn's first appointment was to our Mercantile Marine department which was outhoused in a scruffy building behind Victoria Street, and the work was uninspiring – not at all the stuff of history that I had promised her. It consisted

largely in dealing with applications from members of the public
for permission to use the foreshores round the coast, and of
dunning the users for rent. However, her principal was my friend
Felix Hooper who quickly became her friend too: sometimes
they could see the funny side of the work together. One of their
most awkward tenants happened to be the father of Sir Philip
Cunliffe-Lister, who was then our President. He persisted in
arguing that no rent was payable or, if payable, was too high –
until the day that a number of whales stranded themselves on one
of 'his' beaches. Then an immediate telegram arrived at the office:

'Kindly remove dead whales from your foreshore.'

Sadly, Felix Hooper was killed in an avalanche with all his
party on a skiing holiday in 1927. Evelyn was then left to report
direct to her assistant-secretary, an ageing and susceptible
bachelor. She found herself sent for to his office increasingly
often to discuss points of no importance, and then invited out to
lunch:

'Do you know, my dear,' he said, to her considerable alarm,
'this is the first time I have ever been alone in a taxi with a woman
other than my mother. I should so like to introduce you to her.
Perhaps you would come to lunch with us one Sunday? We
always have a glass of port after lunch on Sundays.'

'What *am* I to do?' Evelyn asked me. 'I can't plead another
engagement for every Sunday.'

'You must invent an invalid sister that you have to look after
every weekend,' I said at once – a ploy which proved successful
except that Evelyn was less skilled than I was at deceit and kept
forgetting the existence of her invalid sister when her health was
enquired after.

Before long Evelyn managed to obtain a transfer to the
Ministry of Health. It was housed in the same group of
Government offices as the Board of Trade, and since connecting
passages ran through the whole building, she and I could now
often slip away together unnoticed when we had problems or
gossip we wanted to exchange, or for a quick cup of coffee. We
used to meet in this way almost daily if only for a few minutes at a
time; and outside the office so close a friendship developed
between us that she became almost like one of the family. She
shared a room with three male colleagues and naturally she was

very quickly the centre of admiration and rivalry: 'Met Evelyn who is having trouble over S who can't understand that she doesn't want to philander. "Have I done it?" she asks. She's never wanted to but is unwilling to end a friendship. And, a day or two later, Evelyn's difficulties with S increase. From which I conclude: Such is the fate of women in the Civil Service: they ought not to sit in the same room with men.' (*Diary 22nd February 1929.*)

Nevertheless, because she was a somewhat angular dancer and the friends I introduced to her preferred talking to her to dancing with her, I tended not to realise fully at the time how attractive she was. Nor was she ever at a loss for a quick retort – or for words even when she didn't fully understand them: 'Balls,' she responded once to a roomful of male colleagues and then, at their shocked expressions, 'All right then, "bollocks" if you prefer it.' She could always see the funny side, even when (as she once told me) she had been met on her return to the office after my first appearance there by a pregnant silence, broken by one of her sturdy admirers with the unfortunate words: 'Well, at least your legs are better than hers.' 'I felt', she said with her infectious laugh and with no hint of jealousy, 'that the general verdict had been that the Board of Trade had got the best of the bargain'.

Evelyn's first principal at the Ministry of Health was determined to treat her exactly as he would have treated a man in her place. He took her to lunch at the 'Escargot' in Soho, gave her port to drink and told her risqué stories, and he sent her alone to represent her ministry at a meeting of a Midlands town council to settle a dispute about some items in the ministry's building regulations. When she arrived, the hall porter wouldn't let her in, refusing to believe her story that she was the Minister's Inspector. 'The Town Clerk,' she told me, 'said he could not take the responsibility of introducing me as the Minister's Representative; he thought it must be some kind of joke. "Very well," I said, "I'll introduce myself," and I pushed open the door of the Council Chamber and announced in a rather high squeak that I was the Minister's Inspector. . . . There was a shocked silence until the Chairman said, "We didn't expect a lass but you're very welcome," and pocketed the large cigar lying beside the place on his right that had been reserved for the Minister's Inspector.'

That experience started the love affair that was to develop over the years between Evelyn and local government, to the extent that, when she died in 1985, *The Times* obituary could say of her that: 'She did more than anyone else in this country to bring local and central government closely together. In local government circles, she earned a personal trust that was unique.'

On my first day I am sure Mr Hutchinson must have done his best to explain to me the duties of our department – broadly to be the link between industry and Government generally, and specifically on any matter affecting the home market – but I doubt if his words meant much to me, wholly ignorant as I was of the work of a Government department. However, it didn't take me long to discover both the scope of our department and the delicate lines between the duties and responsibilities of the various Civil Service grades and for that matter, between the Civil Service and their political masters. Before many days had passed Sir Percy Ashley had pointed out to me with a rare twinkle in his eye, that by addressing a letter to an M.P. at the House of Commons, *Whitehall* instead of *Westminster*, I was 'shaking the foundations of the British Constitution'!

In the first weeks I spent a little time working with Mr Fieldhouse, a senior clerical officer whose duty it was to 'process' Parliamentary Questions which begin the business of Parliament each day. Those who don't know the inside of Government offices would be surprised at the stir that these Parliamentary Questions make there. With Mr Fieldhouse I saw the whole procedure.

'You will find that we are always in a hurry here,' he said as together we began each morning by studying the House of Commons 'Order Paper' and cutting out any questions addressed to our President which appeared there. 'Remember that questions with a star against them are the urgent ones,' he went on. 'We deal with them first because they have to be answered orally and M.P.s are obliged only to give as little as thirty-six hours' notice before they must be answered. The other questions are for answer in writing and there is more time for them.'

When we had pasted the questions on to separate sheets of foolscap, they were rushed down to the Central Registry where they were put in an official file, with a large blue label declaring them to be P.Q.s which everyone knew must be dealt with before anything else. When I got back to my department, these files with their blue labels began to arrive on my desk. I quickly learned that the procedure in a Government office is for the most junior officer to have the first stab at a new file, after which it progresses upwards from rank to superior rank, commented upon and often being altered many times on the way.

Later that day, it would be Mr Fieldhouse's job to see that all these P.Q. files reached him in time for him to get them to the President's Private Office for approval. Which is where the private secretary would come in: the President might not like what he was being asked to say or he or his private secretary might expect a supplementary question for which no answer had been suggested. Most of the questions for oral answer were put by members of the Opposition with the intention of trying to embarrass the Government by a 'supplementary' that had not been prepared for; so knowing enough about the subject to anticipate the right questions could become quite a battle of wits. And how exciting when 'supplementary no. 2' (which could have foot-faulted your Minister, had he not been prepared) turned out to be just the one to be asked!

Though I saw it all from the inside and therefore knew how skilled civil servants and Ministers can be in dealing with awkward questions, I came to regard Question Time as being in very truth one of the bastions of our system of Parliamentary democracy. They have an importance far greater than say the President's press conferences in the United States as a means of making Government accountable, for under our Parliamentary system – so long at any rate as we have a Government formed by a single political party – the Executive is in complete control of the Legislature on matters of policy. By means of Parliamentary Questions, any member of the Legislature, however humble and of whatever party, can call the Executive to account in small but cumulatively vital ways on matters of interest to individual constituents relating to the application of policy. I learned that unless the security of the State is involved, questions must be answered, whether they have been put down in a genuine desire for information or in the hope of favourable publicity for the M.P. or simply to embarrass the Government. Further, however awkward the questions, the answers must not lie, though the truth may be wrapped up or not told in full.

The general run of Government business proceeded at a more moderate pace than the P.Q.s and most of it – at any rate most of that part of it which came to the desk of an assistant principal – was never seen by Ministers. True, our official letters began with the words:– 'I am directed by the Board of Trade to say', but that was Civil Service jargon; it was only the policy on which the letters were based, not its application in our letters that had been 'directed' with such formality. I did not realise until years later that new Ministers arriving in office didn't always find this basic fact of Government business easy to understand. Evelyn told me that when Richard Crossman first became Minister of Housing in 1964 and she was his permanent secretary, he had announced that he must personally approve every decision stated to be authorised by him. She only convinced him of the impossibility of his request by having all the files containing decisions for approval on a single day brought up to his room and piled high on every possible surface in his office.

After my first relatively idle months, Mr Hutchinson sent for me to tell me about the work I would chiefly be doing:

'Your main job', he said, 'will be to work on our new policy for examining the many complaints we're getting from our manufacturers that they are suffering from competition here, in their home market. They claim it is unfair competition because wages are lower and hours of work longer in the competing industries than they are here, or they are helped by subsidies – or, in the case of Germany, by her post-war currency depreciation. As we are basically a Free Trade country, they have no tariff protection.' He went on to explain that the new policy evolved by the Government to deal with these complaints was to appoint Committees of Enquiry to vet the claims being made, industry by industry, and to recommend whether a special protective duty should be imposed. It was no doubt this policy which had resulted in the Board of Trade getting another assistant principal added to their staff – who turned out to be me.

It became my job to make the first comments on the applications we received from various industries under this new policy; and that meant preparing a memorandum (with the help of the staff officer who was a specialist in the applicant industry) which discussed whether or not a *prima facie* case had been made out for the appointment of a Committee of Enquiry. My draft would be considered – and usually largely rewritten – by Mr Hutchinson (who might well ask the industry for more information) and, if he thought a case had been made out, the memorandum would progress upwards from him to Sir Percy Ashley and thence via Sir Horace Hamilton (the permanent secretary) to the President himself who would approve it for circulation to the Cabinet.

Those who do not know the Civil Service may think that this drafting and redrafting is a waste of time. But it is one of the chief ways in which young officers get their training in administration and, more importantly, it prevents errors. I had a salutary example of the risk of error very early in my official life when it was discovered that I had arrived at some percentages by multiplying where I should have divided, and a precious Cabinet paper I had been very proud of had to be withdrawn in disgrace.

I had a second early embarrassment on this work. A case had come to us from the Small Arms industry and, knowing my father's interest in what I was doing and his knowledge of guns, I asked him to explain the difference between the various kinds of sporting guns. He, as anxious to help me as I was to find an interest that we could share, discussed the case with his local gunsmith. I was appalled. On top of having a paper of mine ignominiously withdrawn from circulation to the Cabinet, I was now guilty of discussing confidential Government business with an outsider; worse, by proxy, with someone in the trade concerned. Could I even be guilty under the Official Secrets Act? . . . . I poured out my anxieties to the comforting ear of my cousin (Sir) Oscar Dowson, my mother's first cousin, who was Legal Adviser at the Home Office. He and his wife Eva had befriended Bimbi and me when we first came to London. Oscar had come to the Home Office after a period in Ireland during 'the troubles'; the most gentle of people, he was the last who should have been connected in any way with the 'Black and Tans'. He was a devoted classicist and was, I believe, as much responsible as anyone for developing the conception at the time of the Ottawa Agreements of British citizenship for all citizens of the British Empire, which he saw as following the pattern of citizenship of the Roman Empire.

The two embarrassments I have described seemed large to me, but they were never seen as serious by the powers-that-be at the Board. And I got a public form of official approval when on 13th September 1926 (less than a year after I joined) a Minute of Appointment by the Board of Trade announcing a Committee of Enquiry for the Light Leather Goods Industry, concluded with the words:

> The Secretary to the Committee is Miss A. Kilroy, Board of Trade, Great George Street, London, SW1, to whom all communications relating to the work of the Committee should be addressed.

Had I been a man, this would have been an obvious and inevitable appointment but it was probably the first of its kind to a woman anywhere in Government: it was certainly the first in the Board of Trade, and Percy Ashley must have taken a big breath before asking the President to appoint me.

A year later – 30th September 1927 – the Board were 'pleased to appoint Miss A. H. M. Kilroy to be Secretary' to another Committee of Enquiry, this time into applications made jointly by the manufacturers of 'Buttons, Pins, Hooks and Eyes and Snap Fasteners'.

I don't remember that I got much guidance about how to run my committees but I thoroughly enjoyed myself and took to the work as 'to the manner born'. As the only representative of the Board of Trade on the committees, I didn't hesitate to speak for my department at our private meetings; I saw it as my job to make sure that members heard all the evidence that they ought to hear in order to be fair to both sides, and that neither side's case was affected more than could be helped by the cleverness of Counsel; at the public hearings I used to pass little notes to the Chairman suggesting questions that might usefully be asked from the Chair.

Applicants were given a far from easy ride under the policy:

they must prove that their industry was of substantial importance because of the amount of employment given or the type of goods made, and that foreign goods were coming in at lower prices and in abnormal quantities and were seriously threatening employment in this country; and further that the competition was 'unfair' in specified ways. Having got that far they must also convince the Committee that their industry was carried on with 'reasonable efficiency and economy'. I don't know how many industries got through all these hoops. Neither of mine did.

The applications were always opposed by the importers of the goods, the hearings were in public and the parties were usually represented by Counsel. I was still planning to become a barrister and this was my first contact with the law in action. I found the experience exciting as well as interesting, as I listened to the vigorous and often merciless cross-examination that witnesses were subjected to. It seemed to me that Counsel sometimes forgot that they were not dealing with criminals. Naturally, I also got a thrill from being deferred to as the Committee's secretary by K.C.s, the 'great' men of the law. No doubt they made a special show of deference because a woman in my position was so rare, but they certainly added to my sense of importance.

It was my job to receive all communications in connection with the Enquiries and it fell to me to provide the members of Committees with any official information they needed such as trade and production statistics, to make arrangements for a shorthand note to be taken and to book a suitable room for the public hearings. Occasionally we met in the Law Courts and it was with an added sense of importance that I arrived, well ahead of time, to prepare for our first meeting in these august premises. I was quickly put in my place when a shocked functionary made me change the seats I had planned for my Committee because I had presumed to place my chairman in the seat reserved for His Majesty's judges!

Meetings in the Law Courts had a personal interest for me because there was always a chance that I might catch sight there of Garrow of whom I had seen little since his visit to Oxford. He had asked me to get in touch when I came to London but we had only met once, when my excuse had been that I would like him to show me round the Inns of Court. It had been an uncomfortable occasion; I had gone to meet him at his flat which I had felt was not quite proper. And when he took me to a cheapish place for lunch he had kept leaving me to my steak-and-kidney pudding while he went 'to telephone to someone'. Probably he was just then involved in another 'affair' and my attitude of extreme priggishness must have been discouraging after the first 'charm' of astonishment at my innocence had worn off. I had taken him home to meet my mother and he had delighted her by playing the piano to us and by saying that he thought that, of all the virtues, kindness was the most important, but there had been no follow-up and we had not seen each other for months. Our relationship was to develop very much in fits and starts with long gaps between, and I looked forward now – in vain as it happened – to a chance meeting when I would be clothed with the importance of my new job.

At the end of my first Enquiry the applicants presented me with a fine brown leather handbag made by one of their members. It seemed rather absurd that I couldn't accept it until it had been decided by my superiors that I might keep it without suspicion of bribery, particularly as we had decided that the applicants had failed to establish their claim. However, I met difficulties of a different kind in the second Committee: my chairman, a fat, elderly man of absolutely no charm, insisted on my sitting next to him so that he could seize my hand under the table. I was not at all clever in dealing with this problem.

After these two Committees I experienced one of those complete changes of work which is common in the Civil Service and which makes it such an interesting career; in all my thirty years at the Board of Trade I was never to be more than four years on the same job. This time I was given an individual assignment quite unconnected with the work of my department, on which I had neither guidance nor the usual overseeing by a superior. This was to sort through the Board of Trade files from the First World War and to prepare a memorandum analysing them and suggesting which should be preserved. I was left entirely free to make my own plan of work and each morning I went down to the vaults below our offices where these old files were kept, and stayed for two hours at a time. The ceiling was low and the area was badly ventilated, very dusty and largely filled with great pipes. The files

ABOVE: Aunt Maud on holiday
with us at Argentières

ABOVE: Uncle Will playing the
cello, circa 1920

BELOW: The twin uncles, Chin and Axie, on one of their world trips

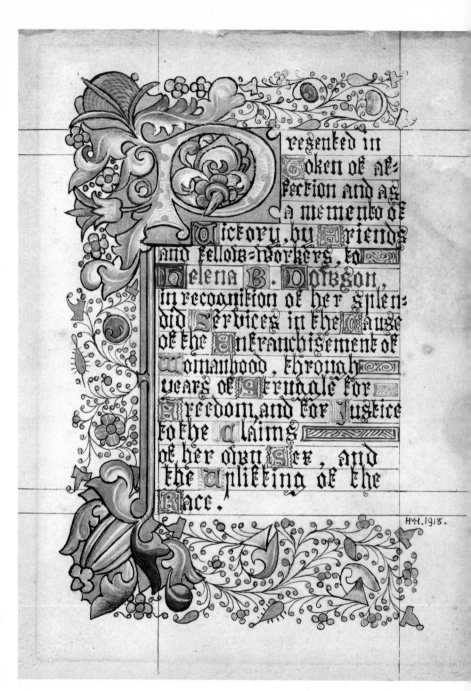

resented in Token of affection and as a memento of Victory, by Friends and fellow-workers, to Helena B. Dobson, in recognition of her splendid Services in the Cause of the Enfranchisement of Womanhood, through years of Struggle for Freedom, and for Justice to the Claims of her own Sex, and the uplifting of the Race.

HMH. 1918.

Illuminated address presented to aunt Nellie by the Suffragists of Nottingham were on rough wood shelves and were bound together between sheets of cardboard, in batches about half-a-foot thick. There were no tables or chairs or other furniture of any kind down there. I took with me my office duster, dusted off two batches of files to make a seat and three to make a table, and opened one batch in ten.

I came upon a lot of fascinating material including minutes by Cabinet Ministers of the time – there was certainly one by Lloyd George – but I concluded that, since no index appeared to exist, the files should all be destroyed. I don't know what was done with this document. My experience while writing this book of the disappearance of so many Board of Trade files of the Thirties, makes me fear that my simplistic advice may have been acted upon.

It was a relief to get back to my department after weeks on this solitary task and to be able to work above ground again. But once more I was in for a big change: I was now to work on the fast-growing difficulties of the still great Lancashire cotton industry, always in those days the Board's 'favourite child' as well as my personal interest. I had to study the emerging young cotton industries of the East and my diary records that 'Hutchinson actually said my memo on the Chinese cotton industry was excellent!' My sources were the reports sent back by our Commercial Counsellors in those countries but I also used my own and my uncle's personal knowledge. I spent all one Sunday at Broughton writing a memorandum on cotton and found uncle Axie very helpful in explaining some of the finer points.

But soon there was yet another change: 'Heavens I am angry! And very near to tears. Ashley has just called me into his room and told me I shall be moved into another department in a day or two!! I can't bear to leave all this interesting work on cotton just in *medias res* and probably it means being passed over for promotion. Instantly went and fired it all off at Evelyn and later I let off at "Hutch". At lunch Mona and I comforted ourselves by buying me rather a dream of a red skating dress.' (*Diary*, 21st November 1929)

But far from being passed over, I was now to get my first promotion. The following morning I was told that Sir Horace Hamilton wished to see me. I was to become personal secretary to Sir Charles Hipwood, who was then the second secretary (deputy official head of the Board of Trade) and head of the Mercantile Marine department: I was told that Hipwood had resisted strongly the idea of having a woman as his private secretary, giving as his reason that he wanted to be free to use strong language. I don't suppose for a moment that this was his real reason; he was just rather old to take to the new idea that a woman could do responsible work.

My appointment was certainly the first of its kind in Whitehall.

I sat in Sir Charles Hipwood's outer office and there was a personal secretary to take dictation and type letters and drafts for me as well as for my boss who looked a little like a kindly albino eagle. His only quirk was that he wanted his private secretary to keep from the public eye the fact that he liked to snooze after lunch on his Civil Service regulation black horsehair sofa. We got on very well together. I don't think it was long before he changed his mind about having a woman p.s. which was just as well for a private secretaryship in the Civil Service carried a financial allowance for extra responsibility and the longer hours, and is recognised by custom as being a quite definite step towards promotion to the next rank up. The service is very unwilling to take away a pay increase once given.

I thoroughly enjoyed making myself acquainted with all the papers that came on to my desk for the second secretary, undoubtedly, the most interesting of which was a request from the City for the Government to help in insuring the first projected super-liner, the *Queen Mary*. This was a much more expensive ship than had ever been built before and the City, remembering no doubt the fate of the 'unsinkable' *Titanic*, were not prepared to insure it unless the Government would re-insure it. There were many meetings in Sir Charles' room and I was always present to take a note recording the proceedings. I believe the proposal broke quite new ground in Government involvement in the City, and (together with the new subsidies then being given to agriculture) it was the subject of a cartoon by Low.

Concurrently with this job I was for a time also part-time p.s. to the Minister for Overseas Trade, a department which was an offshoot of the Board of Trade and which dealt directly with questions of trade promotion. My job there was to look after the

Low's Bargain Basement. I was involved with the reinsurance of the first 'Queen' (see p. 98) and with quotas for agriculture (see p. 187). Walter Runciman, President on the board of Trade on left; Walter Elliot, Minister of Agriculture on right

Parliamentary Questions that the Minister would have to answer. I regret to say that the D.O.T. was rather looked down upon by the officials at headquarters because it did not deal in policy matters, but it could be a stepping-stone to higher office for politicians.

Both the Ministers whom I served at the D.O.T. were men of stature and both made a lasting impression on me. The first was Sir Edward Hilton-Young, who was only at the department for a month before he left to become Minister of Health. He had a brilliant intellect and I had to think fast indeed not to be left too far behind to be able to carry out his instructions. In official life the only difference I have noticed in the way men and women work is that women tend to arrive at a point before men; this does not mean that they are more intelligent, only that their minds often work in jumps, whereas men will go painstakingly from point to point. I have found that only Lord Bridges and Sir Stafford Cripps have left me behind in the way that Hilton-Young did.

My other D.O.T. chief was Colonel John Colville. Work with him was still strenuous but it was less like a flash of lightning. When I left him on my promotion to the rank of principal, he wrote me a most charming letter: 'My university, unlike yours, has sternly refused to give degrees to women, in a laudable attempt to keep them down, but after seeing your work, I feel inclined to let the Chancellor of Cambridge know that the game is up!'

One of my anxieties on being moved to a new job had been the fear that my plans for winter sports at Christmas might fall through. Long holidays were among the great advantages of the Civil Service as a career. Until the last war administrative officers were entitled to six weeks at once, rising to eight weeks after ten years' service. I always took every day of my holidays (usually abroad) in periods of two weeks at a time, so that I could get one winter holiday and two summer holidays every year. I even had the temerity to raise the matter of my winter leave on my second day as private secretary. Hipwood said I could take three weeks.

I had passed my Bar exams during my first three years at the Board of Trade with relatively little difficulty; they were then chiefly a feat of memory. But though I was now qualified to take up a legal career, I had no hesitation at all in abandoning it for the Civil Service. I had discovered that I was likely to be dealing in that career almost always with subjects that were interesting and were often of national concern, and that there was immense variety in the work. Moreover, the Board of Trade had accepted me from the first with complete fairness and equality. I should certainly have had a much harder time making my way as a woman barrister. I had also realised by now that I was much more suited to be a civil servant than a barrister. I was better with my pen than with my tongue and contact with the law through my two Committees had convinced me that I could never have excelled at Counsel's opening and summing-up speeches.

So, I stayed in the Civil Service, a profession I am very proud

to have belonged to. There were anxious – even unpleasant –
hours in my thirty years at the Board of Trade, but there were
very few and I can look back and say that I enjoyed every day of
the rest.

7

First Loves, First Grief

'Twenty-six, nearly thirty,' chanted Mona. It was 2nd February 1929 – my birthday. Mona and I were now sharing the flat in Nevern Square, Bimbi having married the previous summer. Mona was very far from realising that her greeting had touched on a nagging secret fear that 'Life' was passing me by. Bimbi's marriage may have had a good deal to do with the fact that I saw twenty-six rather than twenty-five or twenty-seven as a watershed; she was only fourteen months my senior and there was no marriage in sight for me.

'Perhaps you will be like me and care for other people's children instead of having your own,' Maudy had once said to me and I had dreaded ever since that she might be right. I wanted a career, yes, but I very much wanted marriage as well. 'Just now,' I confided in my diary that year, 'I seem to want very badly to see some chance of matrimony in the future – for children and the physical side too. How women in Trollope novels bear the uncertainty and indeed improbability of matrimony I don't know.' That summer I had gone to Argentières alone with Mum, and, as on other Argentières holidays, had secret longings, which I didn't share even with Bimbi, for companionship other than undiluted family.

On one of our expeditions it suddenly became of terrible importance to me that a mountain stream in which Bimbi and I had bathed delightedly the previous year should still be there and not dried up as often happened in summer; it was a hot thundery afternoon and as I hurried up the steep mountain path ahead of my mother, 'my thoughts dwelt on minimised matrimonial chances and the passing years. My throat was tight and I couldn't have trusted myself to speak', my diary records. When I got to the place and found only a dry stream bed I sat down and wept. However, quite contrary to my forebodings, 1929 proved to be a momentous life-opening year for me: I was to deepen my relationship with Garrow and at last to lose my virginity to him; I was to meet my future husband Francis Meynell (though only as a casual acquaintance) and, on the same occasion, the man with whom I was to have my only romantic affair; it was in that year that I received my first promotion; and in that year Mona and I were to build and enjoy a unique relationship.

There was certainly nothing in the outward circumstances of my life at this time to justify my anxieties and depressions. I was busy and interested both at work and after work. I was usually among the most sought-after girls in any gathering and there were a number of young men who seemed ready to fall in love with me. I could keep myself on what I earned, run a car (admittedly not new) and afford more than one holiday abroad each year – a rarity then; and I could even afford sometimes to help out one or other of my younger sisters when she needed it.

But with the evidence of my diaries I can see that I was struggling with the problem of waking up very late indeed to adult life. At twenty-six I was still almost as inexperienced as I had been five years earlier when I first met Garrow: I had never knowingly been 'in love'; I still believed that sex, in the sense of bed, belonged only with marriage; and I was still a virgin though I had plenty of what we called 'It' or 'S.A.'. An unfortunate side-effect of my very loving family ties had been to inhibit me from other close relationships. I measured young men against the men of my family and found them wanting. 'Uncle Will is something of a pattern where men are concerned. They all have to be compared to him sooner or later,' and 'How could I ever love anyone, even Garrow, as much as I love Robin?' are quotes from my diary at this time. I was always hoping and expecting to fall in love in the story-book way but I simply didn't.

Garrow's life before we met had been as different as possible from my sheltered existence. He had joined the Navy as a young boy and had been old enough to command a mine-sweeper in the Great War. Before becoming a barrister, he had spent two years in South America with an oil-drilling team who, he said, 'made work with English seamen appear like attendance at a church fête'. Garrow was also subject to black depressions which I never understood because they were wholly outside my experience. He was undergoing a course of daily psycho-analysis for these bouts and this too I did not understand or sympathise with. 'Surely,' I said, 'concentrating on yourself in these sessions once a day could make you worse, because they will make you feel still more that you are different from other people. I don't believe you have what you call a "kink".' He did not appear to resent my simplistic approach and in due course he gave up his analysis but his reason – 'I have decided that I am hopeless and incurable' – was not, I noted, 'a very satisfactory one'.

Garrow had joined our family party at Maloja for our winter holiday in 1928/9. It included my uncle Axie and cousin Oscar and though they were both of the older generation, Garrow had quickly established himself as leader on the ski-slopes, taking us on unusual runs over untracked snow and teaching us wood-running using the 'telemark' – a turn in which you had to plunge downhill with one ski well ahead of the other in a position of maximum instability, hoping to finish up in a neat skid at right angles. My uncle still used the 'stick' turn round a long pole held across his body that had been the method of his youth in the 1890s.

I doubt if anyone who has not experienced it can have any idea of the delights of a skiing holiday. For me it had a unique kind of happiness compounded of physical effort, a spice of fear and an overall feeling of joyous freedom from the responsibilities of ordinary life: every morning spent climbing uphill with strips of fur-skin attached to our skis which prevented them (when correctly used) from slipping backwards; lunch out-of-doors in hot sun surrounded by snow and mountain views; back at the hotel hungry for tea with cherry jam and pâtisseries, with a pleasant sense of achievement; and then dancing far into the night. The return to work was always hard and after this particular holiday I found 'the tedium of the first day at the office and the thought of others still out on the slopes almost more than I could bear'. I should certainly have said 'yes' if Garrow had asked me to marry him then. I told my mother about my feelings and she thought he would make a suitable husband for me.

But marriage was far from being Garrow's intention. As our friendship developed, I realised increasingly how different were our attitudes to social conventions and sexual behaviour.

Looking back now, it is clear that he had no intention of entering into any single-partner relationship. He probably intended from the first to get me into bed; according to his code, it was a pleasant and natural part of friendship, and not to be kept for one partner only. He gave me full warning: 'I am definitely polygamous at present'; and, 'If you were to become dependent on me, I know I should be quite horrid to you'. Again and again he warned me. And I did not allow myself to realise that I was in love because I was so busy hiding the fact from him.

Mona and I were very happy to be keeping house together. We had always had interests not shared by the rest of the family. As children we had preferred listening to the grown-ups talking about a mysterious thing called 'business' to playing tennis or croquet. It might be uncle Will telling us about his visits to Switzerland to buy machinery for his embroidery factory in Nottingham, or uncle Axie describing his plans for his mill in Stockport, or uncle Robin enthusiastically discussing his engineering business in South Africa. Mona came to Oxford to be with me at weekends whenever she could and she had followed me in taking Modern Greats at Oxford. Now she found work in London first as assistant to the Conservative agent in Bethnal Green, not pleasant or easy work in that poverty stricken area with its strongly socialist sympathies, then as administrative assistant to BEAMA, the prestigious Electrical Trades Association, to get which she had to conceal the fact that she could type. 'It's typical of the unfairness of men,' she said, 'that if a woman can make herself useful by being able to type, it's assumed she can't do anything else.' Later she did not hesitate to take a job as shop-assistant with John Lewis quickly rising to be one of their chief buyers.

Our flat in Nevern Square was very much the London centre for all the family, uncles and aunts as well as parents, sisters and brother and my diary for this year is as full of their doings and problems as my flat was of them: Robin getting a picture accepted by the Royal Academy; Mona falling in and out of love; and Bimbi with her first baby, torn between loyalties to husband, mother and baby and choosing the baby; the uncles staying with us while they go to the newly instituted Motor Show; my father (just retired from the Navy) spending the evening with us before

going for a long fishing holiday in France; my mother following
him to France; Robin again, being fêted in Madrid for rescuing
General Franco's airforce brother from the sea.

So on this morning of my twenty-sixth birthday, my mother
and sister Toto were also staying at our flat. I was to join them
there for lunch but, though it was a Saturday, I had to go to work
that morning. There was still technically a full six-day working
week in the Civil Service; it was a concession, not a right, that
work stopped at midday, and if you took that morning off, it
counted as a whole day of annual leave. From the moment that I
became a working girl in London, weekends assumed the
immense importance that is so hauntingly expressed in Harold
Munro's poem on the title page of the Nonesuch *Weekend Book*:
'The train! the twelve o'clock to paradise'. On this birthday I
took the afternoon train from St Pancras to Melton Mowbray,
there to be met by 'the uncles' and driven to Broughton. I had to
go back on Sunday night but it was all very much worth while:
when we arrived at Broughton, there was my aunt's fond
welcome and the 'most lovely flowers and meal for my birthday';
there were presents and tea by the fire in the drawing-room,
followed by chess with the uncles, and reading aloud by aunt
Maudy; and on Sunday there was the traditional walk with Kim,
the black labrador. Over the whole visit there was an atmosphere
of delighted welcome and the warming assurance that I was the
favourite guest.

When we didn't go to Broughton, we would often spend the
weekend with our cousins Oscar and Eva Dowson; they had a
tennis court, two gentle Alsatian dogs and plenty of strawberries
and raspberries, and they kept open house for young civil
servants from Oscar's office, and for us and Evelyn. It was here
that Bimbi met her husband, David, and it was in the happy
atmosphere of this house that other marriages were hatched:
uncle Will's protégée Katharine met her husband Laurence
Cornford there; and Norman Brook (later Lord Normanbrook)
who joined the civil service in the same year as I and who was to
be Churchill's right-hand man during the war, was another who
found his wife at these weekend parties. 'Have you heard the bad
news? Another good man gone!' reported Mona when she saw
his engagement in *The Times*.

But for my absorption with Garrow, I too might have married within that group. Bimbi's husband had been one of four Scottish bachelor civil servants who had rooms together in Earls Court and, given encouragement, each of the other three would have liked to marry me. These three were often our companions for dancing and tennis and for winter sports. I fear we were ruthless in arranging parties for our winter holidays because dancing was an important part of them and if you had no partner you simply did not dance. It was then the hey-day of the 'Charleston' and of the 'Black Bottom' which followed it and whenever two or three couples were gathered together, there would be dancing, if only to the gramophone on the sitting room carpet.

When we went out to dance in London it was sometimes to the Hammersmith Palais which had its 'sixpennies' (girls and men ready to partner anyone for hire), but was not then at all rowdy; it was just a large hall with a good floor and an excellent band given over to serious dancing at a low price. More often we went to a night club in Covent Garden called 'Chez Henri'. You reached it up a narrow flight of stairs and there was just room for a tiny dance floor. The band was led by Charlie Kunz whose playing will be remembered by anyone who danced to his music. I preferred it when the band was resting and he improvised alone on the piano. When we four sisters went together, the cloakroom attendant would hold up her hands in delighted surprise and remark how alike we were. Later, Francis was to call us 'the Kilrush'.

Whenever our brother Robin was in London on leave, he would join us and then there was keen rivalry, for we all wanted to dance with him. To celebrate the sale of one of his pictures that summer – 'for 12 guineas!' – he took all his sisters and partners to dance at the Thames Riviera Hotel at Hampton Court: The waiter mistook me for Dorothy Dickson, a musical comedy star. Who would not remember that!

Mona and I not only shared a flat, we shared our lives. We had no secrets from each other as we worked out together our developing attitude to life and to personal relationships and sex. It was an unusual friendship and certainly the closest except marriage I ever had. Our relationship was not an unequal one but I was the acknowledged senior partner by right of our shared childhood and of the generous young hero-worship that Mona gave me. 'You know, don't you, that you are my conscience?' she said one day. 'You wouldn't give me any peace if I behaved in a way you disapproved of.' I had thought that I believed firmly that people ought to decide moral issues for themselves. 'I can't believe I'm like that,' I said. 'You make me feel like a moral tyrant.' In fact, I was as much guided by her as she by me for as I told myself 'her conscience was really better and clearer than mine', and her judgements were always more spontaneous and single-minded. She looked you straight in the face and said just what she thought, but she had an uncanny capacity to know what people needed and to set people at their ease.

It was inevitable in all the circumstances that Mona should share my admiration for Garrow and he became almost as much a life-opener for her as for me. 'If ever I was in any serious difficulty I think that, like you, I should want his advice more than anyone else's,' she said once. We were not alone in falling under his spell. He had been a close friend of both Francis and his wife Vera long before I met them, and he was liked and welcomed even by all my clannish family.

In a way, Mona and I were both 'Eliza Dolittles' to Garrow's 'Professor Higgins'. In all the years of our friendship he and I had never tired of discussion and argument about anything and everything under the sun from Einstein's Theory of Relativity to experiments for getting power from the tides, free will and predestination. As was quite usual then, Mona and I had left school and college with scarcely a trace of scientific knowledge. Garrow introduced us to Eddington's *Nature of the Physical World* (a copy of it was Mona's twenty-sixth-birthday present to me), and he gave me H. G. Wells's *Science of Life* and articles by Einstein with the comment, 'please note and observe'. He didn't manage to instil much scientific knowledge into either of us but he did greatly interest us. 'G came to dinner,' says my diary for 30th January 1929. 'We got on to Einstein and argued till we were exhausted.'

We were on more of an equal footing when it came to philosophy and there we were often joined by John Macmurray. He had been Mona's tutor at Oxford as well as mine and we were now seeing a good deal of him and his wife Betty. But I already found that I was beginning to feel that I had had my fill of pure speculation.

Ready as I was in those days to discuss and argue with Garrow, I was shy and uncertain, even tongue-tied, in strange company, and when he took me to what I called a 'Bloomsbury party' I would find nothing to say. I was sitting silent at one of these, thinking how awful it would be if I were married to Garrow and had to give parties like this, and to have friends like these, when one of the company said suddenly – 'But you don't talk. Why?' Of course I knew I had been a dismal social failure but Garrow reassured me: 'It's only a knack,' he said, 'and I don't think there was anyone there I should much have wanted you to like.' Taking me home in a taxi that evening he put his hand on my breast: 'I used to think it was bold and wrong to hold hands,' I said.

'Then there's no knowing what you may be brought to,' he said. 'I believe you think that everything pleasant must be wrong. Your breast is lovely, just the right shape for my hand. I should like to come up now and undress you and put you to bed.'

That idea was so far from my imaginings that I didn't even consider taking it seriously. In fact Garrow delighted in my lack of sophistication for I remember his laughing with his friends at that party when I didn't know who Dr Marie Stopes was; and when, at another party, I asked him to fill up my glass because 'everyone was more drunk than I was', he wasn't at all pleased.

A chance remark of his had destroyed my religious faith very early in our friendship. We were standing outside the cinema in Lower Regent Street waiting for a bus and as usual we were talking, arguing, discussing. This time it was about immortality: 'Last week I fainted,' he said. 'I don't see why death should be any different from that complete unconsciousness, indefinitely extended.' From that moment my belief in an after-life simply left me and I have never recovered it.

With Garrow we also started to doubt and explore in literature. Until then my tastes had been rather solemn – the Russians, Samuel Butler, Hardy and Conrad (under uncle Will's influence), George Meredith and the other nineteenth-century classics (under Maudy's and Granny's). And, of course, I had read and admired the two very different works that made such an impression on my generation: Virginia Woolf's *A Room of One's Own* and Keynes's *Economic Consequences of the Peace*. Garrow now introduced us to the delights of H. G. Wells's Mr Kipps and Mr Polly and taught us an adult enjoyment in *Alice in Wonderland*. Garrow enjoyed reading aloud as much as we did and we spent many evenings reading to each other.

We used to go to at least one concert a week at this time: to the L.S.O. under Hamilton Harty, or to the Promenade Concerts under Henry Wood – plump, short and black-bearded – and occasionally also to the opera. It is surprising that I could afford this on my salary as an assistant principal. Of course we went to Covent Garden in the cheapest seats 'the gods'. You had to queue for many hours to get them which was possible if you were a working girl only because you could get 'messenger boys' to queue for you. I enjoyed all opera, but when Evelyn and Mona came with me for a performance of *The Valkyrie* the evening was not a complete success. Mona was too shocked by the large bulk of Brunhilde to appreciate her singing and Evelyn was 'in the wrong mood': never one to mince her words, she said that the Valkyries were 'like an out-of-hand suffragette meeting' and I could only agree that this was true.

Once I heard Chaliapin. I was a bit disappointed at the time but on a recent visit to opera in Leningrad I was instantly transported back to the splendour of that voice heard distantly from 'the gods' that long ago night at Covent Garden. Of course we enjoyed the musical comedies of the time too. There was one's first introduction to Fred Astaire when he and his sister Adèle came over from America and took London by storm, doing the 'Oompah Trot' side-by-side round and round the stage, faster and faster – in *Lady be Good* I think; there was Jack Buchanan with his romantically hoarse voice and sophisticated good looks whom I remember (wrongly as I find) in *No, No, Nanette* with its unforgettable lyrics –'Tea for two' and 'I want to be happy'; and in 1928, there had been Noel Coward's *This year of Grace* at the Empire in Piccadilly Circus, of which an indelible memory for me is a crowded night club with the girls all holding up masks of pale exhausted faces, to the lyric of 'Dance, dance, dance little lady'.

But concert music came first: 'To think', said Mona after a first hearing of Tchaikovsky's 5th Symphony, 'that there was a time when I preferred the theatre to a concert'. I was as much moved as she was. I remember feeling that the repetitive hammering theme in the symphony represented the harsh mechanical power of *my* modern world, from which the older gentler generation ought to be protected – almost that it was unsuitable music for them to hear! Schnäbel had my greatest admiration, the more for the fact that he looked like a bank manager rather than a musician and played without any of the usual showmanship. I was furious with the critics when they didn't give him rave reviews.

When there was no concert, there was always the cinema. I welcomed it as a place to spend the evening with Garrow away from the intimacies of his flat which I was still trying to resist. These were the days of the silent film when you could talk as well as watch. I see that I went to my very first 'talkie' in January 1929. I found it 'surprisingly good' but decided that 'talkies would never replace the silent film since the spoken language could not be international and young people would not want to be deprived of one of the few places where they could meet and talk in private.' A nice lesson in the fact that theory needs to be checked by practice!

I had always been enough of a liberated woman to shrink from the idea of marriage in which 'the little woman' is content to run her husband's house, to wave him off to work in the morning and have his slippers and his dinner ready for him in the evening. In my picture of marriage, I was to have a job as well as my husband but I was shocked not only by Garrow's assumption that 'bed' should be a part of a number of relationships but also by his unemotional, almost scientific approach to it. He nearly convinced me that he thought sex should be divorced from emotion as well as from marriage. 'I should like', he told me once, 'to have twelve children, all by different mothers and watch how they grow up'.

Mine was a much less unusual attitude then than might be thought from all that is written about the Twenties. Bloomsbury apart, it was not expected that, when you went out with a man, he would want to do more than hold your hand or at most kiss you in a taxi when he took you home. Our approach to sex was not far removed from my early *faux pas* in assuming that Bimbi was engaged to be married because she had been kissed. Indeed, Francis has told me that his engagement to his first wife came when it did from just such a misunderstanding on her part.

Added to this was the effect on both of us of Garrow's almost pathological fear of having anyone dependent on him or he on them that I have already mentioned:

> Spent the evening at [Garrow's] flat. He said he wanted to talk about me and we had a complete heart-to-hearter. He has a kink (which he is trying to cure by psychoanalysis) that he can't have anyone relying on him and must always be free to bolt. He can't bear 'passionate women lashing out and demanding to be loved'. He had once been in love with Frances Marshall* and had pursued her insistently, unreasonably and jealously. 'Never again will I make the nuisance of myself that I did then,' he said. 'I like your quietness and peacefulness but if you ever began to rely on me I know my behaviour would be horrid!' (*Diary Jan 28th/Feb 6th 1929*)

The inevitable result was to make me pretend a remoteness I did not feel. It did not occur to me that, because I normally made such a point to him of honesty and plain-speaking, he never saw through my excuses or realised that the calmness and remoteness he liked in me was largely simulated. Often we didn't see each other for months on end and I felt that my feelings were exactly expressed in Irving Berlin's famous song 'All alone, by the telephone. Waiting for a call from you.'

I was determined not to be the first to telephone. I told myself that I was content to wait for us to meet by chance. So I would go to a concert as much in the hope of seeing him as for the music, and once or twice I did meet him in this way. Another time I saw him at a dinner at Lincoln's Inn. I found that I was facing him across a number of long refectory tables. We did no more than bow to each other, but I got a postcard next day: 'It was nice to see your cheerful face again. Have you a free evening?' And there was a tantalising occasion in Switzerland when I caught sight of him in a train which drew up alongside mine, and I searched for him in vain at the next station as in a nightmare. When he did take the initiative, there was 'joy in the home' (an expression of delight

---

*Mrs Frances Partridge.

that Mona and I used) but, although my heart would be beating and my hands shaking, I would tell him calmly that I was booked up for days ahead. 'You must be a very popular young woman,' he would say and I would be punished by hearing no more from him for weeks.

And so, one way and another, it was five years from the beginning of our friendship before we finally went to bed together. What was it that decided me at last? Probably it was that twenty-sixth-birthday-feeling. Unfortunately, but maybe inevitably after all the argument, he presented that first occasion more as a liberation from my past attitudes to morality and social behaviour than as an act of love, and he neither said nor for a moment implied those precious words 'I love you'. So, as I went back to Earls Court in the Underground train that night, I wondered whether I felt happy, depressed or ashamed – or even whether I felt anything at all. I found that Mona had not gone to bed and I hurried to tell her that at last I had 'gone all the way'. As usual her comments were wise as well as comforting: 'I don't think one should regret anything provided you feel right about it at the time,' she said. 'You would probably be sorry in the future if you hadn't lived fully instead of only thinking about it and deciding not to.'

The result next day was depression and guilt rather than elation and pride, and things were not made better by Garrow feeling it his duty to repeat again his lesson that sex should be nothing more than a part of friendship:

> He thinks the danger of sex is that it can create illusions about the other person and that could possibly be unfair to me. At the moment there are two other girls he likes as much and in the same way as me. Told me to clear off if I felt I ought to but he'd be sorry.

I had no intention of clearing off. I came more and more to feel that sex with him must be right because it felt right, though what I called my 'inherited conscience' continued to be shocked by the separation between bed and marriage – or at least love. 'You know I'm very fond of you' is as far as he (or consequently I) ever went in terms of endearment. And so, almost a year after that first time of sleeping together, I could still write in my diary:

I feel definitely shocked and sit here at 1.00 a.m. fulminating.
He says if I deny him the physical he will probably avoid me.
And if I cease to see him, will it be out of sight out of mind? Is
he really attracted to me at all except physically? and how
much do I really feel myself? (*Diary November 1929*)

Personal inclination apart, there were considerable social and
practical difficulties in the way of 'free love'. There was no
general acceptance of the idea of sex outside marriage and
contraception for women was new and clumsy and by no means
easy to come by. *Married Love*, Dr Marie Stopes's first revolutionary book on birth control, was not published until 1918
(interestingly by my husband-to-be, at his Pelican Press) and the
first birth control clinic was opened in London only in 1921 – of
course only for married women. A single woman had to shop
around to find a doctor who would provide her with the feminine
means of birth control, which was then only the 'dutch cap'. I
think Garrow must have introduced me to the charming and
intelligent Dr Joanna Malleson who was a friend of his and of
Francis and became mine. She was one of the few doctors
specialising in contraception for women at that time. Abortion
was a criminal offence both for the doctor and the woman, and
the social stigma made the option of keeping your baby out of
wedlock pretty well unthinkable. So you lived with the fear of
becoming pregnant, when you would have to resort either to a
very expensive (but safe) operation in a very private nursing
home, if you could find one of the few doctors prepared to risk
going to prison *and* if you could afford the price (£100 was the
going rate); or to the cheaper but dangerous back-street 'old
woman with a knitting-needle' variety. Fortunately I never
became pregnant and so did not have to make this choice. Just
about this time, there was much publicity about the trial of a girl
for murder because she had helped her sister to get a back-street
abortion and the sister had died. Mona and I knew that we would
not have hesitated to do as much for each other.

It was rarely that I could be sure of having my flat to myself so
our love-making usually took place in Garrow's flat which
consisted of a small sitting-room and bedroom on the first floor
of 31 Great James Street, one of the row of eighteenth-century

houses that still flank both sides of that beautiful street. It was a
severe bachelor's apartment reflecting his lack of taste in clothes
rather than his many-sided mind: the bedroom made no pretence
to comfort – just an iron bedstead and a chest-of-drawers with
linoleum on the floor – and the sitting-room was decorated in
cold nondescript colours – the curtains a dead office brown. But
there was a gramophone with a large horn, a harpsichord and a
guitar on which Garrow played and sang when we were not
disputing or philandering; and there was an armchair big enough
to hold us both. I came to prefer hours spent in that room to the
best concert or film.

The first time we spent a weekend together, Mona came too
and it was Mona and I who shared a room. 'The Bear' at
Hungerford would not have accepted Garrow and me staying
alone unless I had worn a wedding ring, and I hadn't yet
discovered that these could be bought at Woolworth's. 'The
Bear' was then an old-fashioned coaching inn with the dining-
room in dark oak and double beds in the double rooms. I was too
inexperienced to make my way to Garrow's room so he joined us
in our double bed, while Mona made a great show of sleeping. It
was a curiously innocent arrangement and it certainly demonstrated the deepness of the sisterly relationship between Mona
and me.

Quite apart from our need for 'a room of one's own' now that
we were experimenting with sex, Mona and I were feeling
increasingly that we wanted to be able to have our flat to
ourselves for parties which could be confined to our own
generation. I find it easier now than I did then to understand that
our mother did not realise this. She was after all only sixty-two
and we were still the centre of her world; the concerts we went to
were as much a joy to her as to us and she was interested in our
friends and our discussions and knew that she was helpful in the
preparation of pleasant meals for which we had little time or skill.
In the severe winter of 1929 she sometimes even joined our
skating parties on the Wimbledon ponds.

What finally happened was that we asked our mother to take a
room for herself in London where she would be near us but
would not any longer live with us. I think the step we took was
natural and inevitable but it must have been very painful for her. I

can judge the distress that it caused me by the fact that my unconscious has buried it so deep that I cannot actually remember the fact of our doing this, even now more than fifty years later. I only learned of it because I happened to tell Mona that I have a dream every few years that our mother is still alive and I am conscious of a pervasive sense of guilt because I have forgotten, week after week, to go and see her. I have not had the dream since.

Garrow had always felt that I was too much surrounded by my family and too much dependent on their views: 'You ought to take a holiday alone or with friends and learn to make your own judgements,' he said. He got on well himself with 'my' older generation but he could cause me agonising embarrassment in his behaviour towards them. There was one especially painful evening when Maudy had come to London and arranged a theatre party in order that she might meet him. I was uncomfortable about the whole occasion and anxious lest she should make too much of it in the belief that this was the man I was going to marry – for I knew that he didn't think he was and I still believed that I wasn't sure about my own feelings. We went to see Mrs Patrick Campbell in Ibsen's *John Gabriel Borkman* which in itself must have made the occasion special for both my mother and Maudy. All I remember is my hot embarrassment because Garrow insisted on reading a newspaper in the intervals. I see now that he was probably reacting to being looked upon as a future husband for me, but I didn't think of that at the time. Maudy was wise enough to see through his rudeness and to write to me afterwards: 'What a splendid forward look into life there is in the carriage of his head.' But at such times I began to think that he and I could not be really suited to each other. 'Does everyone have to break with the ideal when they marry?' I asked myself.

In September of that year, 1929, I decided – at the urging of Mona and even Mum – that for once I would take the initiative instead of waiting for Garrow to approach me. I invited him to come with me for a weekend in Nottingham with my revered uncle Will. To my delight he accepted in spite of my warning that we should have to be circumspect and would not be able to sleep together. The weekend was a memorable success and of course I wrote a full account of it in my diary. Garrow and my uncle 'got along admirably over Trollope, cigars and chess and both enjoyed driving my uncle's motor boat at full speed up and down the Trent'. The final accolade was when 'I heard uncle W tell G he hoped he would come again'. I allowed myself to think I might really be in love as we held hands in the early train back to London on Monday but by lunchtime I began to wake up and told myself 'he meant nothing by it; he has never suggested that he confines himself to one girl at a time'. He told me later that he had indeed been carrying on another affair at this time.

Nevertheless, Garrow's and my relationship continued to develop after this weekend, although (as always) with stops and starts. Leaving another girl-friend, he came half-across Switzerland to join me at Mürren when he heard that I had broken my leg skiing; and told me (but not until some time later) that he had felt real discomfort himself when he heard of my accident. Since he also said that he thought being in love was when you felt a part of you had got into the other person so that you experienced their pain, I conclude now that this was his way of making a declaration of love. But I was too much conditioned then by his earlier warnings to take it as such.

The following August Mona and I invited him to join us on holiday, camping on the cliffs near Salcombe.

'I can't come unless you will be happy for me to be on the same physical terms with Mona as with you; a threesome could be very uncomfortable otherwise,' he said.

With my newly acquired Bloomsbury principles, I didn't feel I could object, but when Garrow asked Mona out without me I found that I didn't like it at all:

> I find myself jealous and miserable. The situation will be difficult both for Mona and me if he really means to desert me for her. She understands him better and always knows what to say and says it, and I don't and that's that. In fact I'm really an empty bottle if people knew. Am longing to hear what they say to each other. Getting on the shelf is really damnable.

I confided my fears to Bimbi who didn't improve matters by saying she had always thought Mona a better foil for Garrow than me. I ought to have known my loyal sister better. She spent the evening 'ticking G off for jumping from one to the other'.

Thanks to her careful tact, our trio always made very good company and especially so on this camping holiday: 'G was of course more with me than M but he was very charming with her and she with him; they raise the "gamin" in each other and always have the right retort. There was none of the heart-burning I had feared. I think we three could have got on a long time together with satisfaction all round, though it was sometimes a bit of a strain to both Mona and me to find ourselves suddenly as it were "married"; learnt how maddening men can be because they are stronger physically and he in argument as well; decided that honeymoons must be a great strain at times, however devoted. Mona and I enjoy the same things but G sometimes got bored with the comfortable repetition of anything that came into our heads – mainly views, weather and the next meal.'

I can still see the white sails of our tent amongst the yellow and green gorse, still walk in that contented company along coast-guard paths marked by whitewashed stones, taste the unique flavour of food cooked and eaten in the open air, smell the sea and feel again the special pleasure of water and air on limbs as we bathed naked; 'we laughed for sheer enjoyment'. Our tent was pitched by a stream on the cliffs above 'Shingle' cove (called so because the beach was made of tiny white and silver stones instead of sand). Our only company was the occasional sheep. We would wake to an early morning bathe, and run down to the sea through grass wet with dew, and back to breakfast by our camp fire. In the day, we would go for long walks and bathe and climb among the rocks and lie in the sun by the water, and at night would sit late, talking by the light of the fire. My diary does not say and, curiously, I don't remember whether or how often we managed to sleep together in these circumstances.

We were all three reluctant to go back to London and 'real life'. Mona said that she felt like a lost sheep without Garrow and he that it had been 'perfectly lovely'. He paid me the unique compliment the next day of taking me to see 'a great friend of his, a former parlour-maid who had been "his only friend" when he was trying to live at home after he came back from S. America.'

Feeling very homesick for our menage à trois. Morning brilliantly sunny and wanted to wake up to camp and not to

London. We've got to wait a whole year before it comes again and it seems too long.

We never did have that second camp and at the end of the following year Garrow was dead.

Garrow had not been the only man in my life. I had swallowed whole the teaching of my 'Professor Higgins' about sex, and that autumn I put it into practice with a young man with whom I all but fell in love because he was in love with me – and said so. I had met him at a dinner party given by a school friend Eileen Wilson. It had been very much a matter of chance whether I accepted the invitation. Yet it was at this dinner, at No. 3 Boundary Road, Hampstead, that I also first met [my future husband] Francis. So little did I realise the importance of this meeting that I cannot find it mentioned in my diary but I can date it by the only piece of conversation I remember from the evening: 'What would be the best news you could hear from me?' Francis asked Eileen. 'That Vera is pregnant,' she answered without hesitation. 'That is my news,' said Francis. Vera was Francis's second wife, and their son Benedict was born in February 1930, so the dinner must have been in the summer or autumn of 1929.

Later that same evening, Francis took me to a dance at Grosvenor House where we found that we both enjoyed dancing and also each other's company. But he seemed so much older and in every way so much my superior – and married to boot – that it did not occur to me for one moment that I had met the love and companion of my life. He was tall and notably good-looking and he had a confident man-of-the-world manner which was a little awe-inspiring to me. He used to say that his grandmother had told him that he had 'the profile of a Roman Emperor' at which he had felt flattered until she added 'of the decadent period'. His features were clear-cut and he had a slightly protruding intellectual forehead over a smallish mouth and what is called a Roman nose. But there was no haughtiness in his expression, which was always gentle and kindly. At forty, when I first met him, he was already going a little bald.

The young man, that I met at this same dinner, was a Scot of about my age called David. He had come to London in the hope of making a living as a painter. It was only later that I learned that was already engaged to a girl in Scotland. He not only fell passionately in love with me, he told me so at every opportunity good and bad, even once at Westminster Underground station as I arrived for work. He wooed me with Andrew Marvell's *Ode to his Coy Mistress*, with Siegfried Sassoon's poems in *The Heart's Journey* and with love poems of his own to me. He sent me flowers and pursued me with invitations; he told me that I was everything lovely and beautiful as well as desirable; he rang me up every day and said those words 'I love you' over and over again. Starved as I was of all this from Garrow I suppose I was rather easy prey, especially as I found him physically attractive – and he was a good dancer. I was certainly much moved emotionally as well as physically and it was with David, again at 'The Bear' at Hungerford, that I spent the only 'white night' of my life.

True to my view that one ought to be honest about relationships that threatened to be serious, I told Garrow about this other involvement. I was astonished, as I think he was, to find that he was jealous. 'Have I behaved abominably?' I asked my diary. 'By all conventional standards I have; but then I believe most nice people of our generation have. I have deceived Mum and injured S [D's fiancée] and probably D too; and myself less than all, so everything points to it having been wrong. And what of G? Could he be most hurt? I don't think so. Heavens, where am I? I believe I really am an empty shell and a pretty unpleasant one at that.'

Though David's passionate pursuit of me no doubt formed the largest part of my feelings towards him, it would be quite wrong to say that what I felt was not love. 'This is my ROMANCE,' I told Mum who had asked me the question I had asked myself: 'What about Garrow?' I found that, alarmed on his behalf and mine, she had written to him in disguised handwriting (which did not deceive him) sending extracts from Tennyson's 'Maud' which included the words:

> O let the solid ground
>   Not fail beneath my feet
> Before my life has found
>   What some have found so sweet
>
> Before I am quite quite sure
>   That there is none to love me

He told me that he had been greatly touched and had found the words 'particularly apt'. And on top of this I had to come with my tale about David. 'I should have been really angry if you hadn't told me,' Garrow said, 'and I want to give the next lesson.' This time we went alone to a small hotel on the Dorset coast. It was not a success. It poured with rain and a wet cold mist hid the sea. The contrast to the expressions of love I had been receiving from David was very painful and I went out by myself and wept and wept while Garrow read the newspaper. 'Obviously I am no use to you,' he said. 'I only make you cry.' He appeared to have no idea why.

I was finishing breakfast on Monday morning, 14th December 1931, when the telephone rang. It was Evelyn: 'Oh Bay. Have you seen the papers? It's terrible. Garrow has been killed.' I knew that he had been learning to fly, and once or twice, including that very weekend, he had asked me to go with him, saying that he would send me up with an instructor. The newspaper account said that he had been flying solo and practising spins. He had successfully completed one from 2,000 feet but a minute or two later had gone into another and crashed straight to earth.

I could feel the tears physically in my heart as well as in my eyes and I had the sensation that everything feminine in me was drying up. 'Everything has smashed,' I told my diary. 'Felt it was a turning point in my life between youth and middle-age, making me permanently unmarried and childless.' I sent a message to the office that I was ill and fled with Mum to spend the day with Bimbi, who was now living in the country near Epsom. On the journey, I told Mum I had slept with Garrow 'as I felt that in her place I shouldn't want to feel my child had missed perhaps finally one of the most important experiences'. That night I dreamt that Garrow and Robin had both been in an aeroplane accident and that Robin came in with his head all bandaged up and said that Garrow too had been saved. 'He has a beautiful face,' he said.

I learnt then how shatteringly self-absorbed and selfish acute personal sorrow can make you. In the first fury of my grief my one thought was to get to Broughton and Maudy. I had to be reminded by Mum not to let Mona feel that her devotion took second place. Of course it didn't; her quiet unquestioning,

wholly selfless support and companionship whenever she sensed
that I wanted it, was all important and, in retrospect, painfully
touching. Writing about me to Maudy she said: 'There is so very
little one can do for people when they are unhappy except be there
and watch all the time how one can save them something or keep
them interested. . . .' I realise only now that I probably hurt my
mother too. They both wrote to Maudy who put their letters in an
envelope marked 'Keep re Bay Dec/31'. I have them now and it has
been sadly touching to me to read them for the first time: Mona
thinking only of how she can look after me on the winter holiday
we are to take together – and Mum writing that 'I loved him like a
real son and always expected it to come to that – so full of life
though doubtful how best to live . . . if only they could have
come together on this earth. How vain it seems sometimes to
speak of the hereafter when it's the dear eyes and hands and hair
that we love. . . . It seems as if it was not for nothing those long
uncontrollable sobbings she had as a baby before she could even
speak. . . .'

My instinct in sorrow has always been to write about it – to try to
'write out' my calamity. Is it the same with other people I wonder?
In later life, on the deaths of my brother and my husband, I tried to
put my grief into verse; on Garrow's death, I wrote down every
incident I could remember of our years together and tried to turn
my feelings into words. But: 'What's the use even of remembering, when it is NEVER? The sudden door shut by death is so not a part
of anything else we experience. At times it is difficult to realise he
was ever alive and I'm terrified because I don't seem to mind
enough. And next it doesn't seem possible that anything so terrible
could have happened to me – that the personality I depend on most
in my own generation should have just gone. The only thing is to
believe in destiny; it can't just be an accident.'

Uncle Chin had written in the same vein: 'One can only cling to
the belief that even accidents of this sort have their meaning,' but
David Garnett, who had often been Garrow's companion in
taking flying lessons, allowed no such comfort: 'I don't feel there
was any fitness in his death', he said. 'I wanted to warn him not to
experiment in the air as I knew he was doing but . . . it seemed too
much like coming the heavy father.'

As I went over each moment together, there was a desperate sadness in the remembrance that I had refused to go to bed with him on what turned out to be the last evening we spent together. 'Is there any special reason,' he asked, 'or have you just decided I am a hopeless person?' 'No,' I said. 'There's nothing permanent or special about it. It's just that I don't feel like it.' He accepted that but 'At least let's bath together,' he said and when I refused – 'Pig. Why not?' My excuse had not been wholly ingenuous. I still did not want a relationship of sex without marriage to become permanent: 'I don't want to be that kind of person,' I told him. And so from time to time I made resolutions not to yield on a particular occasion and this had been one such. I was acting a part – the old, old, woman's part of the spider and the fly. I don't see how he was supposed to know. The following Sunday I was already planning, as I took the train back to London from my weekend at Broughton, how soon I could sleep with him again: 'Thought of calling in on him that evening but decided not; never liked to interrupt him or phone him unexpectedly for fear of disturbing him with some woman.' – But of course by then he was dead.

I had another reason for refusing him – in retrospect even less acceptable – that I wanted to avoid giving pain to David with whom my affair had continued all through this year. I had never hidden the fact from Garrow, any more than he had hidden his continuing involvements from me. On Garrow's death I lost completely and immediately all interest in David both physically and emotionally. This is not to say that the emotion I had felt was not love. I have learned that more than one love can exist at the same time between men and women, just as can other forms of human love – for mother, siblings, friends. Why not? A verse from a poem by Edna St Vincent Millay seems to me to say all that needs to be said about this love of mine for David.

> After all, my erstwhile dear,
> My no longer cherished,
> Need we say it was not love,
> Now that love is perished?

Reading my account of the last weeks of that year, it seems very clear that by then Garrow's feelings for me had come pretty near to love. He took every opportunity to demonstrate before his friends what Jane Austen would have called 'the particularity of his feelings towards me' and he even brought himself once to go as far as the unfinished sentence, 'You know that if only I could get rid of my knots. . . .' But I did not allow myself to draw the conclusion I longed for at the time, or even on his death. I was determined not to claim for myself (or *from* my family) the sympathy due, as it were, to a *grande passion*. But, judging by the letters I received, my family and friends were not so deceived as I was about my feelings.

Uncle Will said two wise things in his letter. The first was that I should find someday 'that what is of most value in life is not the love one can inspire in others but how much love one is capable of giving'. The second was a quote from George Meredith who 'says somewhere a compensation for misfortune is that "one gathers the worthiest around one"'. The first is a lesson I learned only as death reduced the wealth of love poured on my fortunate head. The second was true at once, for it brought me Francis's understanding sympathy. David had added to our estrangement by taking me at my word and saying how much worse it would have been for me if I had been in love with Garrow. Francis comforted me by showing me in every way that Garrow's friends looked on me as chief mourner: he said that he and Vera would leave it to me to decide whether they went to the funeral; he kept me company during the time of the cremation; he told me that 'everyone' agreed that Garrow had been 'much better' this last year and 'I put this down to you'.

Francis and Vera drove me to the funeral which was at Ash in Kent. What I remember about it are trivialities like the specially delicious egg sandwiches they had brought for lunch and the large black Daimler big enough to hold David Garnett and Barbara (Garrow's other girl friend at that time) as well as the three of us. But this is my diary account:

> Sun shining, a churchyard on a hill, the ground falling away from it; otherwise everything G had always tried to avoid (family and religion) and I couldn't make the connection between it and G. Wanted some of his real friends to be there with him as well as his family – though of course don't believe he was there. . . . Shan't soon forget the look of real sympathy

that Vera gave me. Thought how futile popular morals are, according to which G behaved abominably. There were we three, Vera, Barbara and me, with all of whom G had slept and all felt we had lost perhaps the most worth-while person we'd known. And the sleeping was, as he always maintained, merely a part of a relationship, not a thing for one person only.

That evening we went to 'the Meynell's' house in Gordon Square for dinner and Francis talked to me about Garrow who, he said, had been his chief male friend and had remained such even when he had been jealous of him over Vera. Their friendship had been he said 'only deepened by knowing the same women'.

Christmas came only a fortnight later. I spent it in a family party at winter sports in Austria and found that the activity and the need to contribute to the success of the holiday for the others helped for the time to damp down my grief. Francis told me that the Meynell Christmas party at Toppesfield had been over-shadowed by Garrow's death and that Vera had said – 'any of our visitors could have been spared; there would at once have been a million others to take his place. . . .'

It is possible, even probable, that but for my life-opening friendship with Garrow, I should have kept the attitudes and conventions of my upbringing and generation. I wonder if Francis and I would then have 'recognised' each other.

Verses of the poem Francis wrote for Garrow seem the right ending for this chapter.

The Palace at Spalato; in memory of G. T.

Like weeds the hovels grow against this wall
Once ring and finger of far-reaching Rome.
Beggars and builders in the long interval
Have filched and fumbled away great Caesar's home . . .

. . . You other city, dust that was my friend –
Of all the principalities and powers
Which your rich senses lorded, there's an end:
Scarcely the name of the city now endures.

Before the last defences break and rust
I make this tenement of your dear dust.

8

Young Mandarin

'Now, Miss Kilroy,' asked Mr Leak. 'Do you remember the story of Puss-in-Boots?'

As Mr Leak was the rather solemn head of our Statistical Department, I found the question a bit odd but agreed that I did remember that Puss-in-Boots was the companion of Dick Whittington, who became Lord Mayor of London.

'And of course,' continued Mr Leak, 'you are familiar with the United Kingdom Trade Returns?'

'Yes,' I said surprised at the sudden change of subject. I did indeed know those great tomes with their dark blue paper covers that recorded the value and quantity of all goods imported and exported each year. I had spent many hours studying them for my Safeguarding Committees.

'Well now,' and my questioner leant forward to deliver, as it were, his *coup de grace* –

'You may also remember that Puss-in-Boots was given a bag of jewels as a reward for getting rid of a plague of rats in a far country. What I want you to tell me, is how those jewels would have been dealt with today in the Trade Returns?'

The occasion was a Promotions Board at which my suitability for promotion to the rank of principal was being judged by three senior colleagues, two principals and an assistant secretary as Chairman, who was this same Mr Leak; he looked every inch the statistician, with gold-rimmed spectacles, and the pale complexion of someone who hasn't much time to be out-of-doors. One of the two principals was Gilmour Jenkins* who later became a friend. His great interest outside the office was singing. The other was a brilliant chess-player in his spare time.

*Later Sir Gilmour Jenkins, and head of the Ministry of Transport.

As for the question, I couldn't decide – and I still can't – what the right answer was. I realised that Puss's jewels were no ordinary import to be included under 'Imports: Raw Materials or Semi-manufactured goods', sub-heading – 'Precious Stones'. Mr Leak may well have hoped that I would say this was not strictly trade at all and so did not belong in the Trade Returns; but I did not think of that. So, I simply said lamely that I did not know.

'No, you didn't do very well on that,' agreed Jenkins. But evidently I did well enough on other questions, since my promotion followed on 19th May 1932.

In the aftermath of Garrow's death, my mother had written to Maudy asking her to spend some time in London to help comfort me as she felt I should find it hard to get back to the humdrum of work 'in which at present she has lost all zest'. But in this she was wrong. I found that the old adage 'Men must work and women must weep' was quite true for me – a surrogate man for this purpose. The office meant company, before whom I must put on a face, as well as occupation that absolutely demanded thought. I found then, as all my life, that work, people and interests, unconnected with the source of grief, are healers no less powerful than time.

However, my very full private life must sometimes have interfered with my work and my diary shows I had taken myself to task about it, so when in 1932 the warning came that I 'burn the candle at both ends' to the detriment of my work, my first instinct was to say that 'I quite understood'. My next to defend myself: 'I do my work to support my private life and not for the sake of the work,' I said angrily. I knew that I was being disingenuous. I had to earn my living since I had no private income and most of the time I enjoyed the work for its own sake and had a strong sense of duty about it. The adult reality of my childhood ambition to spend my working life 'sitting behind a desk' had not disappointed me.

Some weeks later, the authorities really frightened me by hinting that at the end of my private-secretaryship I might be sent back to a department without being promoted. This would have been tantamount to being 'passed over' for promotion. Next day, more alarming still, I was sent for by Sir Horace Hamilton, the permanent secretary, that is the Civil Service head of the

Board of Trade. 'H.P.H. sent for me to explain that I am near promotion but not fit for it unless I have more departmental experience. Couldn't but agree and only got annoyed when I began to think about it later.'

Urged on by Mona and by supportive well-wishers at the Board, I asked for another interview with the great man: 'Ominous and terrifying interview. Think I had made a good impression yesterday and spoilt it today and nothing gained.' But I was wrong. Those interviews must have convinced my permanent secretary that I should at least be given the chance of going before that Promotions Board.

I must explain here that promotions to the rank of principal were also made from the executive grade. Even in my day, the British Civil Service was not the 'elitist' service it appeared from the outside. Yes, it had complete career structures in the various grades based on examination – in the Administrative for university graduates like me, in the Executive for eighteen-year-old secondary school leavers and in the Clerical for others. But there was always provision for class-to-class promotion on merit. As early as the Thirties, upwards of half the administrative class in the Board of Trade consisted of colleagues promoted from the executive and clerical grades: I have already mentioned our (Sir) William Palmer as being one of these; examples from other departments were the late Sir Horace Wilson (in the Ministry of Labour) and the late Sir Arthur Street (in the Ministry of Agriculture) both promoted from the executive and both heads of departments. The executive and clerical examinations were opened to women some considerable time earlier.

I suspect that promotion would have been a foregone conclusion for a man in my place. The argument that I had not had enough departmental experience was really a nonsense for I had been a number of years in the I and M Department where I had carried considerable responsibility with my two public Committees, and Mr Hutchinson, my boss during that time, had made it quite clear to me that he gave me high marks. My subsequent private-secretaryships were formal indications of official approval. I only had to nag a little to get fair treatment because I was a woman. I enjoyed being a pioneer but also took

Mum, high up amongst the mountains where she was happiest, with Mona, circa 1929

Garrow Tomlin and self during our Salcombe camp in 1929

it very much as a matter of course – of being born in the right year – and did not flatter myself that it indicated any exceptional merit on my part.

Brought up in feminist families and armed (I now realise) with the self-confidence of the English middle-class 'Oxbridge' graduate, both Evelyn and I simply assumed that we should get the equality that the job promised. That very assumption may have influenced our reception and treatment. Maybe our looks helped too. We were certainly not at all like the then popular picture of a 'blue-stocking'. The treatment we received was in the best fair-minded traditions of the Civil Service. The Civil Service was in the forefront of providing equality of opportunity for women university graduates in the years between the wars.

However, our male colleagues did show considerable generosity of spirit in those early days. I was never made aware of any objections or difficulties they may have felt about working with me on a basis of equality. Evelyn received the same scrupulously fair and equal treatment but one of her colleagues did confess to her that he could not conceive of serving under a woman and would certainly 'not be able to tell his wife' if he ever had to. 'In any case,' he said, 'what do you think you're doing here? A pretty girl like you wasting your time? You'll never get anywhere.' Evelyn's reply – 'Me? I'm going to be permanent secretary' – surprised herself, and was met with wholly disbelieving laughter.

In the circumstances, my permanent secretary was perhaps not to be blamed for a few weeks' hesitation in the role of pioneer to which Government policy had committed him, before he took the step of extending the frontiers of the top ranks of the Service to a woman. For in May 1932 I was the first woman ever to be promoted a principal in the Board of Trade and also was the first in the whole Civil Service from among examination entrants. The event rated a mention in *The Times*:

> Miss Kilroy, who chose logic as one of her subjects at her examination in 1925, has been promoted to be Principal in the Board of Trade. . . . The highest appointments are open to women successful in this examination. A woman can fill Sir Warren Fisher's place as Permanent Secretary of the Treasury, or become Permanent Secretary of the Board of Trade.

Few women had been promoted to the rank of principal before me, mainly in the Ministry of Labour. But they had reached this rank late in their careers with little prospect of going further, whereas my promotion came at the beginning of my career.

I now earned £740 a year, more than double my salary as an A.P., and I felt rich. As well as my salary I had £50 a year from £1000 debentures in R. Greg and Co given to each of us by Axie years earlier with freedom to spend the income but not the capital without his consent. My first act on promotion was to give a party; my second to buy a car. (Because few people had cars in those days, there was always room for me to park in the area reserved for the cars of officials). I regret that my diary is silent about my party but I remember that it took the form of a dinner-dance at the Savoy and I am sure that all available sisters and their partners were there, and, of course, Francis and Evelyn. This was the only occasion on which I reached a rung of the Civil Service ladder before Evelyn and she got a joking card from our mutual friend Dick Plummer: 'Poor old Evie! Never mind. Your turn next.' Thereafter, it was I who got the postcards.

I watched the economic and political upheaval of 1931 with the detachment of the bureaucrat who must serve equally any party in power, and also with the 'house' interest of those who see the changes from the inside. I had no expectation that it would affect me personally but it did, for my first appointment as a principal was in connection with the foreign trade negotiations that followed our introduction of an import tariff in 1931.

My detachment did not spell lack of interest. I had supported the Labour Government and then voted for Ramsay Macdonald's National Government. After hearing his election broadcast, I write that 'I should have no doubt now about following his lead . . . Reasonable to prop up the house, before remodelling it. But would it ever be possible to remodel it when it is in good repair?' My early interest in politics had waned while I was at Oxford and I had left university with the simple philosophical concept that the aim of national policy should be 'the greatest happiness of the greatest number'. I seem to have been shockingly insensitive to the miseries of the depression of the Twenties, and the General Strike of 1926 had filled me with a real sense of outrage because it was an attack on Parliamentary democracy. But by 1929 when for the first time women had the vote on the same terms as men, I was a Labour supporter though commenting in my diary that 'it would be better to wait till the country is a bit richer before making socialist experiments'. There happened to be no Labour candidate in our constituency, for that election so Mona and I had voted for the breakaway Conservative who had been dropped as official candidate because he had been divorced – 'Ridiculous,' said I.

Many discussions with Garrow and John Macmurray and with David, whose views were openly revolutionary, had since drawn me leftwards though I was highly resistant (then as now) to argument by exaggeration and always inclined to moderation 'in John's eyes nothing the Labour Government does or doesn't do is wrong', I exclaim in exasperation, in October 1929. In an argument with Garrow two years later, 'got a bit annoyed because he will say that *all* politicians are unfit for their job and not honest'.

I had been an A.P. for six and a half years when I was promoted, but some of my older colleagues who (like Gilmour Jenkins) had entered through the Reconstruction examination at the end of the First World War, had had to wait even longer because there was little growth in the work of the Department while we remained the Free Trade country we had been since the Repeal of the Corn Laws in 1843. It was the economic crisis of 1931 which resulted in the abandonment of that policy and so caused a big increase in the work of the Board of Trade, which had to make preparations for negotiating Trade Agreements containing mutually acceptable import tariffs, with every important trading country.

The full title of my new department was 'Commercial Relations and Treaties Department' but it was always called C.R.T. It was in charge of all Government-to-Government policy on commercial and trade relations and of the negotiations of any treaties about trade – a job normally done in other countries by their Foreign Office. So it fell to this department to undertake the negotiations for the Trade Agreements we were now to embark upon. There were three other principals in C.R.T. including (I was glad to find) my friend Gilmour Jenkins.

It was the normal custom then for officers of principal rank to have a room to themselves, but we four all sat in one large room. At once a small problem arose. We took it in turns for one of us usually to stay late at the end of the day to sign all the letters which did not need the signature of the head of the department. Official letters still began 'I am directed by the Board of Trade to say. . . .' and ended 'I am, Sir, your obedient servant'. There was no problem there. But what of the many letters exchanged between colleagues, or with individuals outside the Service who were known well enough for the 'Mr' to be dropped? In those days it was the custom for gentlemen (and of course all senior officers were gentlemen!) to address each other by their surname without the Mr (as in public school of course); no one used Christian names then except in their private lives. Inevitably, I fell into the habit of dropping the Mr too, so in my memory of colleagues, they are always just 'Jenkins', 'Elliot' or 'Hutchinson'. When it came to signing letters I continued the same policy; otherwise the typing pool would have had to alter all personal letters when I was to be the signatory. I myself was never addressed by surname alone but no one used my Christian name. I was either Miss Kilroy or 'A.K.'

I must explain, for those who may be interested, that the import tariffs introduced by the National Government in November 1931 subsequently applied to all manufactured goods imported from foreign countries, but goods from the Commonwealth remained duty free. So foreign countries had an interest in obtaining reductions in duties where their manufacturers were in competition with Commonwealth goods, as well as where they competed with the home product. The overall plan was to make a series of bilateral agreements with our foreign trading partners, in which we would exchange tariff advantages on goods of most interest in the trade of each. It followed that a lot of preliminary work had to be done by officials before we could decide what to ask for and what to give.

The cotton industry, still 'King Cotton' and one of our major industries, would be chief candidate for concessions and Raymond Streat, who was then Secretary of the Manchester Chamber of Commerce, has left a vivid description in the diary he kept during these years, * of the many discussions he had with

---

*Now published by Manchester University Press.

the Board of Trade at this time and so, incidentally, of the kind and amount of work which fell on its officials:

> Every foreign tariff has to be scrutinised in the greatest detail and each home industry asked for its views. The officers are almost overwhelmed. Extra officials are being drafted in. Last Thursday I found for the first time, a woman official with executive responsibility – a mere girl, *Miss Kilroy*, who has been given charge of Sweden.

For, new-fledged principal that I was, I had been given the responsibility of preparing for the negotiations for our Trade Agreement with Sweden – of course under the general supervision of my assistant secretary. So now I had to become thoroughly acquainted with the Swedish tariff, prepare notes for discussions with British industries which were seeking tariff changes in Sweden, talk to my old department (I. & M.) who would be responsible for advising about what changes might be made in our tariffs in return, and arrange for the Dominions and Colonial Offices and the India Office to be given the opportunity to comment on the effect upon Commonwealth trade of any changes we might offer.

At my first meeting with Raymond Streat to discuss what he called 'the cotton schedules' (which listed the concessions Lancashire wanted in Scandinavia) we must also have talked about the problem of m.f.n. which his diary shows to have been greatly exercising his mind. This was a principle very dear to the heart of the Board of Trade and over many years it had been enshrined in all our commercial treaties. Under it any country that we had normal trading relations with could claim treatment for their exports as good as that given to the *most favoured nation*. It followed that changes agreed in the forthcoming negotiations would apply to the goods of all other countries which had m.f.n. Bewailing what he saw as the 'closed minds of officials to any suggestion that m.f.n. may no longer be the desirable sheet anchor of British policy', Streat writes despairingly (November 1932) that: 'over it all looms the most-favoured-nation clause. What Sweden gives to us she must give to thirty other countries and vice versa. . . . The officials are so thronged, it is perhaps unfair to criticise but whether consciously or otherwise, these men are forming a policy of international commerical relationships which will be the basis of England's foreign trade for, shall we say, the next decade or two. . . .'

I am sure that he was right about the conviction of the Board of Trade officials on the value of m.f.n.; and essentially that they remained wedded to a basic belief in the merits and almost moral rightness of free trade. But he was wrong in thinking that we should get nothing out of the negotiations. In practice, bargains were possible because the concessions asked for would be those calculated to give most benefit to the country that was prepared to pay for them by giving concessions in return. Sweden might get a reduction in the British import duty on ball-bearings, knowing that few were made except in Sweden; and in exchange, she might agree to reduce the duty on types of cotton yarn or cloth that were chiefly made in Lancashire.

Raymond Streat and I were to meet often in the future and to become personal friends. Whenever I went to Manchester on official business (which was as often as possible because I liked to see problems on the ground) I would stay with him and his wife Doris and would benefit from his wide knowledge of Lancashire and its industries. He had a pleasing way of talking and a gentle voice with a slight north-country accent. I realise now that I enjoyed merely listening to him because his speech was like uncle Will's with the short 'a' for 'bath' and 'path'.

His diaries include percipient comments on a number of the men under whom I worked: Sir Henry Fountain (our deputy secretary) discussing tariffs in China and Egypt, 'dismal as usual about everything; but our duty to put up a show of doing something'; and Sir Horace Wilson (then Chief Industrial Adviser to the Treasury) approached about the cotton industry's problems of redundant machinery, saying 'Let's see whether we can't do something which will enable our masters to make progress.' – a remark which delighted me as I have always divided civil servants between the 'doers' and the 'non-doers'. Horace Wilson became notorious to our generation as one of Churchill's 'guilty men' but I have always felt the judgement to be very unfair. It was not his fault that he was called on to be Neville Chamberlain's personal adviser in a sphere of policy about which he had no previous knowledge or experience of any kind – and on the reaction to Hitler of all things. His whole training, knowledge and excellence had been in the sphere of conciliation in the Ministry of Labour and the Board of Trade.

It is fortunate for future economic historians that Raymond Streat recorded as much as he did in his diaries since I find that scarcely any C.R.T. files survive in the Public Record Office. I too have become for this reason a one-person historical record. The texts of the Trade Agreements survive, since they were published but there are no departmental policy files relating to them.

So it is from Streat's diaries and not from public records that I learn that it was the considered strategy of the Board of Trade to negotiate first with countries like the Scandinavians which had fairly low tariffs and only later with high tariff countries; that by the end of 1932, negotiations had opened in London simultaneously with Sweden, Norway and Denmark; and that by the end of the following year, we were negotiating with seven other European countries and with Argentina. Included in this total were Finland and the three Baltic States, Latvia, Estonia and Lithuania, which were then independent States. When the Swedish negotiations were complete, I was given similar responsibilities for Finland.

We principals were given a good deal of responsibility for our particular country. The department would never have got through the work otherwise; before I had been a full four months in the department, I was sufficiently trusted to be sent alone 'to discuss Sweden' with Sir Henry Fountain. Though the formal hours of work were absurdly short in those pre-war days – ten to five – you actually worked as long as was necessary and most senior officers (I included) regularly stayed at their desks long after the official hours and also took work home. 'I'm afraid I shall have much less time now for our lunches and evenings together,' I warned Francis.

Only six months elapsed between my appointment to C.R.T. and the opening of the negotiations with Sweden. Then it became my job to do the 'dog'sbody' work of arranging the meetings, seeing that everyone had the documents they should have, that the results of each day's discussions were recorded and that consultations were arranged with officials and/or the representatives of our industries, where points had been raised by the Swedish delegation which needed further consideration before the next day's discussions. The meetings were held in the large Board of Trade Conference Room with its long windows looking out on to Parliament Square. The Swedish delegation, headed by Björn Prytz, sat on one side of the conference table with their backs to the windows. For the first meeting the chair was taken by Sir Henry Fountain but often my assistant secretary would have been in the chair.

The Foreign Office were involved only if some point of protocol arose, but they were usually represented, and always by a charming character called Sir Ashton Gwatkin. He had started his official life in the Consular Service but at this time he was head of the first ever Economic Division of the Foreign Office. I know him to have been a man of considerable charm and intellect – it was rumoured that he spoke Japanese fluently enough to be able to write melodramas in Japanese – but he had nothing to contribute to our discussions and could have had little interest in them. With his very pale complexion and prominent nose he seemed to me to have a remarkable physical resemblance to the White Knight in *Alice-in-Wonderland* and I always thought of him as surveying our discussions with quiet humour, metaphorically from his horse.

'It has come to our notice that you have an unpalatable vegetable which you call a "Swede",' said Mr Prytz, opening the negotiations. 'You will understand I am sure, Sir Henry, how insulting this is to us. I hope I may have an undertaking that this despised vegetable will be renamed.'

I can see him now in my mind's eye, his shoulders shaking with laughter even before he could get his words out, and then getting down with hardly a pause to serious business.

He told me after the negotiations were over, that he had decided at the outset that we should have to be given something on coal and cotton, and had conducted the negotiations from the start on this basis. He was quite right in assuming that these were our priorities. Perhaps cotton goods came first with us, but he was to find that we were also very anxious to obtain a lower tariff for the small cars which were the chief product of our young motor car industry; we wanted them to have a tariff advantage over the large cars in which the United States industry was becoming predominant.

After the first few days of our negotiations, all the members of our delegation (including me, the most junior) were invited to a reception at the Swedish Legation. I was shocked to find that there were no plans for us to return their hospitality. At the time, there was no provision for entertainment allowances or expense accounts in the Home Civil Service. I decided to do my part at least, for the honour of the department. So, I boldly invited Mr Prytz to lunch with me at The Ivy Restaurant, then one of the best in London. I was still feeling rich after my so recent promotion. It happened that our discussions on this morning had been about our request for a reduced duty on small cars and that Mr Prytz had been arguing that there would be no point in this because small cars were unsuitable for Swedish roads. I took him to lunch in my small British car and unfortunately the engine stalled half-way up St James's Street. 'Of course,' he said, as he struggled to crank it (it had no self-starter), 'we do not have precipices like this in Sweden!'

This was a joke after his own heart but I certainly did not appreciate it as much as he did. I was distinctly anxious about having invited him to lunch rather than my opposite number at the bottom of the Swedish delegation. Fortunately for my peace of mind, I did not know that, as well as leading for his country in these negotiations, Prytz was one of the richest and most influential men in Sweden. Needless to say, he did not for a moment let me see how much more at home he was at The Ivy than I was.

Out of this lunch a life-long friendship grew between Björn Prytz and me. I think he was attracted to me because I was a wholly strange phenomenon to him, a young woman who talked eagerly and with some knowledge about the business world of men, but who was good-looking and attractive in a feminine way and yet never made up her face or appeared to have any of the concern about dress and appearance that he expected in women – and came out to lunch with him straight from her office desk as a man might have done. 'I like your inky fingers,' he said. And Björn was quite as strange a phenomenon to me as I was to him. His talk about the business world in which he was so obviously pre-eminent, excited me. And I was fascinated by what I can only call the glamour of his personality and of our rare meetings when he happened to be in London and would take me out to dine and dance; he would pay the bill with one – or even two – of those large old-fashioned five-pound notes printed on thin rag paper, and we seem in retrospect always to have had pink champagne.

On one of these evenings, I happened to tell Björn that Mona and I were planning to hire a boat and spend a sailing holiday on the Norwegian Fjords that summer.

'Why don't you come to Sweden and sail up the coast to Oslo?' he said. 'It is a lovely area. I can make enquiries for you about a boat and help you to work out a route and give you introductions too.'

Who would say no to such a proposition? We forgot that we had no practical knowledge of sailing. Ever since, as children, we had fantasised about the Girl's Navy and listened at Salcombe to our uncles reading to us that classic of sailing and adventure, *The Riddle of the Sands*, we had built castles-in-the-air about sailing holidays. But we had not learnt to sail as children and our only adult experience had been rare occasions on the Broads or the River Waveney at Geldeston. Neither of us had any experience or knowledge of sailing or navigation at sea and the third member of the party (an architect friend called Guy Morgan) was equally ignorant. Björn probably sensed something of this. At any rate he saw to it that we were not put to the test, for when we arrived in Gothenburg on a blustery July morning, we were staggered to have Björn point out to us as 'ours' a large yacht which even our ignorant eyes could see would need a professional crew to run it.

'It's quite all right,' he said. 'There won't be anything for you to pay. This boat has been lent to me by a business friend and isn't costing me anything either.'

I don't think it occurred to us not to accept his story at its face value then but we had really no choice for the S.S.S. *Mariska* was a very long way out of our financial class in life: she had a crew of four, had been built for racing at Cowes and was, as our log of the trip records, 'quite the grandest yacht in those waters'. It was a wholly personal arrangement between Björn and me having no relation to our official connection, which in any case had ceased months earlier, but I tremble to think what *Private Eye* would have made of it today.

I still have the log of that trip, written by each of us in turn. Guy was bowled over by his first sight of 'the light and fresh touch of Swedish architecture which seems to have missed the Victorian industrial age of cast-iron band-stands and back-to-back houses'. And we were all charmed by Ainö, our hostess, who welcomed us to the luxury of the Prytz house in Gothenburg and to their equally luxurious island house at Rösenlund. And I was given a formal dinner at which Björn made a speech of welcome thanking me 'for services to Anglo-Swedish trade'.

'Our host and hostess appear to have everything this world can offer' wrote Guy. 'Both are young still and extremely attractive, as finished as their surroundings and altogether most lovable.'

He was wrong about Björn's age. Ainö Prytz was about my age and very pretty and chic; Prytz was handsome with a prominent 'beaky' nose, and a high forehead but he was already slightly balding with hair grey to white and at this time his age was nearer fifty than forty.

The trip itself was wholly planned and provisioned by Björn. Unfortunately, the wine he had chosen in consultation with Mona disappeared mysteriously after the first evening; we assumed that it had been unloaded – or drunk – by the crew while we were at Rösenlund. But the trip was idyllic in every other way: the sea was scattered with small islands, some tiny and smooth like whales, planted alone in the midst of the sea, others with small villages that looked as if plastered to the rock, where brown children waved and drying fish hung all around. We learned about the courtesies of yachting: as the largest yacht in these waters, we did not wave until waved to, and we did not accept as equals 'yachts with motors and a false parade of sail'.

Wherever we went, introductions to Prytz's friends went before us, and twice he joined us himself, sailing after us with a friend who had a yacht only a little less grand and fast than ours; and at Oslo he came by seaplane like the dashing gentleman in today's advertisements who arrives by hang-glider with a box of chocolates.

We sailed part-way back from Oslo with Björn before taking a train to Stockholm and, during lazy hours at sea, I learned something of his personal story. Though he carried his wealth with the naturalness of one born to it, he had not been rich in his youth and had indeed known real poverty; in the days before the First World War, he had found that London was the worst of the three great cities – New York, London and Paris – to be poor in. His mother had been English and he had been at Dulwich school when, at the age of fifteen, he had had to leave on the death of his father. He had found many ways of making a living from sardine-packing in Portugal to strolling-player in the United States and it was from these difficult beginnings that he had pulled himself up to be the leading industrialist in Sweden, head of S.K.F. (the largest ball-bearing concern) and also of the Swedish Match cartel which owned or controlled the match industries of all Europe, including Bryant & May. When Kreuger (the Swedish industrialist who had built up the international match cartel) had shot himself in 1932 leaving huge public debts and 'a network of fraud and forgery', it had been Prytz whom the Swedish Government had called in to sort out the mess. On the day in 1937 that he was able to boast that he had managed to pay off every one of Kreuger's debts, he gave me a lovely French ring, which he said was 'paste'. It is a treasured possession and is not paste.

There was perhaps a sense in which I – and Mona too – were just a little 'in love' with Björn in the heady atmosphere of that holiday, but it was his exciting personality and zest for life and the glamour of his position in national and international industry that fascinated us; there was no emotional depth or physical aspect to the relationship on our side. I ought of course to have realised that the same might not be true of Björn. At this time my relationship with my future husband Francis was paramount for me but I felt bound to dissemble about it in the circumstances of both my private and my official life and was too little aware of the misunderstanding that might be caused in others. Björn and Ainö were, I knew, recently married (he had absented himself from the trade negotiations for his wedding – a second marriage for him) and it simply did not occur to me that Ainö might be jealous. When she did not come with Björn to join us on the yacht I simply assumed that she didn't like sailing. So it was a considerable shock to find her less than welcoming when we went to see her before leaving for England.

Back at my desk I found that my sphere of work had been changed again: instead of the Scandinavian countries and the Baltic States, my job now was the British Colonies desk. This was no small assignment for it was really true then that 'the sun never set. . .'.

My new boss was Arnold Overton, then assistant secretary in charge of all British countries and South America, later to be our permanent secretary from 1941 to 1945. He was a rather reserved and private man with a mannerism, when thinking hard, of clutching at the hair on top of his head; a man of outstanding intellect and integrity and, with his staff, fair to a fault. There was an occasion when I had sent him a minute arguing against a view he had taken. 'What you're trying to say is that I've made a fool of myself, aren't you?' he said with such charm that neither of us was embarrassed.

On my first day back from holiday, Overton asked me to prepare a paper on Japanese competition with our exports of cotton cloth to the British Colonies: 'See if you can suggest changes in their tariffs that will give Lancashire advantages over Japan,' I hear him say. 'The President has promised a deputation from Manchester that we will make this study and if we can't come up with something on these lines, we may have to consider taking away Japan's m.f.n. on these goods and we don't at all want to do that.'

I learned from Nash (our textile expert in my old department) as well as from the reports of our Trade Commissioners that Japanese competition was keenest in Lancashire's traditional trade, the gaily coloured prints that were the normal wear of the colonial populations; it was said that sometimes they even copied Lancashire's designs. It didn't take me long to realise that the only way to help Lancashire would be by replacing the prevailing *ad valorem* duties (where the amount paid was based on the import price) by specific duties (so many pence a yard) which would mean that cheap Japanese cloth would pay as much duty as the more expensive Lancashire cloth. This of course would mean higher prices for the very poor indigenous populations.

There was a special problem in Africa where a series of 'Congo Basin Treaties' (which became quite old friends of mine) provided that the Imperial signatories – Britain, France, Belgium and Portugal – would not impose in their dependent territories any barriers to trade which favoured the trade of the Imperial power. These pacts could not be ended or altered because the signatories had failed to provide any clause allowing for it.

Taking all these considerations together, I wrote a memorandum which offered a wholly different approach to the problem. [Having set out these facts] I suggested that Lancashire should be persuaded to make an industry-to-industry approach to the Japanese to try to agree on voluntary market shares, instead of relying upon having her markets protected by tariffs. 'Surely,' I argued, 'there must be room for the products of both in the huge markets of the British Empire, without having to put up high protective tariff walls that will harm the indigenous populations?'

My memorandum was sent forward by Overton to Sir Henry Fountain and by him to the President, with the recommendation that, in view of the difficulties about tariff protection, my idea should be tried – and the President agreed.

Contrary to the condition of infighting and confusion so amusingly suggested in the T.V. serial *Yes, Minister*, the spheres of the two arms of Government, politicians and civil servants, are quite clear from the inside, and normally work smoothly together – or did in my day: policies are the sphere of the politician, administration of the bureaucrat; but it is a valuable and treasured role of the senior Civil Service to advise and suggest at points such as I have described (which must not of course run counter to the political strategy of the party in power) where the application of policy can verge on policy itself. These occasions are rare but very satisfying.

Sir Horace Wilson was asked to take charge of 'my' policy and I was instructed to arrange a meeting in his room at which there would be representatives of all the interested departments – the Colonial Office, the Ministry of Labour our own I & M and C.R.T. the Treasury and, inevitably, my 'White Knight', Sir Ashton Gwatkin, on his watching brief for the Foreign Office. Sir Horace Wilson was then Industrial Adviser to the Board of Trade and he had an imposing office on the prestigious second floor. At that meeting I was very much the most junior and I expected to have no part in it except to take a note, for Overton was there to speak for C.R.T. We assembled and waited for Horace Wilson to open the meeting and I was appalled to hear him say: 'I understand this policy is your idea, Miss Kilroy. Perhaps you would begin by outlining it for us and telling us how you suggest we should proceed?'

No record of this meeting survives in the Public Records Office among the few Board of Trade files of this period. All I have found there is one file dated September/October 1933 about a request to the Foreign Office from the Japanese Ambassador for a tariff truce in the British Colonies in order to create the best atmosphere for the industrial discussions. The reply (drafted by me and heavily amended by Overton) explains that we can give no absolute guarantee but 'will avoid for the time being, as far as practicable . . . any action . . . which might tend to prejudice the industrial discussions.' There is also a minute in which I say that I 'have explained to the F.O. that the forthcoming negotiations are industrial not governmental' so it is clear that 'my' policy is being referred to. Again, therefore, it is a matter of making bricks without straw, or rather history without documents, and once more I find myself to be a piece of living history.

I learn from Streat's diaries that Lancashire had been in pretty constant touch with its opposite numbers in Japan from 1931 onwards and also with India, so 'my' policy cannot have appeared as new to them as it seemed to the Board of Trade. However, following that first meeting with Horace Wilson, Manchester agreed to give the policy a try and there is the following note in Streat's diary for May 1933: 'Discussed with Miss Kilroy whether Runciman* should make a statement on the Anglo-Japanese talks. If so to what effect.'

A year later (January 1934) my diary describes a meeting at the India Office in which 'I agreed with them and had to argue with Overton who left it to me a good deal. He is straight from Manchester where they have had a regular gruelling on Japan, India etc.' I have no personal recollection of the outcome but Streat records that the discussions opened with visits both to Japan and India by a delegation from Lancashire, and that they

---

*He had replaced Cunliffe-Lister as President, subsequently Lord Swinton.

finally broke down in March 1934, after which the Government imposed quotas on Japanese imports into certain of the British Colonies.

So ended my first steps as an aspiring young mandarin.

9

Francis – The Early Years

In the two years since our first meeting in 1929, Francis and I had developed a mainly dancing friendship and, on my part at least, it was quite casual. I had been absorbed in working out my relationships with Garrow and with David – though David was enough awake to the danger from Francis to say earnestly to me 'there must not be three' – meaning himself, Garrow and Francis. He had tried to discourage me by denigrating Francis – 'a man, I have heard, of great but waning charm'. It had the reverse effect from the one he had hoped for. In any case, I knew that Francis had other feminine interests besides me and, for his part, he regarded me as Garrow's girl. 'He guessed,' he said, 'that I was in love with Garrow the first time we met,' and he had talked to Garrow of his growing feeling for me and received his 'blessing' – an arm across his shoulder – before he asked me out to dance the first time.

The relationship that now began to grow between us was different in almost all respects from the one I had had with Garrow. We didn't spend our time in discussion and argument or even very much in going to concerts or films, and when Francis read aloud, it would be poetry not prose. As often as possible we danced, usually at The Gargoyle, a club in Dean Street then run by David Tennant and his actress wife Hermione Baddeley, to which many Bloomsburyites belonged and which I joined too. It served lunches as well as dinners and it had the delightful extra of a dance floor on the roof for romantic summer nights. It was reached by the smallest of lifts – a crush for three – and the dance floor appeared to have no windows though the impression was of light because the walls were covered with small panes of glass. I should think it would have been a death trap in a fire.

Francis was as keen a dancer as I was – though it was one of our few differences of opinion that neither thought the other quite as good as we thought ourselves! Even the type of dance was different

– the hectic Charleston was out and the graceful gliding romantic One-step was in. We often dressed for the evening and might dine at an expensive restaurant like The Ivy, which Garrow and I never did. I noted at this time that 'I seem always to be a little drunk when I am out with Francis.' This was a new sensation. We hadn't acquired the aperitif habit at home and Garrow and I seldom drank more than one sherry. Out dancing we drank for thirst. The first time I actually got drunk was in December 1931, when I was nearing twenty-nine. I was out with David and had had two sherries and a glass of absinthe on an empty stomach.

Another big difference in my developing relationship with Francis was the large part played by games. Garrow had been very much a non-games player but Francis loved and excelled at all ball games with the one exception of golf – 'I don't like to hit a sitting ball!' he said. Cricket was his first love. He had captained at least three weekend teams, including his local village team at Toppesfield. And he never could pass a cricket match in the car without stopping to watch 'just one over'. At tennis, I was never as good as he was and was content if I didn't actually disgrace myself on the court; but Francis was a good player, about equal to Toto (our family star performer) and tennis was always to bulk large in our weekends and holidays.

Being town bred, Francis had no childhood knowledge of the outdoor activities that Garrow had been so good at and that I loved, like bathing, walking, camping, making fires and cooking in the open, but he made himself adapt to them and even enjoy them. 'The greatest impromptu picnic cook of all time', Evelyn called him. And he had the remarkable courage to learn to dive at the age of forty plus. Later, he was even to join us in cycling and camping holidays but never in one of the strenuous walking parties we sometimes arranged at weekends at this time.

Emotionally too, my relationship with Francis could not have been more different from my friendship with Garrow, for Francis never missed an opportunity to tell me that he loved me. 'I long to make you feel,' he said one evening. 'I would be satisfied if I could be the shaking of your arm while it gets hot-ache.' He was using a family idiom for the pain that one got at winter sports when fingers came back to warmth after having been very cold. 'That's very apt,' I said. 'I have felt half-dead since Garrow died but I expect I shall settle down to be an ordinary nice unmarried civil servant.' 'You can't,' he said. 'You've got dynamite under your heels.'

I knew that I was not ready yet to give love in return but I recognised my need for the permanence and support of his friendship, his kindness and gentleness and his thoughtfulness for me. On a typical evening in April my diary says, we went back to Gordon Square after dinner at The Ivy and dancing at The Gargoyle and he read poetry – 'by an American lady which seemed written specially for my case' and one of his own 'which seemed very good'. It was 'Tissue of Time' that I have always thought one of his best. But he became a little embarrassed about it with me because it had quite definitely been written to Vera.

I had not met Vera until just before Garrow's death in December 1931 when I had been invited to dinner for the first time at Gordon Square and had found her both beautiful and alarming: 'Felt increasingly terrified at having asked Francis to dinner at our flat especially as it became clear that it ought to be Vera too! She was looking very beautiful and was charming to me but I felt she was wondering all the time what Garrow could see in me. When she said she would come to dinner "if you want me", I became generally embarrassed and gauche and said "Yes, I would but our rooms are so small and full of furniture. . . ."'

That party had never happened because it had been arranged for the Monday after Garrow was killed; he of course was to have been of the company. Now, in the aftermath, I renewed the invitation. Vera had been noticeably kind and sympathetic and, to me, it was an added recommendation that I knew she and Garrow had been lovers. But when our mutual friend Barbara heard of my dinner invitation, her comment was: 'How brave. I have known the Meynells a long time but I have never dared to ask Vera to dinner.' It was, of course, a question of fools stepping in for I knew nothing then of Vera's having been for a while editor of *Vogue* or of her quick mind and the bitter tongue she could use on occasion, or of her reputation for not suffering fools gladly, especially if they were women. Nevertheless, I felt that the evening had been a success. 'Somehow being with Vera seems more like being with G than anything else except being alone outside,' I wrote. I even hoped that her baby son might possibly be Garrow's: 'Wouldn't it be wonderful if it was so?' I confided to my diary – 'When I saw him in his bath I noticed that his hair was fair and that he had a slightly underhung jaw [like Garrow's]'. I was wrong in my surmise and later of course I was far from wishing it. I was simply expressing my own deep and natural emotional longing for Garrow to be continued in the flesh. I was not looking at it at all from Vera's point of view – or Francis's, or considering that my 'hope' might imply a lack of integrity between Vera and Francis. For all I knew then, there could have been an understanding between them – or a genuine 'mistake' on Vera's part.

It is surprising but true that at this time I knew almost nothing of Francis's background and experience before we met, or of his international eminence as a book designer or of his Nonesuch Press. People in love are supposed to question each other endlessly about their lives before they met but it was not so with either of us. I suppose I was too selfishly absorbed with my grief and my growing feeling for Francis – and with my work during the day – to have thought to spare for his separate past; it was the present that concerned me. And Francis was too much in love and anxious to bring me the kind of comfort I most wanted – talk of Garrow – perhaps as well too modest, to talk of Nonesuch until I enquired.

Born in 1891, he was the youngest child of Alice Meynell and Wilfrid her husband, both eminent in their time in literature and journalism, and known too for their discovery of the poet Francis Thompson. Alice Meynell died in 1923, long before we met, but his father lived until after the war and he had one brother and three sisters. By his first wife, Hilda, who was a concert pianist of note, he had a daughter Cynthia, born in 1916. He had divorced Hilda in 1923 and he and Vera had married in 1925. Ben was their only child.

Both Alice and Wilfrid Meynell were Catholics. Like me, therefore, Francis was brought up as a Catholic but he kept his religion longer than I did. From the Catholic public school, Downside, he went to Trinity College, Dublin, but did not stay to get his degree owing to an entanglement of the heart from which his father rescued him by giving him a job at Burns and Oates, of which he was General Manager. Leaving there in 1916,

Francis established his own Pelican Press working in the offices of the *Daily Herald*, and in 1923 he and Vera, joined by David Garnett, started the famous Nonesuch Press.

I had taken it for granted when we met that Francis's politics would be Labour. I don't remember when I learned how fiery and left wing his youth had been – very much further to the left than mine ever was. He had supported the suffragettes, the militant wing of the Votes for Women movement, bravely speaking up for them as a lone voice at a meeting of traders in the Queen's Hall who had gathered to urge severe punishment for them; he had been a conscientious objector in the Great War and a propagandist against it and with Bertrand Russell had formed the No Conscription Fellowship; he had been a prominent member of the board of the *Daily Herald* and friend of George Lansbury and had had to resign in 1920 when it became known that he had smuggled Russian jewels into England partly to finance the Russian Trade Delegation in London and partly in the hope of using some of the money to finance the *Daily Herald*; and he (and Vera) had been active supporters of the General Strike in 1926 which from my belief in Parliamentary democracy I was strongly opposed to.

During his stormy Twenties, Francis developed his interest in good printing. It was an important part of his socialist faith – which was always more emotional than ideological – that art should not be confined to the few but should be for the many, that through the machine and in particular the printing machine, 'good design can enter into every home'.* As a designer of pages of the early *Herald* and through his own Pelican Press, he saw to it that the manifestos of socialist and pacifist faith in those early days were printed as elegantly and with as much care as later would be the books of his Nonesuch Press.

How is it that I resisted him? How is it that I didn't fall in love immediately? Partly, it took me a long time to recover the capacity to feel any deep emotion. But there were other reasons. I really didn't believe he loved me in a permanent way. 'I must tell

*From a lecture given by Francis to a socialist gathering towards the end of the Great War.

him I don't expect men to say that they love me' I had confided to
my diary as lately as April 1932. It seemed to me then quite
extraordinary and quite unlikely – it still does for that matter –
that Francis, with all his gifts, excitingly good-looking and
alarmingly sophisticated both in himself and in his circle of
friends, should choose *me* to love.

And then – and this was very important too – he was married.
According to my code and Mona's it was wrong to endanger a
marriage. I knew that, as Bloomsburyites, both he and Vera had
extra-marital affairs and it did not occur to me that Francis and I
could have more than just such a temporary affair, still less that
his marriage might break up; I did not know how near the rocks it
already was. Divorce had been unknown in my family and
somehow the idea of a second divorce seemed even more
unthinkable than a first. I remember saying jokingly to him –
'You can't go about having one marriage after another, you
know.'

In spite of what I had said about being an ordinary unmarried
civil servant I still hoped to marry. I was not yet reconciled to
having my aunt's prophecy come true. So I developed other
relationships. It is shaming to me now to remember that,
although I had no real feeling left for David, I might have said
'yes' if he had been ready and free to offer marriage, and that I
wanted him at least to say he still loved me – to prove that our
love had been real. Later that year I had a quite serious though
short-lived 'affair' with Wells Coates. I comfort myself when I
remember these doings, by the knowledge that Francis, for his
part, was having a serious relationship at this time with the
charming and beautiful Eleanor Singer, whom I later came to
know and admire.

I had met Wells Coates at a weekend party at 'Bradfields', the
Meynells' house at Toppesfield in Essex. It had been the first of
many weekends that I and Evelyn, and sometimes Mona or other
members of my family, were to spend all through the Thirties, in
that beautiful Essex farmhouse with its tile-floored entrance
hall flanked on both sides by Nonesuch books, its staircase that
was wide enough for three to go up it comfortably side by side,
its long living-room with the wide open fire, and polished
broad-beamed oak floor and refectory table that filled the

window end of the room. I was entranced by the atmosphere of happy freedom from convention within my own generation, of good talk and laughter, good food and drink, games of all sorts, and above all of *fun* that (as I was to find) Francis produced wherever he was.

This first time, Vera was hostess and the small Benedict was there, but it was quite in accordance with the Bloomsbury code that normally Vera should arrange to leave the field clear, once Francis's relationship with me was acknowledged.

Stephen and 'Att' (Mary) Potter and Dick and Beattie Plummer were also of the company, or staying near, on this first visit. Evelyn remembered the 'gales of laughter' that both Stephen and Dick could cause. There was always much tennis; there was ping-pong, at which both Francis and Stephen were brilliant performers and perpetual adversaries; and there was the 'roof game' which Francis had invented to be played on one particular roof at 'Bradfields', it was highly competitive and incredibly strenuous (rules, please note, are to be found in the *Weekend Book*) and it caused much exhaustion and at least one heart attack among Francis's friends over the years. Of the women players, Evelyn was certainly the most energetic. When the weather was right, we bathed in the natural pool that was fed by a spring and overhung by ancient willows. It was naked bathing of course – so incredibly much pleasanter physically than even the skimpiest of swimsuits – and naked sun-bathing too. On this first weekend I let my towel lie carelessly across my body. 'That's against the house rules,' said Francis, and flicked it off.

With Francis, as with Garrow, bathing was always naked if circumstances made it at all possible but it could produce amusing – or embarrassing – situations. One such was my first visit to the parent Meynell country home at Greatham in Sussex, then (as now) a kind of family country club with a tennis court, a lawn for croquet and a bathing pool. Francis had said: 'Let's go over and bathe at Greatham.' 'We haven't got our bathing suits with us,' we said. 'No matter,' said Francis. 'There's no one there except my father and he stays in the house.' It happened, however, that on that day Francis's father was entertaining the Bishop to lunch and that hearing sounds of enjoyment, they strolled down to watch the young people bathing. 'Splash!'

shouted Francis, and we all splashed and went on splashing until
Mr Meynell tactfully led the Bishop away, quietly chatting, as
though he had seen nothing unusual.

Our carriage door opened and Wells Coates put his head in. 'Any
room here?' he asked. It was the Saturday following that
Toppesfield weekend and Toto and I were sitting together in the
train to Newcastle where we were to board the S.S. *Meteor* for a
fortnight's cruise to the Norwegian Fjords.

It was typical of Wells that, having met me only once, he
should manage to get a ticket without a word to me, and appear
suddenly like a genie from a bottle. Naturally I was flattered as I
introduced him to Toto and made room for him in our carriage.
From that moment he ensured that we were a threesome, and we
were very quickly joined by Jack Rendle (later to be Toto's
husband) who had come on the trip with his mother and two
friends. The four of us danced, walked, played deck games and
went everywhere together.

In the unreal atmosphere of shipboard and this happy foursome my 'affair' with Wells flourished. His plans to design a boat
and sail it round the world reminded me of Garrow and I was
interested in his talk of the new architecture for which he became
justly famous. He was proud of the fact that he had been born in
Japan and he told me that the interiors of the rooms he designed
with their moveable screens to form temporary partitions which
could be changed according to need, his low tables and cushions
on the floor in place of chairs, reflected his early impressions of
Japan.

But back in England he and I found that we hadn't really much
in common apart from sex and the fun of the holiday, and it
wasn't long before it ended by mutual consent. 'There's no one to
hold a candle to G,' I told my diary in September 1932.

But there was, of course, for later that year Francis and I began
our serious relationship, though our first weekend away together
was so discouraging in every obvious way as to be funny. He had
borrowed a cottage from a friend and when we got there we
found that there were dirty plates in the sink, an unmade bed and
even an unemptied jerry in the bedroom and there was no oil for
the cooking stove. Add to this that I chose on the way there to

warn Francis most solemnly that he must not expect that I would ever fall in love with him; and that I followed my usual custom at weekends of bringing with me an official bag stuffed with papers and sat in the garden that Sunday morning working on them. Incredibly, Francis managed nevertheless to build us a happy and memorable weekend. I am sure it included some invented game, that the chops cooked on the open fire were deliciously flambé and that there was much laughter, and poetry reading from *The Weekend Book*.

It wasn't long before I discovered how wrong I had been in telling Francis I should never fall in love with him but realisation did not come to me suddenly. No, for me the state of being in love was built up over months. Recently I found what seemed to me some very wise words about love in Morris West's novel, *Harlequin*: 'Falling in love – that's for children. But loving, that's like the best wine . . . to decant slowly and hold gently and savour and sip. You don't grow a great vintage. You create it. . . . Whatever the old theologians taught, you don't make a sacrament by saying words, you make it by commitment and by loving.'

That is how it was with me.

'Wait a moment,' said Francis, 'I think I can see my sister on the platform and I would rather she didn't see us.' It was 7th October 1933 and we were at Victoria Station just about to board the night train for a weekend in Paris. I was filled with astonishment that Francis, who had always seemed so complete and so sure of himself, should be afraid of anyone's opinion. It brought him down momentarily to my level, for I had plucked up courage to tell my mother about this weekend knowing it to be a landmark for me. 'I know it must be right for you to go if you really feel it is,' she said, 'but I would like you to take separate suitcases.' To this day I don't understand why she felt that two suitcases conveyed respectability!

We travelled in a first-class sleeper – a new experience for me – and we stayed at the Hôtel de la Gare des Invalides (then only a bed and breakfast place and now a hotel no longer). There was space in our tiny room for little more than a double bed, but what did we care? Our café complet was brought to us in bed just as if we were the married couple we now longed to be. Again we were dogged by misfortune for I developed a rip-roaring cold, but Francis's spirits appeared to be quite undiminished. He brought me a pile of fine handkerchiefs from a smart Parisian shop, he ordered tea and dosed me with aspirin for my headache and he read to me while I rested. 'I'm practising to be an attentive husband for you,' he said. We visited the school outside Paris designed by le Corbusier which was then making a stir in the architectural world and, my red and running nose notwithstanding, he took me to the good restaurants he had come to know from earlier visits with Vera. At the 'Tour d'Argent' he made me laugh with his story of being served there once with an 'omelette fines herbes' which contained unexplained melon seeds. 'Why is this?' he had asked the waiter. 'A specialité de la maison' was the reply; but Francis was sure that the chef had simply been eating melon while he was cooking. We were supremely happy and always afterwards celebrated 7th October as our private wedding day.

I found that Francis's concern, about being discovered by his sister setting off to Paris with a woman who was not his wife, was not so much about her opinion, but lest his first wife Hilda should learn about us until he was ready to tell her himself. From the moment that we came together, I was to realise that Francis, who seemed so independent, was quite as devoted to his family and as beloved by them as I was to and by mine. He remained closely attached to his first wife and felt concerned and responsible for her to the end of her life and I came to share that concern and to have for her a feeling akin to that of an elder daughter.

The following Christmas, there was a train accident just outside Paris in which many English skiers were killed. We were in the next train and I can still see the long row of black-draped coffins at the Gare de Lyon. Francis was not with us and his letter to me described 'the five minutes of sickening apprehension' before he could ring up the *Sunday Express* and discover it wasn't our train, and 'a new voice said in a new and horrible tone in the pit of my stomach, "But I love her, I love her"'.

He never came on our skiing parties. So now, while I was at winter sports, he wrote me wonderful love letters and composed poems for me – for us. 'Perhaps I have hinted before,' he wrote, 'that I don't feel altogether at home on skis – but last night I dreamt I was joining you at Sils. I had electric skis which took me with incredible speed and never a fall just where I wanted to go.'

Two days later he sent me the first draft of his poem 'On lending a wrist watch' which ends with the line:

'Time stays his flight. Look, Time is on your wrist.'

It was also in this letter that he sent me, most important of all, what he called 'my absurdity of a Christmas card set in the basement of the Nonesuch offices at Great James Street, me assisting'. It is printed on a sheet of paper six inches by three inches and at the foot are the words: 'This edition is limited to one copy, for Bay Christmas 1933.' Here it is:

Autumn 1933

The pear-tree in my orchard now
    Is over-laden so with fruit
That the once taut and sterile bough
    Is bent right back upon the root.

How is it with our ripening love
    With our surprising harvest, how?
Quick with our baskets to the grove
    Lest fall the fruit or break the bough!

We must not go anhungered now.

When (during the war) he first published his poems, he changed the title of this one to 'Last Love' and omitted the italicised line but in the special copy that he caused to be bound in blue leather for me, he wrote in his own hand 'this additional verse for Bay which belongs to her alone':

Stay me with flagons, comfort me
With apples; light the darkening room
My last love! Sum the seasons, be
Sap, flower, fruit and harvest home.

Years later when our love had the sureness of time, this verse too was included in his *Poems & Pieces* published by the Nonesuch Press.

What love letters! What a Christmas card! but alas I was too ignorant of everything to do with publishing and printing and knew too little of Francis's eminence in that world to realise fully then the uniqueness of that edition 'limited to one copy'. And how could I, with my Civil Service training and my stolid matter-of-factness, how could I who had never written a line of poetry even in my teens, begin to match his words in any way? Inevitably, my letters were often very stilted beside his and I know that they sometimes disappointed him sadly in the years when our love was young. Perhaps it is fortunate for my *amour propre* that only two survive. But these are so creased that they almost fall to pieces because Francis carried them about in his pocket book.

We were to have more than forty years together, counting from our private wedding day, so it was early to write of our 'harvest' and to give the poem the title 'Autumn', but Francis was always very conscious of his age and at the time he wrote this poem he had just reached forty. I remember his taking me to play bridge with Harold Hobson (the engineer, not the critic) who was the same age and had been his friend of many years, and that Harold asked, 'How old do you think we are?' When I was too shy to guess, he said, 'Neither of us will see forty again'. They were both crestfallen when I at once assumed that they must be in their fifties.

Once I realised that Francis and I were in love and that he was my future, my private diary began to fade out and after 1936 it ceased altogether. It seems I only needed it for growing pains. One evening in June 1934 we drove out of London together, 'leaving my office in Parliament Square at 5.30 in high spirits not knowing where we were going' but looking vaguely for a country club, the kind that in those days provided dancing as well as food and bed for the motorist. Francis had heard of one at Great Missenden. We never found it, but we cared not at all, for 'the country all along was in its fullest and freshest green, the sun was shining on it and Francis and I were very much in love'. We ended up at 'The Spread Eagle' at Thame which Francis always called 'The Thame Eagle at Spread'. It was eight forty-five and 'because we might be staying I donned my ring' – my Woolworth ring. 'We had a luscious dinner over a bottle of red wine that made us both slightly tight so that we got a regular laughing fit, or rather I did and Francis joined in. We decided to stay and I was very matter-of-fact and wifely until I forgot and consulted Francis as to whether he liked morning tea!' Next morning I didn't get to the office until eleven-fifteen – a very unusual lapse for me – but Francis said 'it was a good deposit in the bank of memory' and I wrote that 'there was something of Paris in it' – meaning of course that Paris weekend in 1933.

There followed, that September, the first of the holidays which from then on until the war we were to take together each year on the Continent, always in a party of four or more – by choice, but also at that time for respectability. Always we went to France, for Italy (and later Spain) were closed to us because they were run by dictatorships of which we both had a horror. This first time we were a four with my sister Toto and our cousin Harry Reikie, a blond giant of a man who was later to be headmaster of Felstead school.

Invariably we went by car. In the Thirties, motoring on the Continent was still unusual and the few cars were hoisted on to the deck of the cross-channel boat with chocks attached to the four wheels; we watched ours poised above our heads, rudely displaying its dusty underside. The journey took much longer than it does now, for many of the roads were very poor, particularly those in the towns. But there were few cars on the road, hotels were never full and the absence of by-passes mattered little because most French towns were still small. In any case, we were in no hurry, for the journey was part of the holiday from the moment we landed in France and drank our first 'vermouth cassis'.

On that first Talloires holiday it was as though I was seeing everything for the first time. The whole Mont Blanc range was clear of cloud with the evening pink glow upon it, as we reached the Col de la Faucille above Geneva – which never happened to us again; there was a cycle race (no doubt the Tour de France of which I had not then even heard); there was my first sight of the Burgundy country from the old Route Nationale No. 7. Francis was perpetually seeing the first bullock, the first vine, the first whatever; there were the green strokable hills of the Jura in sun with autumn crocuses scattered over the meadows; and finally there was the arrival at Talloires in evening light with its unforgettable view of the quiet lake and, across it, the hill with its head in the water that always looked to us like a prehistoric animal.

The Hôtel de L'Abbaye, where we spent all our Talloires holidays before the war, is now a luxury hotel drastically modernised except for its ancient façade, and quite beyond the means of people like us. But at that time it was little changed from its days as an Abbey. The former cells had been turned without alteration into basically furnished small bedrooms and there was only one lavatory and bathroom on each floor; the Abbot's room alone was a show-piece. The whole place in its setting beside the lake had a dignity and an atmosphere that made it uniquely romantic. I think that atmosphere was enhanced for me – and Francis would not have minded – by the fact that I had been there once before with Mum and Maudy when by chance I had found Garrow there.

Each day after an early morning bathe, we had breakfast sitting on the lake wall under a blue sky with the promise of a hot day; and each day we hired a boat and rowed out to the 'Roc de Chère', past grey/green cliffs which reflected the ripples of water made by our passage. There we bathed in the cool green water, and sunbathed and ate lunch provided by the hotel – often they sent us a whole freshly roasted chicken – and lit a fire and made tea; and there would be reading aloud before we rowed back for an afternoon of strenuous tennis, basking in reflected glory when an American guest declared of Toto that she had 'a dandy drive like a national champion' and that her backhand was 'no slush'.

Francis was usually the one to read aloud. He had a notably beautiful reading voice of which later I was to be proud as well as fond. But concern for truth forces me to admit that when I first met him, I did not like his voice. It was higher and more mannered – more 'upper class' I suppose – than I was accustomed to in my circle and I thought it precious – even a bit 'showy'. I suppose that, as with unknown music, I had to become accustomed before I could appreciate.

One more 'first' of that holiday must be recorded because it created a gastronomic tradition for us. On our last evening, Francis treated the party to dinner at the three-star restaurant just along the road from our hotel, owned by Georges Bise. It was called Le Cottage and was a good deal grander in those days than the Abbaye. I went with Francis to order the dinner in advance and my diary records that 'M. Bise himself came out bowing' to conduct the discussion and that 'he was much impressed with Francis as a friend of the McKennas and obviously a good judge of wine'. So much so that he showed us his Visitors Book full of the names of English Cabinet Ministers who had come to his restaurant during sessions of the League of Nations at Geneva. The Savile Club – or was it the Wine and Food Society? (Francis was a member of both) – had fraternal links with the 'Club des Cents' and I am sure that this was felt by M. Bise to be an added justification for including Francis's name in his Golden Book. The rest of us were not asked to sign.

I do not, alas, know what wines we drank; the diary simply records that they were 'the best we had ever drunk or are ever likely to drink', but I was more specific about the food: pâté de foie gras and 'a sort of salmon trout which can only be got in the lakes of Annecy and Aix-les-Bains stupendously cooked – it melted in the mouth'; and then M. Bise came from the kitchen to ask us to take next 'because it was ready and he didn't want our taste spoilt by another course before we ate it', a dish 'que vous n'avez jamais mangé. Pourquoi? Parce que c'est moi qui en est l'auteur.' Sure enough, it was called 'Epinards Georges Bise' and Francis remembered having such a dish at La Perouse in Paris where, it appeared, M. Georges was once chef. It was so delicious that we tried (never quite successfully) to reproduce it at home. When we went back there after the war, we asked for this dish again and told M. Georges (now a proud grandfather but still in charge of the kitchen at Le Cottage) of our attempts to cook it ourselves. He was so delighted at our remembering the dish that he yielded up his secret – the addition of a little French Vermouth to the sauce at the last moment before serving. 'Epinards Georges Bise' has remained a Meynell speciality.

After the closeness and continuity of that idyllic holiday, it was hard to go back to a separate existence in which Francis lived with Vera at Gordon Square and I with Mona at 23 Parkhill Road, Hampstead, to which we had now moved. We kept up a pretence of separateness for my sake and Francis's as well as for Vera's, for it was not then acceptable for unmarried people to acknowledge publicly that they were sleeping together. 'Affairs' were not normally pursued openly even among friends of one's own generation and I should certainly not have wanted my office to know. In fact, the only people I told were Mona, Evelyn and my mother. So successful were we in our deception, that one member of our regular weekend circle discovered the position too late to prevent himself from falling in love with me. I fear he never fully recovered from me; he certainly never married. If I hadn't been so busy establishing my public front with Francis, I should not have allowed this to happen; usually I was quick to discourage people before they had time to feel involved.

No doubt another cause for outside misunderstanding was the fact that, though we had been committed to each other since our Paris weekend in 1933, we did not feel that we had therefore to be sexually exclusive. For us, the important thing was that we knew we were 'one another's best' and were confident that we should tell each other about any other involvement. For Francis, as well as for Garrow physical sex was not exclusive to one person: they saw themselves as pioneers breaking the mould of Victorian taboos about sex. Once I knew that Francis's heart was mine, I was not jealous, or even curious, as to his sexual relations with Vera – or for that matter with others – and my diary records Francis as telling me that 'now that he was sure that I loved him, he didn't mind if I slept with Wells'. We did both sleep with other people from time to time but we never felt that it took anything away from our relationship, though 'non-Bloomsbury' thoughts do show below the surface from time to time in my diary. And as our relationship grew up the times when either of us wanted to exercise our accepted freedom became increasingly rare.

For me, always the questioner of my feelings and motives, things could not be always quite so cut-and-dried as that statement suggests. Even as late as the summer of 1934, there were times, admittedly infrequent, when I still asked myself – was I really in love?

I do not remember any feelings of jealousy in these years – perhaps because I was so certain that I had no cause. From the first, Francis had said, 'You will find me embarrassingly faithful,' and emotionally, which is what mattered to me, it was so.

Our foursome on the
Norwegian cruise.
TOP RIGHT: Wells Coates
and self; LOWER LEFT:
Toto and Jack Rendle

ABOVE: The whole family at Mürren for winter sports, Christmas 1927/8. *Left to right*: Toto, self, Charles MacAlpine (friend of mine and David's from Civil Service), David, cousin Oscar, Mona, Bimbi, Robin. Taken by uncle Axie on the day Bimbi and David became engaged

BELOW LEFT: Self at Mürren, 1927/8

BELOW RIGHT: Robin and Toto at Mürren, 1927/8

The secrecy we had to maintain created problems and tensions with Mum and Mona and even sometimes between us two and it greatly limited the times after work when we could be together. It must be a feature of all worthwhile marriages, or their equivalent, to loosen other intimate ties, but where the relationship has to be kept secret, the consequent hurts and misunderstandings are more and greater because the normal claims of marriage cannot be acknowledged. It was inevitably more often with Vera than with me that Francis attended the many social functions which went with his busy public relations job in the film industry, and I too had public and family commitments to observe, though mine were fewer and less demanding. 'Can we try in future to have at least every other day a date?' I wrote to him,

> I find I hate more and more these long gaps of time when I only see you for short and public occasions and can't feel the assurance of togetherness that I get from being with you alone. It is the difficulty of our kind of life. I'm not grumbling about it – only lamenting – and I don't want all your free time of course, only a reasonable amount of it. . . . Dear love, I wish I could find fitting words to tell you how much you mean to me, how you fill my life and how I look up to and admire you as well as loving you.

Mum had accepted the position 'since you think it right for you' but she also longed for marriage for me and she could not be expected to give way to Francis as she would have to a son-in-law and, notwithstanding her acceptance, I could not expect to share a room with Francis, even in my own flat, if Mum was staying there. The resultant tensions and misunderstandings are well instanced:

> both feeling the parting to come. Got back to the flat to find Mum was coming [to stay contrary to my expectation] after all . . . F stayed but not in my room of course. He thought I hadn't really wanted him and produced a shell which it seemed impossible to get through. . . . I felt the hopeless tangle of our position with me torn between him and Mum and bound to wound one or the other. . . .

Mona, for her part, had never accepted Francis with the warmth she had felt for Garrow. I think now (but did not realise then) that her reason was solely her concern for me and for my interests as she saw them; so far as she could see, there was no reason to suppose that Francis would ever get a divorce and, therefore, that I would get the marriage and family that she knew I wanted. Also I knew that she did not feel my certainty of Francis's constancy. So, though he did his best to establish an easy understanding with her, he was never able to get through a certain barrier of distrust. Inevitably, this reacted on Mona's and my relationship and it is a sad fact that it was never again quite so complete and unquestioning.

And then, a month after I got back from Talloires, I realised that time was not on my side if I was to have children. After an operation for the removal of fibroids, my doctor told me that, if I wanted children, I must have them soon since the fibroids might recur. I had talked glibly about being a modern woman and having children outside marriage but there was never any doubt that I was conventional enough to want them in wedlock, and many discussions followed between Francis and me about whether to press Vera for a divorce. In the draft of a letter to Francis, I set out the pros and cons on Board of Trade rough paper in true Civil Service style:

> What is your idea for the future? Do you mean to raise the question of leaving Vera and of divorce again, or not now, or not at all? and if you were free, would you marry again? And what about children? I want both to marry and to have children as a social experiment: if neither Evelyn nor I marry we shall be looked on as 'sports' whose footsteps young women won't want to follow – rather as our generation looks at blue-stockings. I don't want the present state of affairs to be permanent but if you really think it has to be, I want to know. Whatever happens I would like it to be from choice and not from letting it go from year to year.

It appears from this letter that Francis, Vera and I had discussed the situation together a year earlier and that Vera had said then that she didn't want to encourage Francis to keep up 'what she called a bigamist's existence'. I had not accepted that the 'present' state of affairs might be permanent but I knew that it had made Vera unhappy and I had understood and shared Francis's feeling that we should not take more from her while she was so unhappy and we so happy. Now, however, I wrote that:

It doesn't seem to have made her less unhappy, only to prolong the pain; and the longer we leave it, the more difficult it will become, because she will have less of Ben's wholetime companionship and will also be less likely to take up with anyone else. As for me and us, I fear that circumstances and the years will pull us apart, especially if we have nothing jointly to hold us to the younger generation. What would you think of my having an illegitimate child, supposing I could? I love you and feel lucky in any bit I see of you but I don't like living alone. I don't like having to pretend in public about my relations with you. I don't like being a spinster and a maiden aunt.

I made no record of the discussions which followed but clearly they continued for some time, for while I was away on holiday in the summer of 1937, Francis wrote of a 'dinner-discussion with V' and of feeling that 'you and I are not at the end of our conversation' so he will not attempt to alter the *status quo* 'until we have talked more together'. However, two other considerations must now have begun to weigh heavily with us both.

One was Benedict. Before he was born it had been agreed that Vera should be very much the senior partner in their child. But Ben was now growing out of babyhood and needing his father, and Francis was finding that he had strong paternal feelings. The other consideration must have been the effect of a possible marriage and children on my job. I should, no doubt, have been successful in having the marriage bar waived but what about children? As things were in those days, I might even have to resign, though my idea of marrying and having children 'as a social experiment' suggests that I did not expect that to happen. But, at the least, I should have to get long leave without pay; and with the decline in the fortunes of Nonesuch during the depression, Francis was already having a struggle to earn enough to support his two wives and children – Hilda and Vera, Cynthia and Ben. I knew too that he had real doubts about bringing more children into an uncertain world where Hitler and Mussolini strutted and the League of Nations talked and talked about disarmament and achieved nothing.

According to my memory, it was the need for Benedict to have a home with a father as well as a mother while he was still a child which, more than anything else, decided us not to press Vera for a divorce at this time. But, whether or not I recognised the fact, my own enthusiasm for motherhood must have been reduced by the probable effect on my job which was increasing in interest and importance. Whatever the reasons marriage with children and my fascinating job too was to be one cake I couldn't both have and eat.

10

Mainly for Feminists

In 1925 when I joined, there was still a strictly enforced bar against married women entering the Civil Service, and women officers had to leave it on marriage; women's scales of pay were still lower than men's; and women could not enter the senior ranks of the Diplomatic or Consular Services, which were then separate services. Before I had been more than a few months in my job I had a visit from Beryl Power, a civil servant in the Ministry of Labour, to ask me to join the Council of Women Civil Servants: 'The Council was formed in 1920 to fight for women's causes,' she told me. 'Our first triumph was the opening of the administrative examination to women. You have benefitted from that. Now it's your turn to help.'

Beryl was an alarming character, an obviously highly intelligent woman with pince-nez and a severe expression, and already a principal. Women had been admitted to the clerical and executive grades of the Service for many years and could sometimes reach the administrative grade by promotion. Beryl was one of these who, had she had my early start, would undoubtedly have gone higher in the Service than in fact she did. She also spoke with family authority for she introduced herself as a friend of uncle Will and I remembered sitting tongue-tied at 'Felixstowe' while she talked to him on an equal footing.

My first reaction had been to refuse. I was still resistant to joining organisations or activities that were for women only and I had thought that my own reception as an equal showed that the cause had been won. But put the way Beryl had put it, her request was irresistible. So I joined the Council of Women Civil Servants and was to remain with them, on the Executive for most of the time and for a short part of it as Chairman, until all our three causes were won. I was much younger than the rest of them and I think they looked on me with a kindly proprietary affection as the child of their notable first success. I remember with pleasure Edith Ford referring to me as 'our Benjamin' in her speech at the banquet of jubilation when we finally got equal pay.

Miss (later Dr) Edith Ford was Chairman of the Council of Women Civil Servants when I joined. (I always insisted on using 'Mr Chairman' as a term of art rather than the self-contradictory 'Madam Chairman' but the present 'chair' is better perhaps). Miss D. Ibberson succeeded Edith as Chairman. Both these women were stalwart fighters for the cause of women and gave much of their leisure to it. They should both appear on its roll of honour. They were close friends and became my personal friends and also Francis's. Miss Ibberson was always called 'the Ibb' – I never knew her Christian name; tall, thin, and highly intelligent she had the endearing habit (or was it a physical impediment?) of moving her mouth rather like a rabbit when speaking. Edith Ford was a complete contrast: small in stature, her reddish hair Eton-cropped and mannish in dress, she was a woman of action rather than an academic and enjoyed good food and an evening of bridge with Francis and me. In retrospect, I see 'the Ibb' as a solemn stately penguin and Edith as a busy sprightly robin.

Of our three causes, I contributed most to the fight to have women admitted to the Diplomatic Service and I got deeply involved in it when the first of two enquiries about it under Sir Claude Schuster (the Schuster Committee) was appointed in 1933. Since my work on the Trade Agreements was work which would have been done by Foreign Office staff in other countries, I was obviously the Council's Exhibit 'A': 'I have taken part in negotiations for the Swedish and Finnish Trade Agreements,' I told the Committee, 'and I have not on any occasion felt . . . that the foreign representatives objected to dealing with a woman.'

I wrote a good part of our evidence and I was one of our three representatives to give oral evidence.

We met questions that would surprise today's generation, including the old chestnut about the suitability of women to be Consuls when they might have to deal with drunken sailors. Edith dealt with that: 'We believe that men, drunk or not, will almost always behave better towards a woman than towards a man. Indeed we understand that some brewing companies have a policy of putting women in charge of pubs in dock areas just for this reason. . . .'

I was asked whether I thought it reasonable to press for women diplomats when so many countries would not accept them? 'I don't believe that many countries would not accept them,' I said. . . . 'I believe they would accept a woman then as, for example, the British Commercial Secretary, not as a woman.'

They were inclined to think, they said then that if I could prove that a young woman could successfully do the job of a third secretary in a post abroad, our case would be made: 'Her chief job at that rank will be to collect information . . . she will not have easy entry, or entry at all to the sources a man has, such as local industry and men's clubs and bars. And then, what would the position be if she married and was sent abroad?'

To the first part of this question I argued that women would have more in common with the ordinary people and that all-male clubs were a speciality of this country and not to be found abroad; to the second that the separation of married people through their jobs was as likely to happen to men as to women in the future, since both would have jobs.

'Surely,' commented the Foreign Office member 'women's jobs as wives are more important than any job they might have in the Service?'

'They would have to choose,' I said.

At this the retired ambassador on the Committee went very red in the face: 'I hope I shall not live to see the day when a woman puts her career before her duty to her husband,' he said.

This is probably where we – or at any rate I – lost the sympathy of the majority of the Committee. It is clear that they felt that the Diplomatic Service was what they would have called 'un-womanly'. In their report the reasons they gave against admission were the unanimous opposition of the heads of our Missions abroad (including their wives) and the fact that many foreign countries would not wish to accept women as diplomats. But their final sentence is revealing: 'From the evidence submitted to us, it is by no means clear that the majority of British woman-hood would wish to see this country represented abroad by women.'

As to the views of our Missions abroad, it must be said that they could have had little experience of women in responsible posts. It pleases me to repeat what I am told one head of Mission was heard to say: 'Of course if they were all like that Miss Kilroy . . .' The speaker was our Minister in Helsinki and we had met and worked together during the trade negotiations with Finland.

The Schuster Committee was by no means unanimous. The two women members reported stoutly in favour of the entry of women to both the Consular and the Diplomatic Services. All the men were opposed to women in the Consular Service and all, except two, felt that the Diplomatic Service should also remain closed. But these two were the Chairman and Sir James Rae who thought there should be an experiment for a limited period for: 'If it is found that women can be employed in the Diplomatic Service on equal terms with men, we think that it would be in the public interest that they should be so employed.'

Sir James Rae was an under-secretary at the Treasury. He would have received reports about the women graduates who had so far succeeded in entering the top class of the Home Civil Service through the examination; they might be assumed to be the type and calibre of women who would apply to enter the Diplomatic Service. Sir Claude Schuster was a personal friend of Evelyn Sharp and so must have been well aware of her remarkable capacity and personality.

The Committee heard, of course, many other witnesses including a number of other women's organisations. I should like to be able to say that our Council's evidence had a noticeable influence on Sir Claude and his Treasury colleague but I cannot find specific evidence of it. Their minority report refers to the experience of 'women who have laboured abroad' but not, I regret, to the 'diplomatic' work of the Board of Trade. It is significant, however, that one of the three reasons for their proposed trial period was: 'The campaign in favour of opening the Service to women. . . . If no action is taken . . . the question might one day become a matter of acute political controversy . . . and might result in some less cautious solution.'

Our Council had undoubtedly taken an important part in that campaign.

The advice of the two wise men was not taken so we kept up the pressure even during the Second World War. There is a minute on the Council's files recording a meeting at the Foreign Office in October 1941 when I was Chairman, and we deployed the additional arguments that 'it would be inconsistent with our claim to be fighting for democracy if we persisted in excluding women,' and that the number of countries who would refuse to accept women was growing smaller 'and would be smaller still when victory had been won over the Fascist powers'.

Pressure had also been maintained by the other women's organisations who were banded together into the 'Women Power Committee'. Led by Thelma Cazalet M.P. (later Mrs Cazalet-Keir) they had taken a deputation to Anthony Eden, the Foreign Secretary the previous month. Conservative M.P. for East Islington from 1931–1945, Thelma Cazalet was small, dark-haired, vibrant and could always be relied upon to fight the women's corner with sustained enthusiasm. She is another whom I knew personally and who belongs on the women's roll of honour. She obtained from Eden an assurance that a Committee would be appointed after the war to consider the matter again, and that meantime applications for temporary posts in the Foreign Office would be considered from women as well as from men. These were no empty offers: a number of women were appointed and became permanent in 1946; and the promised Committee was appointed by Ernest Bevin, Foreign Secretary under the reforming Labour Government, as early as the summer of 1945.

This time, our Council was represented by Evelyn Sharp, Mary Smeiton and me. It was all very informal and the three of us sat together side by side on one sofa. We were more exhibits than witnesses for all three of us were under-secretaries by then, Evelyn in the Treasury, Mary in the Ministry of Labour and I in the Board of Trade, and it would have been difficult for the Committee not to take us seriously. They took evidence from a large number of individuals including a joint committee of seventeen women's organisations but managed, nevertheless, to report by January 1946. And on 20th March, Mr Bevin announced to the House of Commons the Government's acceptance of the Committee's unanimous recommendation that women should be eligible equally with men for appointment to the Diplomatic and Consular Services, subject to a marriage bar which could be waived in exceptional circumstances.

Years later, I was sometimes a member of the Board of the Civil Service Commission which conducted the interview for the joint Foreign and Home Service examination, and on one occasion it happened that there came before us a young woman, daughter of a Scottish manse, with flaming red hair and quite outstanding intelligence and personality. All were agreed that she was the best candidate of the day and to my amusement there developed, during our office lunch of unappetising sandwiches and coffee, a keen dispute between the Home Service (represented by the Treasury), and the Foreign Office (represented by their principal establishment officer) as to which of them should have her – the Foreign Office won.

'Would the Foreign Office choose now to put the clock back and exclude women if they could?' I asked. 'Certainly not,' was the reply. 'Women have given us a very healthy shake-up and there has been an unexpected extra advantage: our young men now tend to marry our young women diplomats – so we have fully trained British wives in place of wives who usually came fresh to the diplomatic world, and might be foreign to boot.'

There is no longer a Marriage Bar in the Foreign Service.

The principle of the Marriage Bar in the Home Service was reviewed in 1931 by a Royal Commission on the Civil Service. Our Council gave evidence but I was not involved in preparing it and though the Chairman was Lord Tomlin, the father of my friend Garrow, I have no memory of the business of the Commission being among the innumerable subjects we discussed. The Tomlin Commission reported in favour of keeping the bar but it did recommend that the discretionary power to waive it should be made a reality 'where any disadvantage which may arise from the employment of a married woman is outweighed by her special qualifications or experience,' and they pointed out that this was most likely amongst higher administrative staff, medical officers, and factory inspectors. However, the first case of a waiver in the administrative grade was for a principal in the Ministry of Labour in February 1938 and the fact was unusual enough to be noticed in *The Times* under the heading: 'Married women in the Civil Service – a new precedent'.

The marriage bar was not formally abolished in the Home Service until 15th October 1946, so I still had to apply for a waiver when I married on the 29th August that year.

When Francis and I had discussed the pros and cons of his asking Vera for a divorce before the war, one of my 'pro' arguments had been the wish to show that women could achieve high office in the Service and also marry and have children. An article from *The Times* of 15th September 1958 records that by that date two women (one an under-secretary at the Ministry of Transport and one a third secretary at the Treasury) 'have reached their present positions while bringing up families' and that 36 women assistant secretaries and principals are wives, 'history is not unlikely to repeat itself'. The article continues: 'These figures reflect one of the great advantages of the Home Civil Service to suitably qualified women; namely, that the State is an enlightened employer recognising by generous maternity leaves that a married woman *may* have children in the course of her career and arrange her life so that she can have the best of these two worlds.'

I suppose only someone of my generation would be astonished by this statement or realise in any degree how large an advance it represents from the circumstances that prevailed when I entered the service a generation earlier.

Pressure from the women's organisations had no doubt done much to produce that change but the increasing numbers of women at work in the Service during the war must have done even more. Neither the numbers of women in the senior ranks, nor that degree of enlightenment in the Treasury, would have been achieved so rapidly but for the needs of the Second World War when women were accepted, married or not, because they were *needed* and were in any case not then expected to become a permanent responsibility of the State. And thus the Service gained experience, on the side as it were, about the capacity of women to do a job though married and about the problems involved for their employer.

Equal Pay, our third cause, was not to be fully achieved until 1961 but the true historic date was 1st January, 1955 when R. A. Butler announced in the House that equal pay was to be implemented in seven annual instalments. Once more it had been a long fight, the justice of the case again and again accepted as unarguable but its implementation was always refused by Governments of all parties on the grounds of cost.

Again the obviously equal work of women during the war, must have done more than any argument could do to forward the case for equal pay. It was reported at our A.G.M. in 1942 that a recent Gallup Poll in the *News Chronicle* 'had shown the existence of a sympathetic public', that 'for understandable reasons' various trade unions had accepted the principle of equal pay, and that women in higher posts in the L.C.C. and B.B.C. already had it. However, it was the feeling of the majority of our Council that it would be inappropriate for civil servants to press their claim to equal pay during the war. I was retiring from the chair owing to pressure of work and my confident parting advice was that we should concentrate on building the Council into a 'representative, thinking, informed' body that the authorities would consult after the war because they would expect wise advice and so we should 'have a hand in shaping the future, not only for ourselves but for generations to come'.

I find it interesting to realise that in that May 1942 when we were all looking so boldly and confidently to the future, the war was at almost its lowest point. The Battle of Britain had been won and America had entered the war, but there was no sign yet of the turn of the tide.

I was glad to stay in the background on the equal pay issue because at that time I was not convinced personally of the justice of the cause. I did not have any doubts about women giving equal work. What I felt was that employers faced an economic risk of losing their trained women when they married and had children, or alternatively of being involved in costs due to absences for child-bearing and child-caring; consequently that, looked at purely on economic grounds, there could be justification for *un*equal pay; the normal state of marriage could be expected to lead to greater stability and harder work in a man but the reverse in a woman. However, this argument did not apply to women who were past child-bearing age, so I was led to the conclusion that there was a case for equal pay for older women but not for young ones. Since by the end of the war I belonged to the category of older women, it was obvious that the best thing I could do was to keep my mouth shut.

I have changed my mind since. Partly, the conditions are different: an employer is just as likely these days to lose a promising young man because he thinks he can better himself in another job, as a young woman because she wants to have children. But, more importantly, I don't now think this subject is susceptible to a narrow economic judgement. Since the nation must have children, there should be some responsibility upon it to provide conditions in which women can be mothers without being obliged to sacrifice their careers permanently. And this responsibility seems to me to be especially strong where the State is employer. I think this is now recognised.

My earlier argument on equal pay was also related to my attitude to the feminist cause as a whole. I believed quite passionately – and still do – in the right of women to be treated at work as *persons*, with no disadvantage due to their sex. But I should have been just as upset to receive special consideration as a woman as to have been put at a disadvantage on that account. Equally, I have always thought it wrong that women should get their State pensions earlier than men. Indeed, since they live longer, on strictly economic grounds they should get them later and when I was arranging a pensions scheme for the Monopolies Commission I argued on these lines.

I have no reason to suppose that my views on equal pay were shared by my colleagues on the Council but my general attitude to feminism certainly was. As I have already said, my generation asked only to be accepted as persons in equal competition with our colleagues, whether male or female. I know that some of today's feminists take a different view, believing that positive discrimination in favour of women is needed and justified, if only temporarily, to offset what they regard as the disadvantage they suffer both in education and at work, from the total unfairness in the past of a male-orientated society. I respect this as a seriously held modern view, the more that I have a granddaughter who holds it. But I cannot accept it myself. It seems to me to come dangerously near to a form of denigration – even to being open to misprepresentation as a claim to special treatment for 'the weaker sex'. And it has something in common with a policy there was in my day in the Civil Service of including one women, *qua* woman, on all public boards. When, for example, the first Monopolies Commission was being set up, it was my job to suggest names from which a choice of members could be made: 'You should include at least one woman,' I was told, 'and preferably she should be an economist for we need another one of them, and she should have leftish views to make a political balance with some names already settled. So what we really need is – a slightly pink woman economist.'

What we got was the late Professor Joan Robinson, one of our most prestigious theoretical economists and more than suitable in her own right as a person.

I found that I objected to the position of statutory woman myself when, after I retired, I sometimes served on the interview board of the Civil Service Commission and realised that I was being invited as the one required woman – so much that I refused further invitations from the Commission and told them why.

Obviously, women still have a long way to go before they approach in *numbers* the position and power of men in public life in this country. But this is quite a different thing from *opportunity*. As I see it, we have largely achieved equality of opportunity. This, and the ready acceptance of equality by those one works with (which is quite a different thing and just as important) are now so much taken for granted that my experience in the Twenties will seem light years away to the present generation. Time is still needed to build up numbers, but they will probably never equal those of men because a proportion of women will always choose to remain in the home.

Yes, there are far too few women in Parliament but I should not, nevertheless, be in favour of giving them a special position as women; my gut feeling remains that for a woman to be included on a list for any reason except her suitability as a person is a kind of insult. So, the women's section of the Labour party seems to *me* to be an anachronism these days and I voted against the clause in the SDP constitution which provides that when a Parliamentary candidate is being chosen, the short list must include at least one woman.

I was always treated from the first with scrupulous fairness.

This was true both of the authorities and of colleagues, and for Evelyn quite as much as for me. Ours was a profession whose members genuinely felt it to be a 'service', in which all were accepted with mutual trust and respect according to rank, regardless of class or method of entry. So, when women arrived in the top grade they were accepted the more easily, and all the more so because there was entry by examination (where inevitably there was sex equality). I see no reason to think our experience was any different from that of the other women who entered the Administrative Grade by examination before the Second World War – and I never heard my older colleagues who had been promoted to the grade, suggest that they had received other than even-handed treatment once there.

Our three causes having been achieved with Equal Pay, we closed down the Council of Women Civil Servants in 1958. We thought there was no longer any need for an organisation confined to women, since the normal Civil Service unions could be relied upon to look after the interests of all their members, female equally with male. I hope we were right to kill ourselves off. I know that I had a considerable hand in the decision. Today's feminists would not agree and I am inclined now to have doubts myself. Even in the Civil Service there must still be battles to fight specifically on behalf of women and on the attitude of the male world to them – at the least a need, like Alice in Wonderland, to run fast to keep in the same place.

But, at the time, I think our decision was rather fine. Organisations once started have a way of keeping in being after they have achieved their *raison d'être* and I have always felt this should be resisted. We held a big formal dinner at which we congratulated ourselves and thanked our friends and helpers in Parliament and elsewhere – especially Thelma Cazalet-Keir and (Dame) Irene Ward M.P. – and we announced our imminent demise. Much coached by Francis, I made one of the few public speeches of my career.

Obviously, I can only speak from my own experience and from that of my own generation and colleagues. And, yes, I started with a silver spoon in my mouth and from then onwards was sheltered within the enlightened arms of the senior Civil Service. I never had to fight or campaign for equality; I was given it with an open mind but I have no doubt – indeed I know – that it has often been harder for women in the junior grades of the Service.

In February 1949 when I had just been appointed to the Monopolies Commission, I gave a long interview to the *Weekly Scotsman* and one of my answers is a good summing up about the position of women in the Civil Service, at any rate at that time:

'"Did you find being a woman an advantage in your job?'

'"Who can tell? I've often met the type of man who is so surprised that a woman can have a logical approach to a problem that he is, in fact, quite unduly impressed when he meets one! That gives any competent woman an advantage . . . if you show that you're not necessarily a frump because you can read a graph, you may disarm the man who has an obstinate suspicion of any woman in a responsible post. I have to receive deputations of businessmen, and I have never heard of any of them objecting because I was 'only a woman'. Inside the Civil Service too, there seems to be no prejudice – except financial! That is why the Civil Service is a good career for women."'

I am far from denying too that women face special difficulties because we live in a world which has been male-orientated for so long. But to the extent that this is so, does it not make the storming of the fortress all the more exciting and satisfying? And there is, on the other hand, the fact that women have advantages that men have not: they live longer; they can retire earlier; they have the choice of working for a wage or in the home – or indeed both; they can have the joys of motherhood: they have the heady excitement of pioneering in all the formerly male activities; they even have greater freedom in dress than men. Who would choose to be a man in this century of women?

Storm Clouds of Fascism and Matters Personal

'Here are yesterday's English papers,' said Maudy as she joined my mother and me in the train for Calais at the Gare du Nord. It was a lovely early morning on 17th June 1934, and we were coming back from a holiday in Haute Savoie. As we sat in our hot and crowded second-class carriage speeding through northern France, I read the papers with growing depression. The news was all of the meeting in Venice between Hitler and Mussolini and of Italian nationhood being upheld by the music of the machine-gun.

Hitler had become Chancellor of Germany in January of the previous year and the Reichstag fire had been three months ago in March. During long lazy days on the S.S.S. *Mariska* the previous summer, I had seemed to hear that raucous voice, menacing but still distant, screaming across Europe's air-waves and making a constant background to my eager discussions with Björn Prytz. I was a hopeful socialist and internationalist and Björn's views were only different enough to give spice to our talk; he had to defend himself for voting Conservative because (as he said with truth) Sweden had already achieved much that was worth conserving. His dislike of Hitler's creed was quite as great as mine and no doubt better informed. But as he explained to me later when war came and Sweden stayed neutral, Russia not Germany was Sweden's traditional enemy, the only country she had fought against in the last two hundred years and the only country she feared.

My already kindled interest in foreign affairs was never greater than in the Thirties when we watched the three fascist dictators – Hitler, Mussolini and Franco – bestriding Europe's stage and growing ever stronger. Stalin too, of course, but much as I disliked communism, I felt that basically it was an ideology looking to the future with hope, whereas fascism looked wholly backwards.

When for a short period at about this time, I had been put in charge of the Board of Trade section of the *War Book* (a day-by-day plan of action to be taken on the outbreak of war) the instruction had still been that laid down at the end of the First World War; it assumed no European war for at least twenty years – a remarkably exact forecast. And in that summer of 1933, sailing along the coast of Sweden, I had certainly had no feeling of personal or national involvement in what was happening on the other side of the English Channel or any inkling that the Second World War was in the making. But on this hot morning in June 1934, as I read the newspaper in the train, things began to look different.

I had been in favour of the vote in the Oxford Union in February 1933 which resolved 'that this House will in no circumstances fight for King and Country'. Francis had also applauded it but our reasons were different. I had seen the vote as a simple statement of pacifism; I was fiercely patriotic and a supporter of constitutional monarchy as a 'live flag' which could represent the whole nation without muddling up patriotism with party. Francis was a republican and a socialist. His reason for being a conscientious objector in the Great War had been not so much a belief in pacifism as an objection to supporting an imperialist war. He would not fight 'for King and Country' but he might well think it right to fight against fascism.

However, when it came to the enforced abdication of Edward VIII we were largely at one. We both thought that, as Prince of Wales, he had served the country well in the past especially in highlighting the plight of the miners and the unemployed in South Wales; and we were incensed that in a country where divorce was legal, the King could be prevented – by the national Church – from marrying a divorced woman. The embarrassment caused to the Conservative Government by the King's remarks in South Wales delighted us both at the time. I am not sure nowadays that I, at any rate, would feel he had acted strictly as a constitutional monarch in making a public statement, however painful the conditions he had witnessed.

When Hitler had marched his troops into the Ruhr in June 1934 I had reasoned that Germany was taking back what a basically unfair Versailles Treaty had taken from her, while Francis, to my astonishment, felt that Hitler should be stopped, by force of arms if necessary. We argued hotly about it: 'Lunch with F at 'Diner Francais', F saying wild things about how he wanted an expeditionary force to go into Germany and disarm them. I said he was like an old Tory.' (6th June 1934)

With my pacifist views, I missed a unique opportunity to attend the historic Naval Review for King George V's Jubilee in 1935. Queen Mary had made the enlightened suggestion that as well as the hundreds of big-wigs, two junior civil servants – a man and a woman – should be invited to the celebrations, and I was the chosen woman. I went to the Thanksgiving in St Paul's driving there in my little car along flag-bedecked streets. Cheering crowds stood packed tightly on the pavements. I felt like a Very Important Person indeed. But once inside St Paul's, I saw little from my obscure seat behind a pillar. The Naval Review would certainly have been more fun but because I did not approve of glorifying military force I found an excuse to refuse that invitation too.

And then in the summer of 1936 came the Spanish Civil War to bring me up against the reality of fascism. I felt acutely about the rights and wrongs of the conflict. I was appalled by the atrocities of Franco's forces, supported as they were by my former church. At that time, we knew nothing of the atrocities committed by the Government troops or of the tragic fighting between communists and anarchists.

A letter came from my brother, Robin, in which he took it for granted that the rebel cause in Spain was just. He had his personal reason that he had been the means of Franco's brother being rescued when his plane had come down in the sea. *The Manchester Guardian* at the time (1929) had reported that Robin was 'the idol of the Spanish people'. After being fêted in Madrid and Seville he was given 'the highest medal next to the Captain'. One wonders what atrocities Franco's brother and his fellow airmen lived to commit. In one of the long letters that Robin and I used to exchange I managed to convince him of the rightness of the Spanish Government's cause.

It was also in 1936 that Italy invaded Abyssinia and I was proud that in the League of Nations Britain led the demand for sanctions. I was then acting temporarily as deputy private secretary to Walter Runciman (our President) and was invited to spend a weekend with his family in Northumberland. Sitting on his right at dinner, I launched into an eager appreciation of the Government's policy towards Mussolini. 'Oh', he said. 'So you approve of our imposing sanctions? Do you realise that not one other country is going to do a single thing to enforce them beyond paying lip-service to the policy, and that this country's trade will suffer?' I was shatteringly deflated. It was my first insight into the realities that could lie behind the speeches of politicians.

I was able to talk of politics at dinner because I happened to be the chief guest but thereafter I was treated as a young lady who was not expected to be interested in 'men's talk' – of business or politics – a very general attitude in those days which I always found deeply frustrating. I felt appallingly shy and out of my element in the extremely *stately* Runciman home. I was certain that I had all the wrong clothes and, to my horror, my suitcase with all its deficiencies was unpacked for me.

When we had heard the news of the outbreak of the Spanish Civil War, we had been on holiday at Talloires. Our party that year had included the Potters, Evelyn, my sister Toto and Jack Rendle. The Potters were always delightful holiday companions. They joined enthusiastically in all the games that 'sprouted' wherever Francis was and they were a continuous source of entertainment and laughter: they could be very funny singing songs together, in which they aped brilliantly the voices of choirboys; Stephen gave 'cod' lectures on 'Eng. Lit.'; and Att had a repertoire of ribald songs. On one evening of stars and a full moon that Evelyn and I have often recalled together Stephen sent us into fits of laughter trying to explain the organisation of the heavens to complete ignoramuses. 'The galaxy,' he said, 'is roughly bun-shaped. . . .' I don't know why we found it so very funny – we were perhaps a little drunk but mainly with happiness.

Our high spirits usually lasted until we reached Boulogne on the way home. That year Björn Prytz had joined us for a few days at the end of the holiday. We broke our journey at Chagny in an old hotel and after a somewhat uproarious dinner Stephen came out on the upstairs balcony announcing: 'I have made a wonderful discovery. I have found a new way to brush my teeth. I move my head instead of my toothbrush.' Not to be outdone, Björn appeared in his dressing-gown carrying great strips of wallpaper: 'I don't like the wallpaper in my room,' he said. There was a sudden silence: a joke was a joke but did this northern foreigner not know where to stop? Had he really torn down his wallpaper? He had to reassure us quickly that he had found the extra strips of paper in his wardrobe. . . .

Evelyn and I had first met the Potters as fellow guests of Francis and Vera at Toppesfield and our friendship existed and grew almost exclusively in a holiday atmosphere in which there was rarely serious talk. We learned only later of the scholarship that lay behind those 'cod' lectures of Stephen's. He was then lecturer in English Literature at London University, and had written the first biography of D. H. Lawrence in 1930 as well as edit the Nonesuch Coleridge in 1935; Ben remembers him saying, after *Gamesmanship* had made him a public figure, that he would far rather he were known instead for his Coleridge scholarship. Similarly in the Talloires days, I knew little of Att as an artist, despite the fact that one of Francis's early courting presents to me was her painting *Rain* (1934) in the subtle greens and greys for which she became famous.

I returned from our 1936 holiday at Talloires to a private tragedy, the death of aunt Maudy, my second mother. My grandmother had died in 1927 but though I wept and was sad it was mainly sympathy for my mother. Unlike these others, Maudy's death was a piercing personal sorrow. When I was told that her operation had been for cancer and was unsuccessful, I learnt the literal truth of the Bible words: 'my bowels turned to water'. I feel her loss to this day beyond that of any of my elders. In her last words to me she said: 'I leave them all to you.' She had been the unselfish, caring support and comforter for the whole family and she was seeking to hand on the torch to the next generation. Before her operation, Maudy had written goodbye letters to each of those nearest to her in expectation of death. In mine, addressed to 'My Benjamin', she said she believed that I had now found the love of my life. I had not confided in her, fearing that she would not understand my involvement with a married man, but she had an unerring instinct.

No. 23 Parkhill Road, to which Mona and I had moved in 1934, was very much a step up in our accommodation. It was a two-floor maisonette in a detached house off Haverstock Hill. It had two big rooms on the ground floor a little above street level, and two below the level of the garden which was all ours. We enjoyed furnishing in 'modern' style – 'Finnish bentwood' and very square comfortable armchairs from 'Buoyant'. My room had floor-to-ceiling windows overlooking the garden and it doubled as our sitting-room. My curtains were strips of rough linen in contrasting colours, there was a large divan-bed with many cushions that also served as a sofa, and a rug by Marion Dorn given to me by Francis.

Mona and I took another step-up in the world when we engaged a daily help to come to us regularly in the morning and evening for a weekly wage. Her name was Jean Hix and she was to stay with me for a total of nineteen years. Had she been born into a different social class or, fifty years later, her life would have been very different for she had – has – intelligence and the determination and stalwart fortitude to make much out of little.

Our move finally settled the problem of where, and to what extent with us, our mother was to live. She herself now felt it was time to make a change and establish a home with my father. They took rooms in a farmhouse in Berkshire until they could build themselves a small house in the country, and we kept the garden room in our flat for them when they wanted to be in London. The fact that we had a garden made it easy for them to bring their dog, an old cocker spaniel, but on one of their visits he got through to the street and was lost. Both parents were heartbroken, and my father put an advertisement in the paper offering a reward of £20, a very large sum in those days, and he made himself into a sandwich man carrying his offer and walked about the area round our flat. The dog was never found.

Over the years I had come to recognise and admire my father's un-Dowson qualities and beliefs – those expected then of 'an officer and a gentleman'. I remember one typical incident of him when my brother, then in his late teens, happened to mention that he had driven his car for six months without a road licence and my father sent the sum saved to the Chancellor of the Exchequer anonymously. But the reasoned pessimism which went with his world of absolutes, was completely foreign to me. When I protested to him that his attitude deprived him of pleasant anticipation, his answer was that by his philosophy he was never disappointed. Among his brother officers in the Navy he had had the reputation of being the most impatient of men with an unusually wide command of bad language; it was reported that on one occasion he had smashed the top of his desk to pieces with the ship's telephone. But in contrast he also had a great capacity for patience. When he retired, he took to tying trout and salmon flies which, as any fisherman knows, requires a great deal of patience. His working table would be covered with feathers of all colours and he always knew under which pile lay the feather or the thread or the hook that he needed. When he could not afford to do much fishing himself he turned this hobby into a little money, selling the 'Kilroy' fly through Hardy's in London, and this led to an instance that must find its place in my story. He was extremely fond of a game of bridge and early in 1939 Francis (not then my husband but known I think by my father to be rather more than my close friend, though married to someone else) asked my father to dine with him at his club, the Savile, and play bridge there. 'Thank you, but no,' said my father. 'I cannot enter a gentleman's club because I am in trade.' I have always wondered whether this was a real objection.

I had been right in fearing that the decision Francis and I made not to press Vera for a divorce, with the consequence that our relationship had to remain secret, could create pressures tending to pull us apart. After all, we were living separately, I with Mona, Francis with Vera, and the early months of what we felt to be our marriage had to be conducted in short snatched meetings and such weekends as could be spared from our families and other commitments of our separate social lives.

Those weekends were all important. They lasted only from midday on Saturday until Sunday evening but they were full-packed with living. They might be spent at Toppesfield when Vera made way for us, or at New Cottage, Francis's house in the family enclave at Greatham where Hilda, his first wife, made us welcome; or we might go to a pub or a friend's house. Wherever we spent them, they became increasingly precious because they literally were our life together.

Usually we were a party of friends and perhaps one or other of my sisters, and then costs were carefully shared out on a basis of 'man-days' and 'woman-days', the former being usually higher because the men tended to drink more than the women. The system was invented, I think, by Wells who was still sometimes of the party. Other members might be the Potters or the Dick Plummers or Doyne Bell and his sister, but invariably Evelyn was with us. There were two especially memorable long weekends with her in France, when we added days from our annual leave. One was the first time on bicycles since childhood for all three and our bicycles were borrowed. Mine had no gears and since we cycled all the way from Dieppe to Condrieu the first day, I was so exhausted when I arrived that I couldn't eat any of the delicious dinner of 'quenelles de brochet' and 'fraises des bois'. Francis's bicycle had a loose saddle on which he caught a tender part of his body as he mounted with the clumsiness of a beginner; and next morning he threw the saddle in the Seine and bought a new one. We were very envious of the brand-new bicycle belonging to Basil Davidson, the fourth of our party. It was called 'The Speed King' and had four gears with which he sailed easily past us as we struggled up the hills.

For our second French trip we at least had bicycles that made the going as easy as possible. And this was just as well because it was winter and Evelyn, as so often the leading spirit, had insisted that the roads were suitable though rutted with snow and ice. Francis had a boil on his nose and was thankful for the cold since the pain ceased in the freezing air but we could not keep up with Evelyn's intrepid progress and one day we hired a taxi and hid on its floor as we passed her; we didn't deceive her for she saw our two bicycles on the roof. After a particularly arduous day, we arrived at a café at tea-time and felt we were justified in eating our fill of pâtisseries; when the count was made, we found that four of us had eaten twenty-seven cakes.

Over the more than sixty years of our friendship, until her death in 1985, Evelyn became, both to me and to the rest of my family, more like a sister than a friend, though there was never between us the depth of love and absolute commitment that existed between me and my sisters and brother. Between Evelyn, Francis and me there grew a close three-sided friendship which I took completely for granted. Often and often over the years, we would be a party of three for a weekend or an evening, and feel no whit of surprise that, in our case, contrary to the old adage, three should always be such very good company. It did not occur to me to feel pain when in the early Talloires days Francis asked if I would mind if they sealed their friendship by sleeping together; I was even glad. Evelyn of course knew that I had been consulted or she would not have consented. Thinking now about that long friendship I realise that I was never jealous or felt for a moment threatened by the attachment between Evelyn and Francis and I wonder how much the smooth running of it was due to Evelyn's generous acceptance of second place. 'You know, don't you, that Francis was my Garrow,' she said to me quite recently when I was reading her chapters from this book. It has occurred to me only since her death, that she must always have been a little in love with him. Her copy of Francis's autobiography, *My Lives*, came to me on her death and I am glad to see that it is inscribed –

With all my love through most of them, and now, from Francis

It is time to go back – or rather across, since the happenings were contemporaneous – to my work at the Board of Trade. I was now the No. 2 in a small department confusingly called the 'General' department, its functions being few and fairly specific. Our main object was to negotiate import quotas for agricultural products – chiefly bacon and meat – that were the subject of the new marketing schemes then being set up by the Ministry of Agriculture, we also had a 'General' responsibility for the interests of consumers in the supplies and prices of food and such as it was, which was little, this gave us some say in the severity of the import quotas.

The department had a tiny staff: one assistant secretary (who was the head) – Harold Carlill, and one principal – me. Our two offices were side by side on the prestigious Second Floor. It was the first time I had had an office for myself alone and I revelled in it. It was long and narrow, with the high ceiling of the Second Floor, like a shoe-box on end, but there was room for my desk beside one of the tall windows of that floor and it overlooked Parliament Square with its statues of great men that had so inspired me on my first day as a civil servant.

Moreover I was now allocated an assistant principal to work solely for me. His name was Arthur Burgess, product I think of Manchester Grammar School and Cambridge University and a brilliant mathematician. When we became friends, he told me of his astonished first impression of his boss: 'Not the impressive, solemn man I had expected, but a beautiful young woman with a cocker spaniel curled at her feet.' The dog was my mother's and it was, as it happens, the only time I ever took him to the office.

My new A.P. surprised me quite as much as I had surprised him. When I asked him for comments on the latest proposals made by the Danish Government for an adjustment in their share of the import quota for bacon, he replied with a page of figures. I was not going to be bested or admit that the calculations were double-dutch to me. After a suitable interval I told him gently that his paper was interesting but he must follow civil service not university practice and put his thoughts into words. . . .

Harold Carlill cannot have been far off retirement at that time. Though only an assistant secretary, he seemed to me to be someone without further ambition and wholly satisfied with his job as head of his small department; I am sure it was important to him that he thoroughly approved the policy he was implementing. I was a bit of a sceptic when I arrived at the department but I was won over by his enthusiasm. He told me that Sir Arthur Street (already permanent secretary at the Ministry of Agriculture) had been the inventor of the policy establishing Marketing Boards, with the object of giving farmers combined strength to resist the large buyers who had been able to beat down their prices when they acted singly; so weak had they been, Carlill never tired of telling me, that in some shops bacon was actually given away with a pound of tea – a point that he didn't fail to make dramatically to the Danes and others if they became restive with our quotas. To my argument that our policies for agriculture were costing money and it would be cheaper to import our grain, our meat and our bacon, he answered that

England's farmland was her garden and she should be prepared to pay something for it. He had a soft spot for me: and would often arrive in the morning bringing me the best flowers from his garden – the newest tulip or rose and, what impressed me most, a splendid *lilium regale*. He may well have asked for me as his one principal for he had begun taking me out for an occasional meal before I joined the department.

The policy could not have been in better hands than those of Harold Carlill on our side and Mr Sörenson, the Danish agricultural attaché, on the other. He had a round cherubic face and he wore six-sided metal spectacles that glinted as he smiled, which he did so often that he had as many smile wrinkles as my grandmother. Thanks to what I can only call his benevolent flexibility, and to the undoubted negotiating skill of my boss, our discussions were always successful and pleasant and sometimes fun. The Danes had two-thirds of our bacon quota so it was possible – or at any rate Mr Sörenson made it so – for Denmark to give away a percentage point here or there to smooth disputes or accommodate small or new importers – I remember his doing just that to allow Poland to enter our market for the first time.

I learned much from Carlill about patient negotiation and about keeping your head and your temper with opposing interests round a conference table. But there was one occasion when we had to take part in a shaming exercise in appeasement. It was the summer of 1939. Our department were responsible for the British end of the International Sugar Council which met in London in June to consider a British request for increased imports of sugar. I was secretary of the inter-departmental committee preparing the British case that would be presented by Carlill. At once a snag arose. Czechoslovakia was a member of the Council and the German Government objected that there could be no representative of that country which no longer existed now that it had been absorbed into the German Reich. Enter the big guns of the F.O.: this was important; this was a matter of diplomatic propriety; to give the Czech quota to the Germans, which was what was claimed, would be tantamount to *de jure* recognition of their annexation of Czechoslovakia; it might well result in the Americans walking out. According to documents in the P.R.O.

the formula – accepted by the German delegation was that, 'for simplicity', the territory now commonly known as 'the Protectorate of Bohemia and Moravia and the territory now commonly known as the State of Slovakia, be known in discussions as Territory "A"' – not even *Country* 'A'! When the representative from Territory 'A' came to the rostrum, he was seen to be dressed to look as much like Hitler as possible, with the lock of hair over his forehead and the little moustache. My thought then was 'How could he be so insensitive?' but now I think 'How courageous he was to cock a public snook'.

It must have been almost immediately after this incident that I was moved again, this time to the department responsible for vetting the flood of applications from German refugees to be allowed to settle in this country. The Board of Trade had the deciding voice in the case of people who wanted to set up businesses in our Special Areas; if we could argue that they would be helpful in providing jobs in those depressed areas (as in the event, they certainly were), we could get them admitted. We had no illusions about what the alternative was for these people – the first concentration camp at Büchenwald had been opened in 1934. With one accord we stretched the possibilities for admission to the limit.

At that time, ordinary citizens from Germany could come here if they were guaranteed financial support in this country and Francis and Vera were so generous over this that there were no less than nine German refugees at Toppesfield at the outbreak of war. The young Benedict fiercely resented being, in effect, deprived of his home for the many months they had to stay there at the beginning of the war.

Another scheme was started in 1938 for people to offer temporary homes to German and Austrian Jewish children. Our family took part by making ourselves responsible for one Austrian boy aged eight: my sister Toto and Jack Rendle, who had married the year before, took the big step of saying they would provide him with a home. My uncle Felix undertook to pay for his years at Cressbrook and Evelyn and I agreed to be responsible for the rest of his schooling. We shared responsibility with the Rendles for arranging his holidays. He came from a well-to-do background, and arrived with plenty of luggage and a

smart new bicycle but a passport already stamped 'ISRAEL'. The
only person who was not pleased was my father. 'Why?' I asked.
'I want them to have their own bloody children,' he said – which
quite soon they did.

12

War with Honour

When the air-raid siren wailed on Sunday morning, 3rd September 1939, I was at a garage on the Great West Road with a colleague called Carruthers on my way to Chancery Lane where, over the weekend, an 'Import Licensing' department of the Board of Trade was being set up in the hurriedly transformed old Patent Office. The siren sent the garage hands and Carruthers and me down a narrow flight of stairs into a makeshift shelter. While we waited in expectant silence for the sound of bombs, my only thought was – 'But I don't know Carruthers well enough to die with him.'

I had spent the previous night with my parents in their house in the little village of Bradfield outside Reading, and had listened there to Neville Chamberlain's curiously egoistical statement that 'We are at war with Germany. You can imagine what a disappointment this is to ME. . . .'

A year earlier I had been one of the many who had felt shame rather than relief that Chamberlain's announcement of 'Peace with Honour', meant that the long tale of giving way to fascism was to continue, but I have found notes in my handwriting headed 'Views on War and Peace, October 1938' which show that I wasn't as certain as my memory suggests that I would 'rather die than live in a concentration camp under fascism' and arguing that there must in future be some alternative to war now that the Spanish Civil War had shown men that it attacked women and children instead of protecting them. But a year later my feelings were of total commitment and pride that at last we were confronting fascism – not *Peace* but *War* with *Honour*.

I felt neither understanding nor sympathy for the attitude of my permanent secretary, (Sir) W. B. Brown when I was sent to see him on the Monday after war was declared. He had been gassed in the Great War and could not disguise his frustrated anger that a second world war had not been avoided. For me and for most of his staff, it was not only 'War with Honour' it was inevitable, even the one just war. That is what I still think and I have little patience with latterday commentators who argue that if we had done or not done this or that, we could have 'avoided' the war. In almost a 'controlled' experiment we were to see it justified as well as just, because Hitler with his thousand year Reich and Mussolini with his fascist Empire were destroyed, while Franco's fascist Spain, survived.

My feelings about the war were wholly shared by Francis: 'As I saw it,' he wrote,* 'England had become a partisan of humanity.' Later, when he was working for the Board of Trade, he even volunteered to join their section of the Home Guard. However, he was rejected. The reason given was age but it is very likely that it was quite as much his past political history. Its commander, a younger colleague of mine, showed considerable embarrassment when he told me about it.

I was no longer living in Parkhill Road. Mona had been married the previous September to a friend of our brother's, Flight Lieutenant Geoffrey Middleton, and Evelyn and I were now sharing a house at 19 Cliveden Place near Sloane Square. We needed something larger than Parkhill Road because we wanted separate households, and 19 Cliveden Place was a whole house on the corner at the east end of this Regency terrace. When I first saw it I found it too staid and *un*modern – 'like a doctor's house in the country,' I said. I was quickly and properly overruled by both Francis and Evelyn and she and I took a lease for five years. It did not occur to us to buy.

My father alone was full of doubts and anxieties: 'Did we realise that there was sure to be a war and that since we planned to live so near to the centre of London, we should very likely be left with a smoking ruin for a house?' In the event, 23 Parkhill Road suffered a direct hit, as also did 39 Woburn Square where Francis had lived up to the war – but 19 Cliveden Place sustained only a near miss.

We decided that Evelyn should take the larger part of the house (and the larger rent) since she had a sister living with her and as

My Lives.

yet Francis was still living with Vera. So Evelyn had the upper floors including the 'piano nobile' (which we shared for parties), and I had the ground floor, the garage – a rare possession – which had a room over it, and the basement (part of which we were to share as our makeshift bomb shelter). We found a refrigerator in the kitchen left by the previous tenants. I had never owned one before. I told Evelyn (who also had never had one) that she was most welcome to it.

Francis got Marion Dorn to design the built-in furniture for my bedroom, soon to become ours, and also to manoeuvre a dining-room out of what was really a passage from the room over the garage to the rest of the house. Evelyn furnished her part of the house more in keeping with its period, but I remember that I was shocked by what I saw as her astonishing extravagance over the purchase of the mattress for her bed: not content with an ordinary hair mattress she must have one filled with hair from horses' tails.

Jean's sister, May, came to look after Evelyn and these two stayed with us all through the blitz and until we left Cliveden Place (in 1954). When their age-group of women were called up, they were both released on the ground that they were doing war service in looking after us. It did not occur to us to attempt to do our own chores. But neither Evelyn and I nor Francis could have made quite the contribution we did make during the war without the faithful care of these two.

The Import Licensing Department where Carruthers and I worked consisted of three or four principals under an assistant secretary, (Sir) Laurence Watkinson. He put me in charge of the food section (probably because of my experience in the General Department) and told me to draw up a preliminary list of food imports to be prohibited. 'I suggest you go through the Trade Accounts and start your list with all the things you most enjoy eating,' Watkinson advised.

Years later he recalled those days:

What amazing luck we had during the early years of the war . . . starting with the disgraceful first fortnight of Import Licencing when we 'forgot' to consult Treasury, Cabinet

ABOVE: Bathing at Talloires, Lac d'Annecy. Self
(foreground) and Evelyn Sharp. Taken by Stephen Potter
BELOW: On 'our' rock at Talloires, 1934: Francis, Toto
and self

Press conference at the launch of the Council of Industrial Design in April 1944: Clem Leslie (its first secretary), Sir Thomas Barlow and self

Office and a string of other people including our own
Permanent Secretary. . . . Mind you if we had 'consulted', the
whole thing would have ground to a halt. . . .

It was entirely typical of him to use the 'we' throughout. In fact
all the innovation and boldness were his. He was 'Wattie' to the
whole staff, the most imaginative, inventive, and inspiring boss I
ever worked for. You would not have guessed his quality from
his looks. He was a small dumpy man with kind eyes in a rugged
face, an informal dresser usually in a crumpled pullover. He had
an M.C. and bar from service in France and Italy in the First
World War and had joined the Inland Revenue in 1919 and
transferred to the Board of Trade in 1931. Perhaps his real métier
would have been as a politician but certainly he was the right man
in the right place during the war, when the country's political aim
was so clear that the distinction between the spheres of civil
servants and Ministers was blurred and less important than in
peacetime. He, more than any other single person, was responsible for harnessing the civilian front to the war effort.[*] Import
Licensing was only the first of his highly successful new
departments established with the minimum of 'consultation'
with his bosses. There followed amongst others, the 'Limitation
of Supplies', Clothes Rationing, the Concentration of Industry,
and Furniture Rationing, all of which he either invented himself
or adopted and perfected from the suggestions of others.

Wattie was to teach me many things by example, among the
most valuable for a civil servant, being how to say 'yes' and find a
way, rather than 'no' and block. But the most important was also
the first when, the Monday morning after war was declared, he
took me with him to our Enquiry Room which was crowded
with an anxious public whose business depended on imports. A
long table at one end like a post office counter was staffed by
junior officers who had instructions simply to hand out lists of
prohibited goods and guide those who wanted to know more to
the appropriate section – if food to mine. But as he talked to each

[*] I have been very pleased to see my opinion of Wattie confirmed by Professor
Margaret Gowing, joint author of the Civil Industry and Trade section of the
official *History of the Second World War*. After his death, I was given the copy of
this book that the authors sent to Wattie, and Margaret Gowing's letter to him,
stuck on the fly-leaf says: 'You are one of the great unacknowledged heroes of it.'

of these junior members of his staff and encouraged them to patience with the worried public, I saw Wattie convince them of their unique importance as our first line of troops. Obviously the best in staff management, this worked only because he was seen to be sincere.

One of the first enquirers who came my way was the Portuguese ambassador. I had regarded pineapples as a luxury and had put them on the prohibited list. Unfortunately, September was the beginning of the season for shipping pineapples from the Azores which depended largely on this crop. Because of his rank, the ambassador had been shown straight to Wattie and he often laughed with me afterwards about my only too obvious embarrassment in having to shake hands with the representative of Salazar, already a notorious dictator. Another of my visitors, introduced to my by Francis, was Alan Sainsbury enquiring the fate of a shipment of pigeons from Belgium which was already at sea. I felt I must maintain our rules and they were sent back; I fear that in the end they went bad. Inevitably, there were pressures upon us to yield in individual cases and sometimes these were accompanied by gifts of produce, which were duly reported to me for permission to accept. Near Christmas, there were offers of turkeys to junior staff whose pay would very likely not run to their buying one. It was one of my hardest decisions to have to say 'no'.

Only four months after the Import Licensing Branch opened its doors, Wattie moved on to set up another new department. I went with him, promoted to assistant secretary rank. A part of Fanum House (the home of the Automobile Association in Leicester Square) was requisitioned and transformed, with Wattie's usual speed, to house us.

This time we were putting a limit on inessential goods produced here for the home market, an idea that had come from (Professor Lord) Richard Kahn, then a lecturer in economics at King's College, Cambridge, who had joined the Board of Trade as a temporary principal in December 1939. Wattie had immediately seen the value of his idea and adopted it. The plan (called 'Limitation of Supplies') was to confine the home trade in goods that used imported raw materials – chiefly textiles in the first instance – to fairly low percentage quotas based on the last peace-time year. Thus money and transport would be saved on imported raw materials and at the same time industry and the business world would be encouraged to increase the exports now needed to pay for 'the war effort' – a portmanteau phrase that covered anything from tanks and shells to razor-blades and even sanitary towels, a shipment of which had once to be hurriedly imported from the U.S.A. after the wives of members of the Cabinet had protested that they were becoming unobtainable. An equally important object of the policy was to release labour needed for the factories producing munitions, aircraft etc. However, when Wattie and Kahn went to the Ministry of Labour to explain their plan and get their political support for the necessary Statutory Orders, they were met with opposition. This was the period of the 'phoney war' and the Ministry of Labour were still geared to the relief of the unemployment that had been such a scourge in the depression of the Thirties. That the Board of Trade should plan to create unemployment artificially shocked the Ministry profoundly: men of course would be needed in the Forces but the textile industries (with which the policy started) employed chiefly women and the Ministry saw no prospect of a need for numbers of unskilled women in the war; since they believed that the weapons used would be sophisticated and unlike those of the last war.

So, when Wattie got authority for the policy, it was on the understanding that the release of labour for war production should not be used as one of its justifications.[*] This meant that when his staff received the inevitable deputations of protesting manufacturers and traders, what they saw as a basic reason for the policy could not be used. I still remember with discomfort that I actually sweated physically when I received the hosiery trade with one hand thus tied behind my back.

In the first months of the war, Francis tried at one Government department after another to get some kind of war work and was rejected first by the Ministry of Information, then by the Ministry of Works and finally by the Ministry of Labour where Ernest Bevin (long known to him in the Labour Party) greeted him with –

---

[*]In fact there was no increase in unemployment but a decrease down to almost nil by the autumn of 1940.

'What, YOU my boy?' – and a burst of dismissive laughter. Since his left-wing past had included a short period of membership of the Communist Party and the Russo-German pact was still in force, this was perhaps not a matter for surprise. Wattie, however, knew Francis through me and he could recognise sincerity when he saw it. He needed someone with experience of market research to keep an eye on the possible shortages that our policy might cause and Francis had the necessary qualifications: he was director of the creative department of a large advertising agency and, as well, was already working for the Ministry of Food (*for* not *in* mind you) as editor-in-chief of the advertising campaign, 'Food Facts'. Wattie didn't hesitate and Francis was at last *in*.

So it was that the war which divided so many brought Francis and me the happiness of being together at work. And not only at work; as Vera at once took Benedict out of London, Francis could move in with me at No. 19. We never afterwards lived separately.

Working in the same building provided a special bonus once the bombing started, for it meant quite often that we were in the same group for 'fire-watching'. This duty was shared equally by all staff from the permanent secretary downwards. It was much more uncomfortable than dangerous. It involved spending your evening and night at the office and, when there was no raid, sleeping on a narrow makeshift bed with prickly army blankets and only one pillow. During a raid you took it in turns to keep watch in groups on or near the roof, ready with your primitive little stirrup pump.

Fire-watching at home was organised by air-raid wardens, street by street, and Evelyn and Francis were on duty one night when they saw what looked like an airman hanging from a parachute and coming down over Ebury Street. They started forward together but fortunately had gone only a few paces when the 'airman' touched the ground and turned out to be one of the first landmines – a huge bomb which made the area at the Chelsea end of Ebury Street look as if a giant foot had stepped on it.

I didn't find that I was frightened in the first years of the blitz but this was more through lack of imagination than courage. I saw plenty of bombed buildings after the event, with their rooms open to the sky, but I was never present at an incident when people were killed or injured. Nor was any building destroyed with which I had a close personal connection. That, fear apart, could be a searing emotional experience as I learnt from Mona who arrived for work at John Lewis in Oxford Street one morning to find a still smoking ruin, where the night before she had left a great shop with its carefully laid-out goods, including the women's blouses of her own department.

I was full of admiration for the people whose job it was to be at the scenes of bombing and who had to go back to them night after night. Amongst them my friend Doyne Bell. Though already a consultant paediatrician, he volunteered to be one of the 'blitz doctors' recruited by the Ministry of Health, no doubt through Evelyn. He told me about his shattering fear one evening when he had to go to the help of injured people trapped in a burning house though he realised all too vividly that he risked being burnt to death himself.

Our part of London suffered less from raids than some other parts, but we did have three near-misses – that landmine on Ebury Street, a direct hit on Sloane Square Station when a train had just come in, and a bomb fell in Cliveden Place itself, during the spring raids of 1941. It was just after the birth of Mona's second son, Henry, and they were staying with us. The bomb came down in the road only some twenty yards away. It must have been set to go off some seconds after impact for I had time to make a wholly instinctive dive down the basement stairs to join Mona in leaning our bodies over the baby in his cradle. There was no time at the moment of the bomb dropping for anything but instinctive action – just as on another occasion when the 'imminent' signal caught me in the King's Road, I found myself standing with my face pressed against the plate-glass window of Peter Jones.

No. 19 was entirely undamaged by its bomb except that for some days afterwards we had no gas, electricity, water or telephone. But there was plenty of light outside that night from a jet of flame reaching high in the air out of the ruptured gas main. The front of the house immediately opposite the great hole that the bomb made in the road was demolished but no one in it was killed, though we learnt later that a beautiful young woman whom we used to see taking her Afghan hound for walks had been killed some streets away: a piece of concrete from Cliveden Place had been carried by the blast over a row of houses and in through her bedroom window. The next morning we found another piece in our sitting-room; the windows were closed and unbroken and the blast had blown them open and closed them again leaving the curtains outside and the piece of concrete inside.

I came to the conclusion later that one's store of courage is not infinite. When the VIs (the 'doodle-bugs') began with their warning approach whine and pregnant pause before the crash told you they had fallen somewhere else, my store began to run out. My first experience was especially humiliating: Evelyn and I were both lunching (though separately) at the same place and during the silent pause before the explosion I went down under my table; when I got up I saw that Evelyn was still calmly eating and reading her book. I did not make the same mistake again but at night I found that I simply could not stop my teeth from chattering. It was only through this physical manifestation that I knew how frightened I was and I was ashamed that it happened to me alone and not to Francis or to Evelyn, who shared our bomb shelter. We called it 'the pink-and-silver'; Chelsea Town Council had given it metal struts to the roof which were painted silver and I had had the walls painted in 'shocking pink' to cheer us up. It was probably more a death-trap than a shelter being a store-room partly under the street – and not more than a foot under I should judge, because you could hear people's echoing feet on the pavement outside as you lay in bed. We had also contrived what I called 'the push-through' with some loose bricks between the 'pink-and-silver' and the food cellar where there were extra bunks. We hoped to be able to remove the bricks if either space was buried.

The whole of our shelter area was pretty uncomfortable and damp and after a night there with 'flu I developed jaundice which gave me an attack of depression – a rare thing for me. I couldn't stop crying until Francis made me laugh by going to Peter Jones and buying two dozen little handkerchiefs which he dropped all over my bed like so many tiny white tents.

The black-out troubled me quite as much as the raids. Though we soon got used to the shields on our car lights that let through

only a tiny light in the shape of a cross, the song with the refrain –
'When the lights go on again All over the world' – could bring a
lump to my throat any time. 'Finest hour' or not, I remember
vividly an evening when I was waiting for a train in Piccadilly
Tube station. I was surrounded by sleepers in pathetic small
family groups sheltering there from the bombing and trying to
establish some sense of home and privacy, and I happened to
notice an old 'Robinson's Flour' poster in which a smiling rosy-
cheeked cook offered some homely pre-war pudding: it seemed
an almost impossible hope that life would ever be normal again.

Evelyn had some responsibility at this time for people whose
only resort at night was the platform of a Tube station and on one
evening when she had gone to see for herself what could be done
to make things more comfortable for them, she noticed a little
group of a mother with her child and her old father. They looked,
she said, so lost and so like the Holy Family, that she at once
invited them back to her own flat and installed them in her only
sitting-room. Father proved to have no interest in anything but
pub opening-time and mother to be a tart with absolutely no
housewifely knowledge – and they were very difficult to get rid
of. . . .

The bombs on Ebury Street and Sloane Square Station must
have caused a big loss of life but I believe that ours in Cliveden Place
was more typical in the large amount of physical damage it caused
in relation to the deaths and personal injury. There were rumours
of redundant churches full of redundant plastic coffins. I don't
know what truth there was in these but certainly the Ministry of
Health expected more civilian casualties than in fact there were and
there was a greater need for shelter than for coffins.

In preparation for the assumed need for extra hospital beds,
Evelyn had been promoted to be an assistant secretary and given
the job of organising from scratch a number of temporary
hospitals outside London. She went about it with typical skill and
dash. With the help of the senior Ministry of Health doctor, she
got out a shopping-list of beds, blankets, bandages, drugs, and
operating equipment and advanced confidently with it upon the
medical department of the War Office. They said that they were
fully stretched laying in supplies for military casualties which
alone were their concern and must have priority. They couldn't

help: and they advised her that she would have to get authority from the Treasury for the necessary cash before attempting to buy anything at all, and warned her that she need not think she could get that approval in full or quickly. Typically, she decided to act first and get authority afterwards. She knew that the London County Council was the largest hospital authority in the country and she knew its Clerk personally because he had been a colleague in her ministry before going to the L.C.C. So – cutting down her shopping-list to its bare minimum – she went to him with it. Could he supply these things in the national emergency and even lend some of his staff to help in making ready the hospitals? . . . 'I shall need at least £6 million,' he said. 'Done,' said Evelyn and the country got its hospitals in time. Not long after that, the Treasury took Evelyn on to their own staff – a sufficient comment from Their Lordships on her unconventional action. At the time Evelyn and I knew little about each other's work. When we saw each other in the evenings it was to play bridge or, when the raids were on, Francis would read aloud to us. We got through more than one Dickens in this way.

Though bombing was so much less frightening than we had expected, the war did bring me a very real fear of another kind. I had no doubt of our winning in the end but there had to be the possibility that we should be overrun like the rest of our European allies. In that case we would join the resistance underground and it seemed to me certain that Francis would be among those most at risk from the Gestapo as a former Communist. Wildly, I pictured our having to go underground hiding perhaps in Epping Forest, like the character in *Rogue Male*, that remarkable thriller by Geoffrey Household in which a man who had tried to kill Hitler is chased by a Gestapo agent literally 'to earth' in a Devonshire wood. So real and pervasive was my fear that, even half a century later in peaceful Suffolk, I catch myself looking at hedges and sunken roads as possible hiding places. What I did in the end was to extract a promise from Björn, that I never told Francis about, that if necessary he would give Francis sanctuary in the Swedish Legation.

I assumed as a matter of course that devotion to the cause of winning the war was the general feeling and I remember thinking, when my work at the Board of Trade took me to Stoke-on-Trent, what splendidly steadfast partisans the people of the potteries would make. For me, the spirit of that time is summed up in the attitude of a stalwart English lady I knew who had been cook in great households and who worked for Francis and me occasionally after the war. When war was seen to be imminent, it happened that she was working for some wealthy Americans and they suggested that she should go back to America with them:

'Thank you, Madam, but no.' said Mrs Riley. 'England has been good enough for me in peacetime. I expect it will be in war.'

I put beside that story, my father, buying himself a gun and joining the Home Guard. There were not enough men in my 'Dad's Army' to satisfy his conception of the vigilance necessary, and sometimes there would be no one to replace him on watch in the little village of Bradfield when, from sheer exhaustion, he had to abandon his post on guard duty.

I did have to deal personally with one exception to this unity of feeling when it was reported to me that an important member of the wartime Regional Organisation had been heard to say that the Germans would inevitably occupy this country quite soon and that within six months Russia would turn them out, so we must begin to prepare now to help and to welcome our Russian allies. This was official defeatism and, after some heart-searching, Francis and I went together to report what we had heard to Alan Barlow at the Treasury. Within a few days, the speaker found himself inexplicably rusticated.

In the high mood of national determination, the occupants of 19 Cliveden Place established an evening discussion group to bring together the suggestions that crowded all our thoughts for helping the war effort outside our own particular sphere of work. There must have been many such unofficial groups as there were, of course, many official studies. We called ours 'Say It Now; Do It Now'. We started it at the low point of the war in the beginning of 1942 when it seemed that each day brought a fresh defeat – with Germany in the Channel ports and at the gates of Cairo and Stalingrad, with Japan in Singapore and Burma, and the American fleet destroyed at Pearl Harbour. There was a backs-to-the-wall atmosphere when everything was being tried.

Our fairly large and fluctuating group consisted of a number of senior people who were our friends or colleagues. They included Raymond Streat, Wattie and Wilfrid Anson (Chairman of the Imperial Tobacco Company) and also Hugh Gaitskell who had joined the Board of Trade as a civil servant when Dr Hugh Dalton became President. The intention was to present a document to Churchill urging action based on 'the Cromwellian principle that the citizen soldier must know what he fights for and love what he knows'.

The few records of our discussions that survive* include two early drafts headed 'The People at War' which are almost entirely concerned with the total mobilisation of civilian and military forces for total war and contain criticisms of a kind to be expected of intelligent civilians subjected to old-style military discipline. A draft three months later, however is an ambitious attempt to outline plans both national (on Beveridge lines) and international (including an international police force and key strong points around the world), to implement the Four Freedoms – 'to be made with the co-operation of the U.S.A. and Russia and promulgated NOW' on the basis that 'we must tell our own people and Europe what we are fighting for. . . . The economic past is indefensible'.

In a long letter to me as secretary on lines not so much negative as down-to-earth, this third draft was pulled to pieces by Hugh Gaitskell, and he suggested a different approach under which there would be a closer study of various aspects (on some of which he outlined detailed proposals) before any attempt was made to consider the whole document again. There is no record of any further meeting and my impression is that effectively this brought our discussions to an end, especially as the tide of war was beginning to turn in our favour. Certainly no document was presented.

Looking at the ideas of our 'Say It Now; Do It Now' Group from forty years on, I think the most notable thing about it is its background of simplistic idealism which assumed a world capable of being unselfishly united for the good of all. The fact that this group of sober people embarked upon so large a canvas in that spirit and with such radical and often impractical proposals, is striking evidence of the mood of the time.

*Now in the Francis Meynell Archive in the C.U. Library.

No. 19 Cliveden Place was also involved in the follow-up to Victor Gollancz's celebrated pamphlet 'Let My People Go' which horrifyingly revealed what was then happening to the Jews under Hitler. The only surviving record of this[*] is the detailed report of a meeting chaired by Francis in February 1943, attended by Gollancz, Eleanor Rathbone, Tom Driberg, Alan Sainsbury, Sidney Bernstein and many others. Evelyn and I were both present and the record shows that I took an active part. The object of the meeting was to discuss means of bringing pressure to bear on the British Government and other allied Governments to accept any Jews who could escape from Germany, though the fear of provoking anti-semitism in Britain was felt to be an inhibiting factor. A number of means were envisaged such as arranging for letters to be sent by influential businessmen and others from various parts of the country and from the United States.

It seems to me that the most remarkable of the many remarkable things about the Second World War is that it really was our 'Finest Hour'. There were, of course, some who were 'private-spirited' to use Alan Barlow's neat phrase, but they were never a large number and fewer, I believe, in the bombed south east and north west than elsewhere. It would be interesting to know what the crime figures were during the war; at the Board of Trade we had reason to know that there was very little looting after raids because our regional staff had the duty of visiting bombed areas to ensure a sufficient replacement of goods both in homes and in the shops. In London throughout the war people shared an extraordinary patience and cheerfulness – no doubt fuelled by elation that one had survived so far – and a determination to put up with anything and everything from nightly raids and disturbed sleep to transport discomforts and delays, and shortages of food and of almost all consumer goods. The sound of broken glass being swept up became as insistent as London's starlings, and the tangle of fire hoses on the morning after a raid looked like great snakes lying across the roads. There was a sense of comradeship that spread right across the old class distinctions. I got a thrill of pleasure from the first time one of our office

---

[*]Also in Francis's archive in Cambridge.

cleaners handed me my blanket and pillow for fire-watching duty with the words: 'Here you are dearie.' Their patience and their cheerfulness was outstanding; many spent interrupted nights on deck-chairs in their 'Anderson' shelters and then had to queue for early buses but managed, nevertheless, to get to work in time to keep our offices reasonably clean.

To what extent the morale of the 'Finest Hour' was a prevailing mood to which Churchill gave expression, or an attitude of mind that he created, must be a matter of opinion. I am sure that the behaviour of the first people to be bombed was of great importance in giving courage to the rest of us. But certainly Churchill's words strengthened our resolve, if they did not create it. In one respect, however, Churchill misjudged the public mood. I don't think that it was the usual reaction of people who had been bombed to be comforted by being told that we would 'do it back to them'. It was quite positively not mine. In a strange way, the mood of solidarity which underlay the 'Finest Hour' extended to the individual people who were the enemy. Admittedly, I didn't suffer myself or witness neighbours suffering in a raid, but I would have been aware of a general demand for reprisals.

Again looking back from the 1980s to the 1940s, I think it is worth adding that when Churchill said that this country 'stood alone', there was one important sense in which we have never been less alone. For after the five weeks that followed Hitler's invasion of the Low Countries in May 1940 when that speech was made, this small island became a kind of Noah's Ark filled with people from all the nations of Europe that Hitler had overrun. They were part of our 'Finest Hour' and indeed many had the harder and greater part, for often they had families at desperate risk in the occupied countries. And because in many cases the people who came included the heads of governments who set up governments-in-exile here, London became for those few years in a true sense the capital of Europe.

13

Civilian Front

Meantime at the Board of Trade I had moved on from Fanum House to a department called 'the Control of Factory and Storage Premises'. (C.F. and S. for short), another wholly new function for the Board of Trade. It had begun with Lord Beaverbrook, newly appointed Minister for Aircraft Production, sending his people round the country to slap a requisition order on any factory or large store that they thought could be adapted to produce aircraft. Many of these factories, of course, were important for the production of exports and essential civilian goods so something had to be done to stop the marauders.

A committee of the War Cabinet under Sir Cecil Weir,[*] decided that one department only should be given the right to authorise the requisitioning of space for war purposes and Richard Kahn and I (probably on Wattie's advice) were asked to collaborate in preparing a paper to implement this. We were told we should plan for an operation that would release at least one million square feet of covered space. We worked easily together because we were both determined 'doers', and we became and remained friends. Richard was a brilliant theoretical economist but he preferred administration and he had a real flare for innovation in the sphere of practical policies. When later he was offered the title of Economic Adviser to the Board of Trade, he refused it because he wanted to remain an administrator.

Our instructions were to assume that the control would be exercised by the Ministry of Works but when we consulted the under-secretary in charge of Government buildings, we found him extremely unenthusiastic; the target of one million square feet was quite unrealistic he assured us; requisitioning was a long

---

[*]Sir Cecil Weir K.C.M.G. Initiator, and Chairman of the Administrative Committee, of the Empire Exhibition in Glasgow in 1938 and Civil Defence Commissioner for Western Scotland, 1939.

and difficult business and his department was already fully stretched in finding and equipping space for all the new government departments, not least those for the Board of Trade. Richard and I looked at each other with the same thought. If the job was to be done with the urgency needed, it would have to be done by the Board of Trade. And since the buildings would have to be found from civilian industry and storage the Board of Trade was in any case in the best position to say which could be spared.

Sir Cecil Weir has described* how, in March 1941, he agreed to head the new department, how 'I was given a first-class Civil Servant staff headed by Miss Kilroy, a brilliant representative of women civil servants' (I can't resist quoting that); and how 'There was no delay – within a few hours we got to work.' Though we were technically part of the Board of Trade I had a more than usually independent command under my businessman boss, Cecil Weir. He was a Glaswegian Scot with great charm of manner, white hair and moustache, and winning smile who always seemed to me to be almost too 'good', in the sense of innocently good, to be the successful businessman he was.

It was decided between us on the first day that we should divide the organisation into two sections – factory and storage – each headed by a senior businessman with experience of the needs of those two functions and that we should also need a regional staff to inspect and negotiate the transfer of premises on the spot.

From the first we worked happily and easily as a team of four. Our factory controller, Sir Thomas Barlow, was chairman of one of the largest cotton firms in the country and had for many years been chairman of the Manchester Chamber of Commerce while Raymond Streat was its secretary. He was Alan Barlow's brother and already a personal friend of Francis's when he joined us and I came to know him as Tommy. He had a large handsome face and a mass of greying hair which he tugged at as we argued about, for example, the need for him to set an example to others by moving some immensely heavy and complicated redundant cotton spinning machinery out of an unused part of his own factory to make room for war storage: he yielded but proved his point; the job took too long to be of practical use. His manner in dealing

*In his book, *Civilian Assignment*.

with difficult people or problems was both incisive and dismissive but always charming and ready with a twinkle in the eye. Sir Philip Warter, our storage controller, was already working as wartime director of warehousing at the Ministry of Food when Cecil Weir persuaded the Ministry to release him to us.

Because it was a new departure for the Board of Trade to deal with bricks and mortar, our staff at headquarters included Sadler Forster who had run the first and largest of the Special Areas Trading Estates, and a principal lent from the Factory Inspectorate by the Home Office. I hoped that both would have the practical knowledge of buildings that the Board of Trade lacked. However, undoubtedly my most useful member of staff at the start was a senior staff officer called Middleton who, in the fashion of the time, I knew only by surname, and who exuded calmness and competence. We worked together on our priority task which was to establish a register of the space occupied by civilian factories that might have usable space available; there was a separate storage register. The only list of factories in existence was the one used by the Factory Inspectorate which was found to contain some 70,000 names. We cut out all those employing only ten people or less, those, such as engineering firms, that were likely already to be involved in war production, but that still left 38,000. It sounds a tall order but Middleton approached it as though it was an everyday affair. Between us we drew up a quite simple two-page questionnaire and were rewarded by a very high percentage of returned papers – no less than 32,000 in the first year. It is worth noting here, I think, that like so many guesstimates, the original estimate of one million square feet needed was wildly out.

Our regional controllers were mainly businessmen known to Cecil Weir. They needed to be people of enough calibre to set up their own offices and to work pretty independently on the task of inspecting possible premises which they identified from our register, and then negotiating their transfer to war purposes, by agreement wherever possible. Inevitably, this was usually a painful process for the civilian owner who was faced with the closure or reduction of his business, but the general experience was of ready co-operation once the war need had been demonstrated. I don't remember a single case of serious revolt.

Many of the Regional Controllers became personal friends and I never sensed that they felt any objection to taking instructions from a woman. I did, however, have a difficult moment with one of them: I was summoned to an interview with the Board of Trade Establishment Officer and informed with great formality and secrecy, that this Officer was having an affair with someone who was believed to be a security risk; as his boss, I must tell him to break off the relationship if he was to continue in his job. Our interview, painful already because of our friendship, was made more so by my having to tell him that he must not reveal to the girl the reason for his action.

Alec Cairncross,[*] one of the many economists turned civil servant for the duration, joined the staff for a time during the early months of the Control, having been secretary of Cecil Weir's Cabinet Committee that had outlined our policy. While the rest of us were dealing with current demands for space, his assignment was to try to establish a 'blitz storage' – a rather 'Will-o'-the-wisp' task he has described it as, because anything he found was immediately wanted for current use. He tells me that I left him free to follow his own judgement and he seems to have acted like a flying squad beside the regional controllers, inspecting premises himself and dealing direct with Tommy Barlow. He and I were to become friends and meet again officially when he was Economic Adviser to the Board of Trade after the war.

Our work was greatly helped by one of the Board's most revolutionary policies that had again been suggested by Richard Kahn, and given official life by Wattie. It was called the 'Concentration of Production' and involved arranging 'marriages' between competing firms which produced similar goods, this released premises as well as employees and at the same time keeping the firms alive. It was one of our chief sources of space. It often worked well even between sworn peacetime enemies, because it reduced the costs of the civilian businesses that were drastically cut; and of course it was very helpful for our regional controllers when they could propose something of the kind to ease the pain of a requisition order. But I had one of my few differences with Wattie over a particular case under this policy;

[*]Sir Alec Cairncross K.C.M.G., Fellow of St Anthony's College, Oxford.

the important consideration for me was where the space would
be released, while for him the question was which factories
would be most efficient for producing essential goods. I found
him quite unable to recognise that my need could possibly be
greater than his: 'Really A.K.,' he said, shaking his head. 'You
mustn't get things out of proportion. . . .' I realised then – and
remembered for the future – how single-minded the great (for he
was great) have to be, if they are to achieve greatly.

In April 1941, early in the setting up of the C.F. & S., both my
parents died within a fortnight of each other. My mother's death
from cancer was merciful and, at my request, was 'helped' at the
last by my blitz doctor friend Doyne Bell. I had had to watch her
suffering and to suffer with her when, believing that one must
not lie in answer to the final question, I had told her the truth
about her illness. I saw her face crumple and realised that I had
taken all hope from her. 'All that is left now is courage,' she said.

We had all, Robin included, kept an unusually close relationship with Mum and had taken what opportunities we could to be
with her in her last illness though we knew that she was
professionally and gently nursed. 'It's almost worth being ill to
have this time to myself with you,' she said to me. Her only
request was for music, either Bach or Beethoven. It didn't occur
to us to call a priest and she didn't ask for one. She had given up
her Catholic faith gradually as her children defected one by one
but she kept a basic belief. In her letter to Maudy about me at the
time of Garrow's death she had written that 'she has to trust and
we, too, to the light within and that it comes from something far
beyond our seeing here; it is there.'

My father was desolated. 'It's a terrible thing to lose a wife,' he
said with pathetic simplicity. He remained wholly devoted;
would even follow her to London (to her exasperation, alas) and
walk behind, keeping her in sight, in case there should be a
daylight raid. All his children went with him to Broughton for
the traditional Church of England service in the village church,
he holding tight during the train journey to the brown paper
parcel that contained the ashes. Inexplicably in our dear uncles,
they did not tell us in advance that there was no room for another
urn in the small family monument. We did not argue but buried it

instead in Broughton garden. I cannot understand why we didn't scatter the ashes in the churchyard as Maudy had done with Grandpa's ashes.

It is my lasting regret – shame – that we encouraged Mum to leave their house in trust to Mona and me her executors, instead of direct to Dad 'because' (we felt) 'he would fuss so' – typical, I feel now, of the unintended cruelty of the young in their certainties of what is right for the old. Of course, it saved tax but what is that beside the dignity of possession? I had dealt him another blow by arranging for my mother to give me power of decision in the last stages of her illness. Unforgivable? But then Dad would never have agreed to her being 'helped' to die. 'A kind of murder,' I heard him murmur. I managed to get away to spend the following Saturday evening with Dad and he took pains to hand over any documents he thought important. His last advice to me when I told him I had had an approach from Wilfrid Anson to consider joining the Imperial Tobacco Company after the war, was to stay in the Civil Service and not to be tempted by more money to go into industry. I am surprised that it didn't occur to me that he felt ill; a day or two later he was dead. In late years he had had a weakness of the heart: it was certainly broken.

It was inevitable that the atmosphere and pressures of war should a little soften all individual griefs, and work – war work especially –had to go on. The Control of Factory and Storage Premises began formal operation the next month, on 15th May 1941. So immediately after the funeral I went back to London and to my new job with Cecil Weir.

I find from the records that I was only thirteen months in the C.F. & S. Had I been dependent on memory, I should have said at least two years. I was given an affectionate send-off and a presentation cigarette case with the signatures of my three controllers engraved on it but I could not be sorry to go because I was being promoted again – to be a principal assistant secretary (a grand kind of head of department) – in charge of one of the big departments. It was called I.M.4 and it had general responsibility for most of the non-textile industries and for introducing furniture rationing. Inevitably my boss once more was Wattie.

All my senior staff were men and I met hostility for the first time. I had asked one of my assistant secretaries to be responsible for our knowledge of the retail trade and was taken quite aback when he stormed out of the room saying that this was not sufficient or fit work for someone of his rank. He may have had some justification; I was asking him to be chiefly a repository of technical knowledge in a sphere in which, as I remember, there were no immediate policy questions in sight. I am not certain to this day whether his anger was due to this alone. I wonder now whether an edge was added to his feelings from the fact that his boss was a woman. I set against it words written to me years later by (Sir) Tony Percival who was another of my assistant secretaries at that time: 'You piloted I.M.4 brilliantly and you liked your colleagues because they liked you. You have always raised my morale which is generally round my ankles. . . .'

It is also worth mentioning that I was for a time the elected chairman of the First Division Association for the whole Civil Service – a clear sign of the absence of prejudice.

Hugh Dalton had become President of the Board in 1942 and I saw a good deal of him in my work at I.M.4 for he regarded furniture rationing, and utility furniture its accompaniment, as very much his baby. I was not alone in finding him little pleasure to work for. He appeared to have a distrust of all civil servants and clearly to enjoy 'putting them down' in front of their juniors or the businessmen who occupied advisory positions in the department. The civil servant could not answer back unless he could confront the President in private.

I was never the subject of a public 'put-down' but I often got short shrift on paper, and once when a minute of mine had been peppered all down the side in red ink with 'Rubbish', 'Nonsense', 'Absurd' and similar comments, as if it was an essay by a student at the L.S.E., I asked the private secretary to arrange an interview for me and, rather shaking in my shoes but also with a rare anger, I put the minute in front of him:

'You have, of course, every right to disagree with me,' I said, 'and what you say goes. But you can't treat the head of a department like this and expect to have a happy and efficient staff.'

He was all contrition and gracious apology:

'But surely,' he said, 'this paper will not be seen by your staff?'

'Of course it will,' I said not yet mollified. 'It's part of an official file and can't be removed from it.'

He never tried to bully me again and, thereafter, our official dealings became quite friendly.

I had another difference with Wattie over the kind of scheme we should introduce when he took the advice of the economist Brian Reddaway[*] instead of mine on the form that the rationing should take. It couldn't be like clothes or food rationing because furniture was only an occasional purchase. So people would have to make applications based on need. I argued that successful applicants should be given permits for the specific pieces of furniture – a chair, a bed, a wardrobe – for which they had established a claim. Reddaway (then working in our Statistics Dept) argued that we should allocate points to the various pieces of furniture and grant the appropriate number to successful applicants who could then use them as they wanted.

It was at Dalton's personal insistence that the production of new furniture (to which alone our control applied) was confined to approved utility designs at controlled prices – in this respect unlike utility clothing which never formed more than a proportion of the clothes produced and rationed. We officials argued at first that it would be going too far along the road to state control to limit the production of furniture entirely to approved Government designs but Dalton was right; his was the only way to ensure that the controlled price meant anything – that is attached to an article of the intended quality. It was also the only way to avoid the waste of wood which was largely imported and of skilled labour, on unnecessary frills. We were very keen on 'clean lines and fitness for purpose'; claw feet, so often to be found in Victorian and Edwardian furniture, was our symbol for all that we thought wasteful, *un*beautiful and to be avoided in utility furniture. We started with six main patterns ranging from the best and priciest made by Gordon Russell and usually sold through Heals, to the

[*] Now Professor Reddaway, at Cambridge University.

everyday furniture mass-produced by Harriss Lebus at his modern factory in Tottenham. Both these men worked with and for us as unpaid advisers.

Dalton launched the scheme himself, with me in attendance, and told the Press that he was 'chivvying Miss Kilroy' to get a move on. I didn't mind this – I knew that no offence was meant or would have been justified – but Sir Arnold Overton, (then our permanent secretary and my former boss at C.R.T.) sent for me to apologise formally for the President's discourtesy to me. Those two could never have understood each other. Overton was a tall good-looking man, a classicist, highly intelligent, gentle, quietly spoken and reserved; as different as possible in every way from Dalton who was naturally outgoing and gregarious and could be intimidating with his considerable height, large domed head and loud booming voice. When Dalton left the Board to become Chancellor of the Exchequer, Overton – determined to say nothing that was not truthful at the official leaving party – could find no socially polite word of praise for his political master. But Dalton spoke for half-an-hour without a single note and said something pleasant – even apparently sincere – about each of us. Had we, we wondered, misjudged him?

All this time I could not fail to be aware of what Francis was doing to help Wattie with the launch of clothes rationing. Secrecy had been essential to avoid a run on the shops and it was only through the newspapers that retailers could be told about the scheme and what ration points to charge for individual garments. Whit weekend, May 1941, was chosen for the launch to give the shops the Bank Holiday to mark up their goods and, meantime, two hotels were requisitioned in Bournemouth and a considerable staff engaged, all for an undisclosed purpose until after the shops had closed on Whit Saturday. It was Francis who drafted the technical advertisements explaining the scheme to the shops and Francis who had to persuade the Ministry of Information (who alone had authority for Government advertising) to book blank space in advance. So well was the secret kept, that there was only one run on the shops on Whit Saturday – in Ruislip the home of the Government's confidential printing works. And above all it was Francis who produced the 'fair shares' banner under which the scheme was launched and was made acceptable to the public, and I can count Francis one of the master builders of wartime morale. It could even be said that he influenced the shape of the peace too, for his banner motif of 'Fair Shares' was basically the stuff of socialism. Over the months and years he had become not only the Board's Adviser on Consumer Needs but also its acknowledged though unofficial adviser on the presentation of all policies affecting consumers – one of the first of the now numerous public relations officers. At this time too, he did so much broadcasting that he became effectively broadcaster-in-chief on any matter to do with civilian supplies for the home front. He did not often talk outside this subject but on the day in December 1941 when America entered the war, it was his voice that we all heard on the wireless reading extracts from 'John Brown's Body', Stephen Vincent Benet's moving history in blank verse of the American Civil War.

By a surprising chance, I had been given an extra part-time appointment which had brought Francis and me together as joint heads of the same department. The work of checking shortages begun at Fanum House had grown into a separate section at headquarters called 'Consumer Needs' which had the job of finding and reporting shortages of consumer goods of all kinds except food. It did invaluable service visiting places that had been bombed to ensure that the shelves of the local shops were restocked with essential goods such as clothing, blankets and cooking utensils but their work in reporting shortages from our Board of Trade controls was no less important. It had its own regional staff of Area Distribution Officers (A.D.O.s) and a small headquarters staff, none of whom were career civil servants. No one doubted its efficiency but when Francis was formally appointed to be the Government's 'Adviser on Consumer Needs', it was felt that a modicum of Civil Service system ought to be introduced into his department. To our delight, I was given the job. Apart from Wattie, the Board knew nothing of our relationship when this happened. I think that, when we married, they had the happy belief that they had first brought us together.

I didn't interfere with the staff and friendly family-like organisation already established by Francis and his able deputy, Leonard Skevington, an economist who had worked in industry and journalism; he was 'Skevvie' to everyone and was as important to the organisation and almost as much loved as Francis. Indeed, I did little more as joint head than insist on Civil Service files and records being kept but I made many friends, chief among them Susan (then the wife of Woodrow Wyatt*) and Reg Hicklin† whom she later married. Susan had a mass of unruly corn-yellow hair which was always escaping into her eyes, and an ebullient personality made up of enormous energy and enthusiasm and later she was to be my personal assistant in the Reconstruction Department before she began her family of four.

Consumer Needs were a help on a number of occasions over a policy under which the production of luxuries was limited to the bare minimum needed to avoid killing the trade altogether. When it was applied to jewellery, reports began coming in almost at once from A.D.O.s all over the country, that wedding rings had disappeared from the shops. Not unnaturally (but unforeseen by me) jewellery retailers concentrated their reduced trade on goods on which they could earn the largest margins. We had to give them a special quota for wedding rings and then to avoid profiteering, we had to insist that the quota be filled with 'utility' wedding rings which were price-controlled; they were all that people could get until after the war.

The A.D.O.s also reported a widespread famine in domestic crockery, especially in cups: 'Do you realise,' they asked dramatically, 'that in some places, people are reduced to drinking out of empty sardine tins?'

Without quite believing that example, it was clear that something had to be done, and it would have to be done by me since the pottery industry was one of my responsibilities at I.M.4. I was told that the stores had all been emptied – even the old stock of 'moustache' cups made for Edwardian whiskers had been sold. The industry didn't know the peacetime output of cups and saucers because they kept statistics only by weight. So,

---

*Later M.P., now Lord.
†Advertising Manager of Lever Bros.

could Consumer Needs manage to find out by market research how many cups we must have a year for normal civilian needs? If we knew that, we could add a percentage for bomb damage. A fairly large sample of households was asked how many cups had been broken in the previous year. The result was an astronomical figure.

'Then,' said Francis, 'we will enquire how many cups have been broken in the previous week and ask to see the pieces.'

A very different figure resulted.

I went to Stoke-on-Trent to discuss what could be done, and the result was white, undecorated, domestic crockery and handleless cups. I was unsympathetic to the suggestion that people would burn their fingers; it was a question, I said, of holding by the rim. We got more cups than had been planned because it transpired that since handles had to be added on the day after the cup part was made cups were not normally made on Fridays; without handles, they could be made on all five working days. The cup shortage was over. An amusing example of the wartime policy of fair sharing arose when the Board of Trade slapped a maximum price of one shilling and sixpence on a packet of cigarettes. Our tobacco controller was a good-living out-spoken businessman called Sandy Maxwell and it fell to him to receive the manager of the Savoy Hotel, protesting that they had always felt justified in putting an extra price on their cigarettes because of the special amenities they provided. Sandy interrupted the description of the luxuries of the Savoy, which he knew well from experience, by slamming his hand down on his desk and saying: 'I don't care if you've got two bloody bidets in every bedroom, you aren't going to charge more than one and sixpence for a packet of cigarettes.'

I heard of a similar case from Eric Hooper,[*] a business friend of Francis's who was working at the Ministry of Food. He was chairing a meeting of soft drinks manufacturers to agree quotas for imports of fruit when one maker argued that his company owned big fruit plantations and should have a larger share on that account: 'Right,' said Eric. 'If you insist, you can have all of your company's fruit but you'll have to find your own ships

[*]Later Sir Eric Hooper, Chairman of Schweppes.

and you mustn't expect to have the protection of the British Navy.'

Civil servants would have spoken less picturesquely but to the same effect. The sumptuary restrictions that we imposed on the civilian population and on industry during the war were accepted with remarkable complacency once the war need to save labour and materials was demonstrated. When the Nottingham embroidery industry argued that women would not accept plain underwear, Wattie produced me as his 'secret weapon' to tell them that they were mistaken – and the trade conformed without more argument. But there was one economy on which we were defeated: we never could get the male public to buy the short socks which we persuaded the hosiery industry to produce. It was not until the Americans arrived, that the exposure of an inch or two of male leg between trouser and sock became acceptable.

I doubt, however, if the 'togetherness' of the Finest Hour would have survived – would it even have begun? – but for the certainty that the essentials of life, as well as the dangers and discomforts, were being shared equally, regardless of differences of wealth.

In January 1943 I was moved to yet another job; this time to take charge of a newly formed Reconstruction Department to work out plans for peace-time policies in the home market. The idea was probably once more Wattie's; he was the overseeing deputy secretary and, as usual, we were 'ahead of the field'; the new Government department under Lord Woolton as Minister of Reconstruction, to co-ordinate plans for the Peace, was not established until November. My own appointment was further evidence of Wattie's hand in the setting up of our Reconstruction Department. Yes, I swelled with pride when he told his assembled principal assistant secretaries that I was *primus inter pares*' but I suspect his real reason for choosing me was that he meant to take a big hand in the work himself and knew that I was happy to be his deputy – I had certainly had enough training in that position.

During the following two years we made plans for the unscrambling of the many wartime controls we had imposed on

industry: How long should we have to keep control to ensure
production for the rationing schemes while they lasted? How
could we see fairness done between firms that had closed under
concentration schemes or had opted to turn over to war
production, and those which had not? Should any preference be
given to efficient over inefficient firms? . . . and any number of
similar problems. And we proposed and outlined a considerable
number of new measures, most notably policies to control
monopolies and to help the old and declining industrial areas.
Among the smaller but still important plans which would
become accepted policy were the invention of the Institute of
Management to combine the many associations concerned with
management problems that were then in existence, and a new
Council of Industrial Design. Here, my work again touched
Francis's interests for beauty in the look of things. 'Eye appeal' as
he called it was as near to his heart for consumer goods generally
as for books; he used to demonstrate his point by holding up one
of the streamlined Parker pens just produced in America. I
assembled a small committee to finalise our plans consisting of
Francis, Kenneth Clark,[*] Josiah Wedgwood[†] and Gordon Russell which met in my room on the eighth floor of the I.C.I.
building overlooking the Thames. Dalton didn't wait for the
Peace to set up the new Design Council. *The Times* for 20th
December 1944 announced its appointment and welcomed it
with a leading article. It was headed by Tommy Barlow as
chairman with, amongst its members, the four who had met in
my room to plan it.

I have no doubt that it was Dalton who directed our early
attention to the Special Areas; he was M.P. for Bishop Auckland
(which was in one of them) and the declining old industrial areas
were always a major concern of his. We studied the Barlow
Report that had been published just before the outbreak of war. It
described the drift of industry and population to London and the
south, and highlighted the conditions caused by the high level of
unemployment in the old industrial areas of the north and west:
young men forced to seek work in more prosperous areas; old

---

[*]The late Lord Clark, husband of my College friend Jane, and then Director
of the National Gallery.
[†]Chairman of Wedgwood Potteries.

people left behind in poverty; closed shops; whole communities dying. We not only read about these conditions, we pictured them because our experience during the war had given us some firsthand knowledge of them.

It seemed clear that, if these evils were to be avoided, the emphasis of post-war policy should be in taking the work north and west to the people and not the people south to the work. It had been pre-war policy to attract new industries to the Special Areas with government-sponsored trading estates which gave firms the great advantage of not having to sink capital in bricks and mortar. These estates had prospered but had clearly not been a sufficient answer to the problem. It looked as if some element of compulsion would be needed and our industrial controls during war – in particular the Concentration of Industry policy – had accustomed us to the manipulation of industry for the general good. What emerged was a plan renamed 'Distribution of Industy policy' under which (subject to a minimum size, of the order of 5,000 sq. ft.) no manufacturer would be allowed to extend his factory without an industrial development certificate (an I.D.C.) from the Board of Trade; the Special Areas would become Development Areas; and I.D.C.s would normally be given only in one or other of these areas. Since the main discussions and decisions under this policy would be industrial, it followed that responsibility should be transferred to the Board of Trade from the Ministry of Labour where it had been before the war. I have always suspected that by being well-prepared in advance, we stole a march on the Ministry of Labour over this. But, in any case, it made political sense.

I contributed one idea of my own to support the policy. I think it came to me in that fertile thinking area, my bath. Why not add to the I.D.C. control the inducement of a building licence? The building industry was over-stretched as a result of the enormous destruction during the war, and in consequence the right to build – the right to use building labour and building materials – was strictly rationed. If we could offer building licences with our I.D.C.s, we should get quick industrial expansion in our Development Areas. We might even get people whose factories had been bombed to move away from the south by the bait of an early building licence. I had some difficulty in persuading the Ministry of Works who ran the building licence control but in the end the policy was approved and it must have added to the inducements in favour of the Development Areas in the early years after the war.

Looking back once again from the 1980s to the 1940s, it seems to me pretty obvious that industry would not have accepted, or co-operated with, this policy had it not first grown accustomed to Government controls in war, often administered by its own people, the businessmen who made such a large contribution to the war effort, working within the government departments. It is surely unlikely also that either the I.D.C. control or the Building Licence preference would have been considered politically acceptable outside the atmosphere of the war and the euphoria of the immediate post-war years.

All our plans were included in a memorandum for the Cabinet and most if not all became Board of Trade policy. It was not a matter of surprise to anyone that the wartime Coalition Government should make plans for the Peace or that civil servants should help to prepare them. As it turned out, the policies were implemented under a Labour Government but, in view of their origin, most would probably have been adopted equally under a Conservative administration. Indeed, we began to implement some like the Design Council before the General Election; and I, for example, began work on the drafting of the first Monopolies Bill with Sir David Maxwell-Fyffe (President of the Board of Trade under the Conservative Caretaker administration) which became law under Sir Stafford Cripps (President in the Labour administration). Altogether, an admirable demonstration, it seems to me, of the productive and efficient working of Coalition Government.

I find it very difficult now to believe that the five very different war jobs which have made such an impression on my memory, were crammed into only four and a half years – that two years at Reconstruction was my longest job and that I was only nine months on furniture rationing. But it was also in that short time that I stepped unknowing from youth into middle age: I used quite often to cycle to work and one day as I pedalled up the almost empty road from Hyde Park Corner to the Ritz, I was behind a lorry full of recently arrived American G.I.s. What was their greeting? A wolf-whistle? No. What I heard them shout was – 'Come on Auntie!'

14

Cobbold's Mill

For Sale. Mill house in rural Suffolk on tributary of river
Stour. Suitable for retired city gentleman of sporting
tastes. (from *The Times* personal column, April 1945)

Francis was neither retired nor at all like a city gentleman and
though he was a compulsive player of games, he had absolutely
no sporting tastes; he didn't hunt or fish and he had given up
shooting (he told me) at the age of ten, when he had been taken on
a shoot in Ireland by his uncle and saw all the wounded birds.

But – a *mill* house, and in *Suffolk*. We had to see it, and a week
later Cobbold's Mill was ours. Francis and I had been spending
some of our weekends recently on our bicycles looking for
somewhere in the country where we could 'put our roots down'.
Though there seemed no early prospect that Vera would agree to
a divorce, we both knew that we could not go back after the war
to a pretence of living apart, and my recent discovery of the
advance of middle age upon me had made me feel that there was
no time to lose.

My sisters had all been married for some years now and had
homes and growing families. We also wanted the country for our
weekends; we were no longer content to squander those memories of happiness either at the houses of friends or at Toppesfield
which was so very much Vera's home. Moreover, the war had
added an extra dimension in favour of the country – a longing to
create, to build, to grow things, in contrast to the years of
destruction and of what in one of his poems Francis called 'the
random sluttishness of war'.

We recognised two special attractions about Cobbold's Mill
before we even saw it: first that it was not more than twenty miles
by road from Toppesfield where Benedict still lived with his
mother, and where our friends the Potters and the Plummers,

and later the Sainsburys,[*] had houses; and second that it was east of London and so was served and (as we maintained) protected by the least attractive of all the London railway stations. We delighted to argue that the horrors of Liverpool Street station with its draughts and its wide spread of platforms, plus the cold misery of Marks Tey station (where passengers must change whether going to Toppesfield or Cobbold's) provided a barrier to all but the most hardy travellers and had prevented this part of East Anglia from becoming a fashionable development area for Londoners.

The moment we saw it we knew that Cobbold's was what we wanted. It had a 'Georgian' front painted in Suffolk pink, its own stretch of river running under the house, a possible bathing pool, even its own punt, and a great water-wheel that worked; for the mill had been producing flour commercially as lately as 1938. The house had no fine staircase or 'big' sitting-room like those at Toppesfield but there was a 'big' bedroom with huge beams silvered with age and we could create a 'big' sitting-room by knocking down a wall. It was obvious that we could put our roots down there with great happiness. But could we afford it? And wasn't it much too large and grand for us?

The price that was being asked was more than we had planned to pay. Was it £7,000 or £5,000? I can't remember. All that following week in London the charms of 'Cobbs' were at the back of our minds and that we determined to see it again the next weekend. Evelyn insisted on our telephoning early on Sunday morning from Toppesfield to say at least that we were interested. 'It's as well that you telephoned,' they said. 'We have a possible buyer now in the house but we will wait to decide until we see you since you were here first.' We hurried over feeling more eager at every mile but stopping just before we arrived (at a henceforth memorable stretch of road called Humble Green) to try to be sensible and decide what we could really afford. I had £3,500 of capital and Francis had about the same. It did not occur to us to try for a mortgage so we hadn't much room for manoeuvre, bearing in mind that we must allow for furnishings. The owners said that a provisional offer had been made but they

[*]Alan (now Lord) Sainsbury and his second wife, Babette.

would prefer to sell to us because 'the other people were spending trustee money and were making difficulties about surveys and such. . . . Would we be prepared to offer a little more – say £200?' We threw caution to the winds and said 'Yes'.

We clinched the deal just after V.E. Day, and the Visitors' Book, bound in red Morocco leather, and opened by Francis with an italic flourish, records that we slept there for the first time on 11th August, V.J. Day. Between these dates enough happened both in the world at large and to us personally to fill an ordinary year and more. In June, I was moved from the Reconstruction Department, which I had led for two years, to a challenging new job as head of the two I. and M. Departments, and Francis was honoured by being made one of only forty R.D.I.s (Royal Designers for Industry). In June too there was the excitement of the post-war General Election and in July the thrill of the overwhelming Labour victory.

Why did so many reject Churchill? Why did we, Francis and I? We yielded to no one – either then or later – in our admiration for Churchill and our acknowledgement of him as a war leader who had literally saved Europe, and us individually, from the Nazis. But our politics had been 'Labour' before the war and they had been strengthened in that direction by the sharing and togetherness of the war. Churchill was certainly not the man to win the kind of peace we wanted and had planned in 'Do It Now'. Our gratitude to him was in no way reduced by his right-wing stance in the General Election but we were profoundly shocked by his use of the hated enemy word *Gestapo* in connection with the policies of Labour colleagues with whom, side by side, he had fought the war: they would have (so went the broadcast with which he opened the election campaign on 4th June 1945) 'to fall back on some form of *Gestapo*, no doubt very humanely directed in the first instance'.

When you add to Labour's victory the exhilaration we already felt about Victory in Europe and our personal realisation of the end of fear on the death of Hitler, and add to that again our smaller but still great excitement over Cobbold's Mill, it can be seen that we must have been punch-drunk with euphoria. So perhaps we are to be forgiven for assuming that the war with Japan was as good as over. Robin was then Flight Commander on

ABOVE: The bay of Lerici, oil painting by my brother Robin
BELOW: Group at Lerici. *Left to right*: Self, niece Alice, Martin
Zander and Francis

ABOVE: Francis and self playing chess at Cobbold's Mill, oil
painting by my brother Robin
BELOW LEFT: Francis with Pam Zander at Pisa; BELOW RIGHT:
Francis and Evelyn Sharp at Gordes, May 1971

his ship the aircraft carrier H.M.S. *Illustrious*, in the Far East. It was only after we read John Hersey's report on Hiroshima which entirely filled two consecutive issues of the *New Yorker* that we began to realise the horror that had been released by the invention of the atom bomb. Robin wrote that his life might well have been one of those saved but he would rather have died.

Cobbold's Mill, drawn by Colin Milne

Cobbold's Mill lies exactly on the boundary between Monk's Eleigh and Chelsworth, an even smaller village. We were delighted some years later to find in the 1960 *Shell Guide to Suffolk* under the entry for Chelsworth not only that it was 'a pretty Brett-valley village' but also that – 'Francis Meynell lives at Cobbold's Mill.'

The previous owners had occupied only the part of the building that had been the miller's house. The upper part of the working area where the bags of flour had been stored became a vast and lovely bedroom with windows both east and west. It was occupied largely by bats that we had some difficulty in discouraging. The lower part of the mill where the grain had been stored was also unused, and, as our only structural change before occupation day, we got the local builder to knock down the wall between this area and the dark narrow room next to it, to make our 'big room'. Here we installed a refectory table we had found at Maples, and Arnold Bennett's sofa (bought after his death) to provide the seats on one side. For many years this was where we had meals when there were guests – and there almost always were.

The only other important change we made at once was to install an Aga cooker in place of the old-fashioned kitchen range. Francis's advertising firm had Allied Ironfounders as clients, and they supplied us with an Aga for its advertisement value. We had many struggles with it when it went out during the week and had to be laboriously relit with charcoal, but it was a lasting boon. We both learnt to cook on it; we shared the cooking, soups and sauces were Francis's speciality, puddings mine.

Our first care was to make sure that we could get local help for garden and house. Mrs Fosker (the previous owner's gardener) agreed to stay on. The same answer came from a second village lady called Mrs Stowe. It would not have been the Suffolk way to be, as it were, handed over with the house but we found the Suffolk people in general to be very friendly and both Mrs Fosker and Mrs Stowe stayed with us for the whole of our twenty-one years there. Like our Jean in London, they became friends as well as employees. Mrs Fosker was/is a very small woman with a very large fund of energy. She had been a Salvation Army girl before she married her farm-labourer husband, and it was said that, small as she was, she was quite ready to extract him from the local pub by force if necessary. In her spare time she was the Monks Eleigh correspondent for the local newspaper. Mrs Stowe was a very different kind of person, a big substantial country woman full of country knowledge and superstitions. Somewhere in her ancestry there must have been gypsy blood and Francis used to call her 'the village witch' after he had wondered why Cobbold's had no south windows and she had told him: 'None of those old houses has south windows because the black death came in from the south.' I think Mrs Stowe had some such belief in her powers herself and was proud of it but also a little afraid for she told us that once when she was picking potatoes, she had an altercation with one of the other women who she thought had taken one of her bags. 'I said I hoped she would fall off her bike and hurt herself and that afternoon she did,' she told us in an awed voice. Like many village women, she made extra money by potato-picking and she was very scornful of the stamina of the younger women: 'they wants an upright after only half-an-hour' she said. Assisted through the years by one or other of her daughters, Mrs Stowe was our house help and sometimes cook, who prepared and warmed our freezing house for our arrival and cleared up when we left. She arrived promptly, riding very upright on her bicycle, her bust well to the fore, and would never sit down for a cup of tea because, she said, she came to work not to sit about. There was, however, one occasion when she broke her rule: I was in charge of clothes rationing at the Board of Trade and we had just taken children's shoes off the ration. I knew she didn't think we really did much at our offices in London and I asked her if she was at least pleased about the children's shoes. She sat down and after a pregnant pause she said: 'Well milady. What I said to Stowe, milady, was – "the old girl's done something for us at last"' – and covered her mouth with pretended horror at referring to me thus. I told Harold Wilson who was then our President and thereafter when he wanted my opinion he would say – 'What does the old girl think?'

On buying Cobbold's we acquired some geese for £2 each, and also 1943-hatched hens for 12/6d each. I had got on easy terms with hens when I helped my aunt with them in the days I spent at Broughton. She kept Rhode Island Reds because they produced brown eggs and Light Sussex because they were the comfortable shape to make good mothers. I have a pleasant tactile memory of picking up the Light Sussex hens, unprotesting if held firmly in two hands with their wing feathers closed. I don't think Francis ever developed a liking for hens but he was keen to have geese and ducks; he bought a highly bred drake for the ducks and added three decorative Muskovies that we called Miriam, Merle and Oberon (after the two beautiful film actresses Miriam Hopkins and Merle Oberon whom he had known in his pre-war film days). What we had not realised was that ducks get very firmly attached to their first mates, and when we killed our first ducks for eating the highly-bred drake would have nothing to do with his daughters. A rather similar fate met the Muscovies: Merle flew away and when Miriam died, Oberon put his head down and died too – of a broken heart? Two swans arrived and established their home year after year on our piece of river. Francis christened them Swan and Edgar. We happened to be sitting in the garden in a warm early spring sun when they arrived for the summer; we heard the loud sound of their wings and saw them high up in the sky with their necks stretched out, and then watched them make first a low reconnoitre and then a graceful splash-landing like a flying boat. They had the same nest each year at the far end of the garden, largely made of twigs, close to the river, and they reared some cygnets every year. Edgar learnt to tap, and then to hammer, on our sitting-room window to ask for food and when he judged that the cygnets were old enough, he and Swan led them across the lawn to join the clack for bread. The cygnets were much too heavy for their legs and had to flop down for a rest several times on the way.

It was accepted that I was the gardener and I had the audacity (as I see it now) to put 'gardening' as my hobby when I first entered the pages of *Who's Who*. I had learned the technique of planting from Bimbi and I happened to have 'green fingers' but that was all and Francis and I learnt together from experience 'on the job' – or rather 'on the garden'. On the whole, he did the planning and I the execution: it was his idea to plant a wild rose hedge down one side of the drive (which was most successful because the scent was lovely) and fig trees on the other (which was not, because the soil was too good and they died). It was also his idea to go in for asparagus and to invite a well-known specialist to come and look at our land and advise us about varieties and planting methods. He came bringing down his own shiningly clean spade which he plunged once into the earth and announced that our light sandy soil was specially suited to the growing of asparagus.

One crop that we didn't attempt was honey. We had had quite enough of bee-keeping during the war at Toppesfield. Evelyn had arrived there one weekend carrying a bee-hive and a short book on bee-keeping which she announced with confidence was quite a simple job. A week or two later a 'swarm' obligingly and unexpectedly arrived and was persuaded to stay with much banging of saucepans by Mr and Mrs Suckling, the gardener and house-help; it took up residence in Evelyn's hive and for a time all was well while the bees consumed the sugar provided for bees outside the ration. They even produced some honey. But then came trouble: Evelyn had read in her little book that the season had arrived when the number of females must be reduced to leave the coast clear for the Queen Bee. Veiled and gloved, she advanced confidently on the hive and proceeded to 'pinch out' a number of bees that she judged were females and prospective aspirants for the throne. When, some hours later, Francis went out with the kindly purpose of filling their water trough, he was attacked and stung again and again on his unprotected head by angry bees. He stood his ground at first in the hope/belief that they would stop if he remained still, but after some thirty stings he ran. His face next day was so swollen that he was unrecognisable. While the stings were being removed one by one, Mrs Suckling told of the village people she knew who had died of as few as four stings.

Our asparagus adviser had flattered us by saying that he knew we should find the Suffolk people friendly and welcoming because 'you plan to be real country people and treat the land right, not like city-dwellers. . . .' He had said just the right thing to delight us for, basically ignorant as we were, we did indeed want to become real country people. There was a pig-sty at Cobb's, so we bought a pig, and we had several meadows, so why should we not get a cow and have our own milk and cream? Within months, we had bought for £40 a Red-poll with dark brown coat and eyes, called Clover, in milk and already in calf. It was fortunate that Leo Russell,[*] a wartime colleague and friend, was a local farmer. He realised that we had assumed that cows would live off the land – on grass alone. He supplied us with enough feed for Clover for one day and took us to his own millers in Lavenham to arrange for regular supplies.

We had learnt something about the feelings of animals from our ducks and swans. We got more lessons from our cow and later from the herd of pigs that I built up. It took little understanding to

---

[*]The hon. Leo Russell. Chairman of the Cement Makers Federation.

realise that Clover needed a companion and we bought another
Red-poll to keep her company. She was called Beautiful the
Third and she looked her name but, alas, before many months,
she fell ill. The vet could not discover the cause and advised that
she should be kept away from Clover for fear of infection.
Whether from the illness or, as I thought, from the separation,
real tears trickled out of Beautiful's eyes and down her nose. I was
touched to find that our cat – Puss – kept her company cuddling
up against her every night instead of sleeping in her usual place
until Beautiful died. Years later, I realised that cats have a special
sympathy for distress for, after Francis's death, I found that our
cat knew by instinct whenever I most needed comfort.

We got another lesson from Clover's first calf, Clodia. We
reared her in a converted pig-sty near the house and she saw only
humans until she was six months old. Then we bought another
Red-poll calf and put them together. Next morning Clodia's coat
was bathed in sweat, presumably from fear of the four-footed
creature she had been made to spend the night with. Notwithstanding this lesson, we sent her in due course to join our herd of
cows, and when we visited her, it was like going to see a
homesick child at boarding school.

There were no such traumas for our pigs, or for ourselves in
relation to them, except for the first which we had reared for our
own food. I didn't like sending it off to be slaughtered. We had
visited it each weekend for six months and I had come to enjoy its
contented grunts, so appropriately the opposite of disgrunt-le.
But when the butcher asked me to come and choose which parts
of the carcase I wanted for the table next weekend, I realised that I
couldn't possibly eat any myself. Thereafter, I made friends only
with our sows.

Over the years I built up a herd of pigs for sale to Sainsbury's
for bacon, and pig-weighing became a regular weekend happening that all enjoyed. In the end, we had as many as 100 pigs and six
to eight sows. The sows I preferred – perhaps from childhood
memories of my black and white rats? – were Essex Saddle-
backs. They made the best mothers but were rather short for
bacon pigs. There was a crisis with one large white sow that we
chose for its long back and called Very because it was very
expensive. Her first farrowing was difficult and instead of

welcoming each piglet and pushing it towards her teats, she started to eat them. There was not time to get the vet. 'Give her a feed with a whole bottle of aspirin,' said Francis from his armchair. This was done. She fell fast asleep and took to her piglets happily when she woke up. We used to keep the little pigs in a rearing house across the river until they were ready to move into the fattening house on the near-side. Driving them over was usually easy – they followed the most adventurous – but one day they simply would not cross the bridge. I said I would fetch some food and make a food paper-chase for them. It wasn't necessary, for as soon as I ran ahead, they followed; they knew that Wellington boots meant food.

One of the first things you learn when you keep pigs is that they are naturally clean animals – from the moment of birth they stagger away from the farrowing bed to excrete. And they love water. One hot summer Sunday when I had spent the morning in and out of our river pool and happened to walk past one of the pig houses. I found the six young pig inmates all standing in the full sun, panting. 'I know what I should like if I were you,' I thought. I fetched a hose and as I sprayed them with cold water, the panting stopped and I saw what I insist were smiles spread over their faces. Pigs also love sun-bathing and, in hot weather, Bill Game (our pig and cow-man) had to spend a lot of time rubbing sunburn lotion on the white ones – the black ones didn't appear to get sunburnt.

It may seem surprising that I so much enjoyed keeping pigs whose only end would be the slaughter-house. I argued it out to myself at the time and justified it on the ground that people must be fed and that I gave my pigs a pleasant life if a short one. What I couldn't get used to or justify when the lorry came to take them away, was the manner of their loading: they had to walk up a ramp to the floor of the lorry – often a very steep ramp to the top floor – and when their small trotters slipped, they got frightened. One particular occasion stands out in memory when my sister Bimbi was with me and quietened one frightened pig by a gentle hand on its back. . . . I could see no reason why pigs should be put through this misery instead of being lifted by a back-lift on the lorry as is done, for example, for bales of wool or paper and I started an agitation on the subject. I even dared to address a meeting of working farmers at Bury St Edmunds. I did not prevail but it is a good cause which I gather has since been recognised in some places abroad.

Mrs Fosker had been responsible for our one pig but from the moment we got a cow, we had to employ someone to milk and look after her – and the herd of pigs followed. And so Bill Game had joined our staff and become as important to the health and happiness of Cobbold's Mill as Mrs Fosker and Mrs Stowe. He too stayed with us until we left. He was a small wiry man with an abundance of country and agricultural skills and knowledge that is so *in*adequately described by the term 'agricultural labourer'. Before the war, Game had been employed for a time at Cobbold's when it was a working mill, for thirty shillings a week including overtime. He was so poor then that his children had to stay in bed while their clothes were washed because they had no change of clothing – 'In those days,' he said 'I didn't live, I existed.' He also worked with Mrs Fosker in the garden and – in this specifically under Francis's instruction – looked after the river. Through the centuries, as the old documents back to the sixteenth century showed, the river level had been a matter of contention with neighbours both up and downstream but thanks to Game's skill and Francis's charm, we had very little trouble.

Amongst the most important of the amenities of Cobbs was our river bathing pool and this too we owed largely to Game who built not one but three dams. The first two, built of sandbags filled with cement, were washed away but the third held.

In the 'Fair Shares' atmosphere of the war, and of the socialist Britain of the peace, we could not help some feeling that we were getting more happiness from Cobbold's Mill than was fair. We felt – not ashamed at our joy and pleasure in the beauty and delight of the place – but as if we needed to justify our tenure of it by sharing it. There can hardly ever have been a weekend when we went there alone. When we added up the number of our visitors during our first year and a half we found that we had ninety different guests (a third being family) and that between them they had made two hundred and twelve visits. We felt that was a reasonable balance of fairness.

Our guests could hardly have been more varied in their

personalities, interests and tastes. There were many friends from pre-war days, including the Potters, the Sainsburys, Doyne Bell (the paediatrician) and his sisters and Harold Hobson (the electrical engineer, not the theatre critic), and his second wife, Maggie; and there were Cyril Joad of *Brains Trust* fame, Norman Brook, Secretary to the Cabinet, and his wife Gossie known to me and Mona from early days at Cousin Oscar's, Björn Prytz and his wife, and the Raymond Streats. And there were many whom we had met and made friends with at work during the war; among them Pamela and Martin Zander, Reg and Susan Hicklin, Wattie and his wife, Chips.

Those Cobbs weekends! We could sleep eight, ten at a pinch, and very often did. We would leave the office as early as possible, which meant twelve o'clock on Saturday, and picnic in Epping Forest. Mrs Stowe would have got the house ready and probably have cooked a rabbit pie. There would be bathing in the river pool, tennis at our neighbour's, and boule. Richard Kahn has reminded me of an occasion when one of our set of boule balls was thrown too hard and rolled into the river, and he stepped straight into the mud and retrieved it before it could disappear for ever. Francis who was at the kitchen window wearing his chef's hat, commented: 'A courageous act. But had you done less it would have been cowardice.' Boule balls were not then obtainable in this country; ours which we had brought from France were the old hand-made kind with iron nails hammered into a wooden base to make a continuous surface.

In the evening there was usually reading aloud by Francis. Or there would be indoor games such as 'tishy-toshy' (rules in the *Weekend Book*) and ping-pong played on the refectory table. Francis was always the centre and fun-maker of the party, the initiator of all games; the stimulating talker, the teller of amusing anecdotes. I remember thinking how lucky I was that I had no problems as a hostess; I had only to provide the food since Francis always provided the entertainment. He was the person whom everyone, young and old, wanted to talk to. This is by no means to say that I felt frozen out. Quite the contrary. Francis took every opportunity to draw me out and would often set up my *amour propre* by telling me, how much he had admired what I said and how I said it. I am not sure I did the same for him. I thought it was self-evident. In the last years of his life he lost some of his confidence in company, and it was a pain to me to see him sometimes on the outskirts instead of at the centre of the party. I hated it when people turned to me instead of to him. I found at such times a fellow feeling with Mrs Gladstone who, it is said, silenced the talkers at her dinner table with the admonition, 'Hush, Mr Gladstone is speaking.'

Pamela and Martin Zander must have been our most frequent guests until they built their own house nearby.

Francis and Pamela had first met when she became his secretary at his advertising firm during the war. But she was a far greater help than any ordinary secretary: 'some cells of my brain, almost all my memory and always the fingers of my hand in the planning of Nonesuch books . . .' is how he has described her. She had great sweetness of character and such personal courage that in the long and painful illness from which she eventually died, she managed to an extraordinary degree to hide her own sufferings in her interest in her friends and their concerns. When Nonesuch was being re-established after the war, Martin was Francis's legal adviser and he and Pamela became Francis's chief support in that venture. Born in Danzig Martin had settled in England in the early Thirties, and practised as a solicitor. He always seemed to us to have the eye of an artist as well as the intellectual precision of a scholar: his exact learning and open mind built between us an enduring friendship.

For one memorable weekend houseful, our niece Sylvia had brought with her an American pen-friend, a retired school mistress from the Middle West. Things began badly when Sylvia implored us not to ask her to share a room with her friend who had already eaten up all her store of tinned food only obtainable on rationing 'points'. It became clear that the pen-friend had expected a much less austere Britain and an altogether grander house and ménage. At dinner, she enquired pointedly what the meat was in her helping of pie and, on being told, rabbit, remarked: 'May I have the mustard please? I always say, there's nothing like mustard for making-over a dish.'

Another time when the Potters were guests, Stephen asked Francis to look at a manuscript of his that he thought might possibly make a book. It was the first draft of *Gamesmanship* which was to introduce a new word and a new word-ending to the language. We read it aloud to each other and laughed and laughed. The conception of 'gamesmanship' had been evolved jointly over many years between Stephen and Francis and their friends – Cyril Joad especially – and the first book (the one read in draft at Cobbold's) was published in 1947; it is dedicated to Francis whom Stephen always named 'Gamesman No. 1.' They applied the idea to all sorts of games that they enjoyed together differing only over cricket which Francis always maintained, with solemnity, was too serious a game to joke about.

The general idea is revealed in the sub-title 'the art of winning games without actually cheating' – the word 'actually' having been Francis's contribution – but in case the present generation of readers does not know the book of the series, I will not resist the temptation to quote an early passage in which Stephen and Cyril Joad are pictured playing tennis against two much younger men, 'Smith' and 'Brown', who 'had the advantage not only of age but also decisively in skill'. I quote:

> Now here comes the moment on which not only this match but so much of the future of British sport was to turn. (Smith has just served to Joad whose return hit the back netting *before* touching the ground). Score: forty-love. Smith is about to cross over to serve to me (Potter) when Joad calls across the net, in an even tone: 'Kindly say clearly, please, whether the ball was in or out'.
> SMITH: I'm so sorry – I thought it was out.
> BROWN: I *thought* it was out – but do let's have it again.
> JOAD: No, I don't want to have it again. I only want you to say clearly, if you will, whether the ball is in or out.
> Now, there is nothing more putting off to young university players than a slight suggestion that their sportsmanship is in question. Smith served a double fault to me and another to Joad and we went on to win the match.

When we had read to the end I said, 'Let's go and find Stephen at once and tell him how much we have enjoyed it.' We didn't have far to go because he was listening outside the door.

Sometimes when we had to be elsewhere ourselves, we lent Cobbold's to friends – to the Potters or the Zanders or to Evelyn for a party of her friends – but after visits from the Potters, it was a joke between us that we were apt to dig up pieces of broken cups which Stephen had buried in the garden rather than confess to. Cobbs also provided holidays for people who worked for us – Francis's business chauffeur, and our occasional cook in London and her husband, who said 'No one has ever lent us their house before.'

Our most frequent guests must have been Benedict, our niece Al, daughter of Francis's brother Everard who was very dear to us, and my twin uncles who felt Cobbs to be their 'second home'. Felix (the youngest uncle) also came frequently after he retired from school-mastering. He was the gentlest of men with a wide tolerance, linked with deep convictions. In old age he suffered very much from rheumatoid arthritis and had to become almost wholly sedentary; he bore this with stoic patience and once, after a morning spent sitting alone and watching the birds by our river, said 'Bay, I've been in paradise.' I asked him for a Latin motto for the Visitors' Book. What he produced was: 'Panem Olim Dedi/ Hodie Otium'. Translating this to me, as 'Once I gave bread, now pleasant leisure', he explained, that 'Otium' meant something much deeper than just 'pleasant leisure'.

15

Marriage

During our first year at Cobbold's Mill, two couples had their honeymoons there and on 29th August 1946 we spent the first night of our own honeymoon there too. Vera had written to Francis at the beginning of that year to tell him that she was now prepared to agree to a divorce. Ben was then sixteen and he has told me recently that up until the war, Vera had hoped that Francis would 'come to his senses' and get over what she saw as his 'infatuation'; and that while the war lasted she thought it important for his (Ben's) sake to freeze everything. But when we bought Cobbold's and divided possessions – as Francis kept their car I gave my little car to Vera – she decided not to hold out any longer.

The marriage bar was then still in force in the Civil Service. It was removed altogether that autumn but in any case there was no doubt about my being given permission to remain on marriage under the Tomlin Commission procedure. However, I wanted to be the co-respondent in Francis's divorce since this was the true state of affairs and for this I had to consult my employers; it was after all possible that the fact could be noticed by some journalist and become a matter of public comment. This was still the period when the one divorce you could not have was an agreed one. It was called collusion and, if found out, condemned both parties to their original partner or to living in sin for the foreseeable future. So Francis would have to be the 'guilty' party and go through the indignity of being found *in flagrante delicto*, and Vera, watched by the King's Proctor, must be the 'innocent' party, as white as snow for the six statutory months between the decree nisi and the decree absolute. (Coincidentally, this absurd six months period was reduced to six weeks in August 1946 and so we could be married in August instead of waiting until the end of the year). The system was lampooned by A. P. Herbert in his novel *Holy Deadlock* published in 1934.

I went to see our establishment officer, Harry Lintott,* whom I
met then for the first time and who, with his wife Margaret, were
to become close friends. Without a moment's hesitation or pause
to consult 'higher authority' he said that it was entirely a matter
for me and no business of the Board's whether or not I decided to
be co-respondent. So – 'a little man in a bowler hat' came to 19
Cliveden Place early on a day arranged while we were having
breakfast and assured himself that Francis and I had indeed slept
there together the previous night. An amusing sequel was that, a
year or two later, when the fact of Francis's divorce was noticed
at the Palace, I was informed that I would continue to be invited
in my turn to royal garden parties but that my husband could not
be asked.

We were married at Chelsea Register Office and Björn gave us
a 'wedding breakfast' – lunch in fact – at the Swedish Legation.
Our witnesses were my Cousin Oscar, Mona, Evelyn and
Cynthia, who said 'I know I don't need to ask you to look after
my old Dad.' She (and I think Ben too) always regretted being
brought up to call their parents by their Christian names and on
solemn occasions she seized the opportunity to say 'Dad' or
'Father'. None of Francis's sisters came though they were wholly
supportive, as was his father, who had earlier delighted us by
signing himself in a letter – 'Your father, in and out of law.' I
knew Viola best of the three sisters. I had already developed a
friendship with her. She was the literary one, a superb writer of
short stories, one-time friend of D. H. Lawrence, gentle and
sweet-tempered but with a piercing intelligence.

I had enjoyed buying Cynthia a cameo brooch – as surrogate
bridesmaid – and Francis a leather brush-and-shaving case. He
was a great present-giver on non-present-giving occasions. I had
worn for years the Victorian topaz ring he had given me with
F.M./A.K. engraved on the inside and he showered me with
presents on our wedding trip. But on our wedding day he didn't
even bring 'the ring'. I used my grandmother's 'guard' ring.

Evelyn, Björn and the four Potters came with us to Cobbold's
that evening and Att did a drawing in the Visitors' Book of two
hearts pierced by Cupid's arrow. It was signed by us all and also

*Sir Henry Lintott K.C.M.G.

by Mrs Fosker and Mrs Stowe and her youngest daughter who
were at Cobbold's to greet us and who joined us in the wedding
toast. For once, Francis and I had driven down alone – a fact
sufficiently rare for comment. Evelyn was driven by Björn and
she always maintained afterwards that she had never had such a
frightening journey. Björn was the kind of person who drove
talking all the time like a Paris or New York taxi-driver – but
without their skill. The presents we got were symptomatic:
Mona made me a set of underwear – so no coupons – Evelyn gave
me exquisite white silk pyjamas from Harrods whose value, she
pointed out, lay even more in the clothing coupons she had
sacrificed than in their price.

Because Francis had a business conference to attend in Stockholm, we decided to take our honeymoon in Sweden and Björn
invited us to spend the first few days on his island near
Gothenburg which Mona and I had visited so happily in 1933.
But we would be solely his wife's guests: 'Are you sure she will
be happy to have us?' I asked Björn. 'She'll be glad to see you
married,' he said.

We went by car to Harwich to join the boat for Gothenburg. It
was our first day as a married couple and I have to confess to a
small snobbish thrill of pleasure when I heard myself referred to
by the steward as 'her ladyship' – for Francis had been knighted in
January of this same year. As we were not then married, I did not
go to the investiture and Vera did not go either. Francis's two
family guests were his daughter and son, Cynthia and Ben. At
fifteen Ben had not found Francis's knighthood easy to accept:
'You know I would always rather think of you as a jail-bird,
whose principles were unshakeable' he wrote in his congratulatory letter. 'Still there've got to be knights even under a Labour
Government, so they might as well be good ones.' I think the fact
that the honour was given by the Labour Government of which
we were so proud made it easier for Francis to accept the
knighthood and he knew too that our much admired Wattie must
have been the proposer.

Francis had just become a Director of the Cement and
Concrete Association – the up-and-coming research body for the
cement industry – and he had also been appointed as the first
Honorary Typographical Adviser to H.M.S.O. He believed that

Alan Barlow had invented this post but Evelyn told me recently that the original idea had been hers. She rated it one of the best brain-waves she had ever had. This appointment and his recent R.D.I. led to his and my only meeting with our present Queen and to an unusual conversation with her. When still Princess Elizabeth, she came to an R.D.I. reception and moved from table to table talking to the members and their guests. When she came to Francis, she asked him about his appointment as Typographical Adviser to the Stationery Office. He said that he hoped to make great improvements in Government printing, 'For example, Ma'am,' he said, 'the invitations printed for your wedding looked like an auctioneer's catalogue.' She was not offended and when preparations were being made for her coronation, she instructed that Francis should be consulted on all matters of printing connected with it – much to the annoyance of Garter King of Arms.

Francis used to call our wedding day our 'aggregation of income tax' day because my income was added to Francis's for tax purposes and as his was already at surtax level, the whole of my income became subject to surtax. It cost us £600 a year to be married. The amount was certainly a shock but even if we had calculated it beforehand it would not have deterred us. We wanted the outward sign and public recognition of a so long privately accepted state; we wanted to shout it abroad. Also there were conventions in those times which deprived unmarried couples of pleasant social occasions which as husband and wife they could have enjoyed together. And for me, there was a special reason; I wanted to be Francis's undoubted next-of-kin. It had been an added anxiety for me during the war, that if he had been involved in an 'incident', Vera and not I would have been told and had the right to be with him and be consulted if he was injured or dying. That particular anxiety was over now, but there was still the possibility of peacetime illness or accident.

A year after our marriage, in August 1947, Vera committed suicide. It did not occur to me to link this sad happening with the final end of her marriage, or to feel any guilt about it. This may seem surprising but it is a fact. I don't remember whether I even argued it out to myself at the time. I certainly felt that we had shown Vera all due consideration in the past, given that her marriage to Francis was already on the rocks when he and I met. It was for her sake (though admittedly also for Ben's) that our marriage had been postponed for a whole decade, and that I had given up the possibility of having children of my own. I had seen some of the sad letters that Vera wrote to Francis in the early days, saying that while she had not expected to continue a relationship based on romance, she had hoped for a lasting and stable marriage. But from what I knew and heard of her, I am sure that they were ill-matched for a lasting relationship: he was essentially gentle, considerate, altruistic, above all compassionate to the ordinary, the less fortunate or the less gifted; she was made for youth not age, beautiful, possessive, egoistical. She could appear haughty, be arrogant – intellectually at least – and say the most hurting things. I have never forgiven her for trying to puncture Francis's self-esteem in the days when he was riding high in the film industry by saying – 'It's easy for you; you have a second class mind and are dealing only with people who have third class minds.' Whatever she thought she wanted, I don't believe she would have been able to build and maintain the unromantic comfortable relationship with Francis she had pictured in her letters.

Some weeks before her death she had written to Francis saying 'If, as may be, I have Parkinson's disease, that is not what I shall die of.' He believed that in this she gave the reason for her suicide. Probably it was the main one but she must have been influenced too by her general state of mind. And, as to that, I believed that in recent years she had become an unhappy woman and an over-possessive mother. Ten years earlier, when we had been discussing whether to press for divorce, I had written to Francis pointing out that postponement did not appear to have made Vera any happier; and I had argued that the longer we postponed 'the less able she would be to have Ben's whole-time companionship and less likely to take up with anyone else.' At the time of her death, Ben was seventeen, already old for his age and a student at the University of Geneva. I cannot help thinking that the inevitability of future loneliness must have been the fertile background to her decision. Francis said, 'I'm afraid this will add Ben to your many responsibilities.' He needn't have been afraid. I was very positively happy to acquire a stepson.

The following spring Francis had to go on a business trip to America and his letters were as full of love as those he had written fifteen years earlier – 'I had such joy at receiving your first letter that I sent you a night-letter telegram to say thank you . . . excitement at receiving it gave me diarrhoea!' And – 'Groaned at finding no letter from you . . . TEN DAYS ARE PAST' . . . 'short of one day, today's HALFWAY.' My letters to him have not survived but I do remember that when the previous year, I had had to be away in Havana for the International Trade Conference which followed the war, I left a letter with my will to tell him that heaven (if it existed) could be no better than my life with him had been.

I did not expect marriage to make any difference to our private relationship, and there was none in love or in our enjoyment of each other's company. But there was, I found, a subtle change at first, difficult to pinpoint or express in words, in Francis's attitude to me. I can only describe it as a barely noticeable increased possessiveness, a subtle assumption of responsibility for me – what I did, what I said and how I looked – that was not there while we were separate public people. I wonder if others making the change from extra-legal to legal have felt the same and I wonder if my own attitude changed in any way? If it did, I was not aware of it.

In principle our views about sex did not change when we married. We did not demand exclusiveness. The only accepted compulsion remained the compulsion to be honest with each other, the only accepted assurance, the knowledge that we were one another's best. However, those principles were rarely tested. There was one occasion when I was not only not jealous but glad that Francis should have the pleasure of a flirtation, which I knew to be transitory, with a quite young woman. But there was also one that I knew could have more emotion in it, which Francis gave up as soon as he saw that it caused me pain. When an old friend proposed one to me, I surprised – and discouraged – him by saying – 'only if Francis knows and doesn't mind'.

I don't think I ever attached the importance to physical sex that most people do. I wonder how much I was a disappointment to Francis in this. He used playfully sometimes to accuse me of being a lesbian at heart. Had I thought him serious I should have been deeply offended; I had, I have, nothing against lesbians or lesbianism but on the very few occasions in my life when I have thought I sensed an approach from another woman, I have felt physically repelled – there is no other word for it. Perhaps I was under-sexed; certainly I was not highly sexed for even when I was young, talking and dancing were more important to me than bedding. And in marriage it was the intimacy of love – the words the memories for us two alone, the certain happiness and publicly accepted privacy of the shared bedroom – that I valued far above the physical aspects of sex.

It seems to me that Francis and I had as near perfect a relationship as could be, though I never did quite understand why he was sympathetically amused by James Stephens' poem:

> I have looked him round and looked him through
> Know everything that he will do
>
> He cannot do a thing but I
> Peep to find the reason why.
>
> Yesterday he gripped her tight
> And cut her throat – and serve her right!

but not to be open to the charge of complacency, I remind myself always that our marriage did not have to meet the stresses of many marriages. Because I had a job which, in its way, was as demanding as Francis's and even more time-taking, our needs at the end of the working day did not clash. We did not have the problem that one partner might have been alone all day and needed company and entertainment in the evening while the other, in company all day, might want only rest and quiet. And our marriage was neither tested nor extended by the arrival of the children that, when I was young, I had so much hoped to have. Francis hadn't wanted more children. How would he have reacted to sharing my time – and me – with them? And how should I have coped with having children as well as my job or at the expense of that job? I find I cannot guess whether our relationship would have been deepened or threatened by their arrival.

16

Quiet Revolution

We are embarked on a great adventure – the adventure of
democracy, of civilisation, of social service. . . .

(from Attlee's election victory broadcast, 26th July 1945)

It looked to us as if our dreams in 'Do It Now' were about to be
realised and, on the Home Front, in many respects they were,
with Beveridge and the National Health, and the great utilities –
coal, gas, electricity, and transport – being taken into public
ownership to be run not for profit but for the public good. It
looked as if it was no longer true – in Britain at any rate – that the
poor were always with us. And abroad? The Labour Government began at once the unravelling of Empire which the
Churchill administration would surely have delayed. The only
feeling I can remember about all that was happening outside these
islands just after the war is the exciting day in 1947 when *The
Times* recorded the complete and sudden change in Indian
opinion that came when they realised that, at last, we really did
mean to leave. When Francis and I were invited to the party to
celebrate Hugh Gaitskell's becoming Leader of the Labour Party,
I got Francis to introduce me to Attlee: 'My wife wants to shake
your hand' he said 'because you freed India'. His reply was
typically modest: 'I could not have done it without Mount-
batten.'

At the Board of Trade, our new President was Sir Stafford
Cripps K.C., one of the high-flyers of the Labour Government, a
socialist by moral conviction of such straight-laced integrity that
we began to feel it was almost necessary to prove that a course of
action would be against his personal or political interest before he
could be got to approve it. But he was only austere with himself.
Though he looked like a rather severe headmaster he had a great

deal of charisma; on a one-to-one basis, he could be overwhelming. I remember vividly an occasion when I had to advise him on some point of price control; we were sitting together on one of the red leather benches in the corridor outside the House of Lords Chamber – the House of Commons was still out of action after bombing. 'I think, President, that you should bear in mind such and such,' I said, and I was almost physically knocked backwards by the force of his personality as he turned towards me and asked, 'Do you really think so?' I felt like Annie Oakley meeting Frank Butler in *Annie Get Your Gun* that splendid musical had just stormed London and Francis and I had seen it three times. I think its special popularity at that time was due to its *joie de vivre* and verve, for the people of Britain – especially Londoners – were tired at the end of the war. Francis and I felt it first the night we saw the New York Theatre Ballet in 1946.

Stafford Cripps could dominate a meeting held in a room no larger than the courtroom he was accustomed to, but in a large group his personality seemed to go into eclipse. He opened his Presidency by calling a meeting in Westminster Hall of all 4,000 Board of Trade staff from permanent secretary to messengers. The idea was to tell us about the Brave New World and inspire us to joint effort. It was a complete flop. His next and more successful innovation was a regular ten o'clock meeting in his room attended by all the heads of departments. We called it 'Morning Prayers'. Francis and I were both at the first of these and as we came out, Francis said, 'I have just realised that what we have dreamed for years is really beginning to happen.'

My responsibilities in the new socialist Britain were price control and clothes rationing. There had been a control of prices all through the war and it was the policy of the new Government to continue it for all essential goods. It was administered, within Government policy, by the Central Price Regulation Committee, a semi-independent body with a K.C. as chairman. It was a type of relationship that I had had much experience of and I and the Committee had no serious differences that I remember because we understood our respective spheres.

The policy was successful in preventing the kind of price rises that had occurred after the First World War, but it may well have been kept on too long for the health and growth of industry. For one thing, there could be little price competition because our maximum almost invariably became the minimum; for another, the price strait-jacket discouraged experimentation. I saw one piece of evidence of this myself when we decided to stop controlling the price of nylon cloth and the price promptly fell instead of increasing. When I asked why, the manufacturers explained that they had believed for some time that there would be a large market for this new product at a lower price; but had not dared to try it out while they were still subject to control, lest we should not allow them to put the price up again if the market failed to respond.

At first, a wage increase was accepted without question as a justification for a price increase; wage levels were no business of the Board of Trade's. However, it began to dawn on me that, on this basis, wage negotiations became almost meaningless since manufacturers would have neither excuse nor inclination to resist wage demands, and the consumer would have no protection against price rises. To counter this, I evolved what I called 'the 10% Rule' under which manufacturers would not normally be granted a price increase for more than 90% of the cost of a wage increase; they would have to absorb 10% either by increased productivity or reduced profits.

At this time my deputy secretary was Sir Herbert Hutchinson, the man who had been my first principal in the Twenties. He had spent most of the war in the Ministry of Supply where the established method of fixing prices was 'cost-plus'. I don't think I had consulted either him or my political masters about my 10% Rule and when he heard of it he was not pleased. He asked me to walk across the park with him and told me I had been 'playing politics', an unforgivable sin in a civil servant. I saw that he was right about that, though I think the policy was a good one. Once again my wartime experience had led me to draw an insufficient distinction between civil servant and politician. I had one of the worst half-hours of my official career. I wonder if it appears in my 'personal file'. Even after the more than thirty years since I left the service, I am not allowed to see that file. I think it more likely that 'Hutch' kept it to himself for I was left in no doubt at the time that I was in very good odour both in the Board and the

Treasury. I had recently been sent for by our then permanent
secretary Sir John Woods affectionately known to us all as 'John
Henry', to be congratulated on a policy proposal I had made 'just
at the moment when Ministers most needed it'. Is that perhaps
recorded on my 'personal file'? It certainly should be if the
'wigging' from 'Hutch' is.

The end of the war did not bring the end of shortages of clothes
and other consumer goods any more than of food. I took this
very much for granted at the time. My work in the Reconstruction Department and now as head of the Clothes Rationing
Department meant that I was in a prime position to know the
reasons for continued shortages: the time needed to unscramble
industry fairly from its wartime 'marriages'; the bombed factories to be rebuilt; the demobilised factories and workers to be
redeployed; the millions of demob 'civvy' suits that must take
precedence over any general increase in the clothes ration; and
overall the chronic need for priority for exports that would
provide 'hard' currency. As late as the autumn we even continued
to apply a ration to the Royal family, and one day I had to go to
the Palace to discuss a request for an increase for the then Queen. I
drove my little car into the forecourt and was conducted to a
female dignitary called I think the Mistress of the Bedchamber,
who said that Her Majesty found it difficult to manage on the 300
coupons we had thought would cover her necessarily large
formal wardrobe, and that anyhow she could not understand
why she should be expected to be confined to a ration at all. It
surprised me that the Queen, who had after all not been born
Royal, should expect to be above this kind of law. Very likely it
was not the Queen's view at all but that of her ladies.

And then, in the summer of 1947, the fashion houses of Paris,
led by Christian Dior, added a final blow – the 'New Look' in
women's clothes appeared with its mid-calf hemline, and the
London fashion houses demanded their right to follow suit. In
mid-September, battle was joined with Stafford Cripps arguing
at a press conference that 'this seems an idiotic time to introduce
longer dresses' it could only mean fewer dresses since there was
no more cloth. And on 30th September I held a press conference
for women journalists. It was not the quiet talk to a submissive

audience that we had grown accustomed to during the war; it was an unpleasant confrontation with a lot of very angry women and it was fully reported in the daily and evening papers of the whole country, with me identified by name:

'Coupon Chief in row over knee skirt', reported the *News Chronicle*:

Fifty women journalists and fashion writers heckled Miss Alix Kilroy, head of the Board of Trade's clothing coupon administration, yesterday when she said to them: 'Make us look smart in short skirts.'

I have kept my notes of what I should say at that meeting and they are interesting reading:

Item: I announced a ration of 48 coupons a year which was only 2 more than the wartime figure.

Item: I told them the quantities needed to honour this ration – e.g. 900 million square yards of cloth, 110 million pairs of boots and shoes.

Item: I said the ration could by no means provide for fashion. What was needed was for women to stand out against fashion changes that would make last year's clothes look dowdy.

Item: I explained that sheets and household textiles had been put on the clothes ration. There were not enough to honour a special ration – there would, for example, be less than 1 sheet per household or 1 towel per person – 'We think it is right to let the public choose the form in which they take their cloth – in clothes or curtains or sheets.'

I concluded by asking the assembled company to 'count their blessings' because, forsooth, they could now buy sheets on the clothes ration when before only newly-weds or bombed-outs could get them at all, and because such necessities as saucepans, razor blades, and babies' bottles, were much more plentiful than formerly – though if wanted for export, they could become scarce again.

Some months later an enraged member of the establishment – a General or a Master of Foxhounds at the least – stormed into my office to complain of that decision. It seemed he lived in a minor stately home and that all the sheets were becoming threadbare.

'Do you suppose', he asked, 'that my guests or my grown-up children are going to give us their precious coupons so that my wife can buy sheets? The whole burden will fall on me and my wife. Your fair system is completely unfair.' I couldn't help seeing his point and I have a strong impression that the system was changed because I had been brought in touch with reality by this incident.

No wonder people were angry! It happened that Francis and I had been going to dinner that evening with our old friends Ernestine Carter* and her husband to meet some of her fashion colleagues. She telephoned to ask us not to come because her other guests could not trust themselves to meet us with civility.

A parcel had arrived on my desk on the morning after my press conference. In it were two small packets addressed respectively to me and Stafford Cripps and each contained – a fig leaf. They were described in the letter enclosed with it as 'the most ancient skirts known. . . .' It was signed by H. W. Dinscombe of Bridgewater and includes a sales slogan pointing out that by wearing this style of dress 'people will save cloth, buttons, pins, needles and also manpower'. I find to my regret that I didn't reply to this letter. It was a good joke carried out with taste.

The morning after my press conference, I was also besieged by the evening papers demanding to know how short was short, and taking photographs showing the length of my own dress; I lent them a ruler and it was found to measure eighteen inches from the ground. Of course, we had to be ready with an answer to the question 'How short is short?' We said that we regarded mid-calf as 'long' and 'mid-calf' as fourteen inches from the ground; we were asking for something shorter than that on the home market but, said I, 'We are not dictating fashion, fourteen inches from the ground may well be right for export, our designers are the best judge of this.'

In all this we, and I in particular, must have sounded both arrogant and high-handed. I had been promoted an under-secretary the previous year and I had a lot of power. I suspect I had begun to see myself as larger than life. Certainly I had not adjusted to the fact that civil servants should not take the

*Ernestine Carter O.B.E., Women's Editor for many years of *The Sunday Times*.

prominent part in peace that had been quite acceptable in war. There was perhaps some justification for a letter dated 9th October from an unknown Miss Adcock to Harold Wilson (who had just replaced Stafford Cripps as President). In it she said that she hoped one of his first duties would be to seek a person 'possessing a little more commonsense' to advise him on clothes rationing for 'Miss Kilroy's statements that 4 coupons a month are quite enough have been the talk of the town amongst the "common folk" and we are all VERY TIRED. . . .'

Almost immediately after that press conference in October, 1947, I found myself on a plane to Havana to join the United Kingdom delegation with the job of looking after our end of the discussions on international cartels at the International Trade Conference which led to the General Agreement on Tariffs and Trade (GATT). No doubt most of the very little that was known at that time in the Board of Trade about international cartels was known by me through my work in the wartime Reconstruction Department. However, as I fell ill after a month or two it was fortunate that Ronald McIntosh[*] the assistant principal who came with me, was much abler than his rank and seniority would have suggested: he had only joined the Board that year but he had seen service through the war in the Merchant Navy and also had an Oxford degree and was well able to inherit the U.K. Chair from me.

We arrived to find that it was the cold season in Havana and the Cuban ladies were sporting their fur coats but it was really hot for Europeans coming from the northern winter. I found for the first time that the sun can be an enemy; in the Anglo-American Hospital that I went to when I became ill I found comfort in hugging a bottle filled with ice instead of a hot water bottle.

I soon found that then, as now, the United States regarded the Central and South American countries as very much their preserve. The outline and main detail of the draft document we were discussing had been negotiated among the more important allied countries before the World Conference opened; it stood to reason that countries not in at the beginning would want to make some impression on the text. At one of our meetings, the

[*]Sir Ronald McIntosh K.C.B.

Brazilian delegate argued for an amendment which I thought could be met without difficulty by a small change but when I discussed it, one to one, with my American opposite number, I found him unsympathetic. 'If the change is large,' he said, 'we can't do it. If it is small and unimportant, why should we?' Admittedly, the Americans, unlike ourselves, had been through the process of arguing the draft through Congressional hearings. 'But', I said, 'we must surely be ready to make a few small concessions? Some at least of the representatives will need to be able to swell out their chests when they get back to their own countries and point to something they have achieved?' I realised we couldn't make enough changes to please all but how important was Brazil among the South American nations? What was its population? 'They claim there are 40 million of them,' he said, 'but I don't know how they count them for half of them live in trees.' It was a day or two after this discussion that I fell ill, and I learned with amusement from McIntosh, that my suggested amendment had been put forward with a considerable flourish as a gesture from the great American people to their Brazilian neighbours. This was my first experience of official America and it made me feel very European. In spite of language, I felt much closer to the French than to the Americans in thought-processes as well as in experience and historical background.

The business of the conference left little time to socialise with colleagues working on other sections of the Treaty but there was one evening when McIntosh and I, and Arthur Burgess (my A.P. in the General Department before the war) and Gerald Macmahon, an Irishman with even more than the usual Irish charm, went out together to explore the town. In our wanderings we found ourselves alone in a beautiful, unmistakably Spanish square opposite the Christopher Columbus cathedral built of pale pinkish brown coral, and saw an arm (female we wondered?) beckoning to us from an upper room. We felt as if we had been transported into a scene in Stevenson's *New Arabian Nights*. We climbed the stairs to what turned out, rather unromantically, to be a wine bar where we were encouraged to taste and buy. We came away with bottles of banana liqueur, a taste new to all of us.

We had travelled out to Cuba on a Tudor IV, a comfortable little plane for less than a hundred passengers with only four seats to a row; it had been adapted from the wartime Lancaster bomber. Our only mishap had been a 'boss' landing at Nassau where the pilot found himself coming in on too short a runway and had to roar up into the air again after he had actually touched down, but a month later this same plane disappeared without trace carrying some Board of Trade staff among its passengers. I knew too little about flying to be as alarmed as perhaps I should have been about our landing at Nassau but I was glad that I was sent back by a different route when I left hospital. It was just before Christmas and we travelled via Miami, New York and Gander: New York looked beautiful under snow with lighted Christmas trees all up Park Avenue but the snowstorm was so heavy that we were the last plane to leave from La Guardia Airport where people were sleeping by their baggage all over the small departure lounge. It was quite dark and snowing hard when we walked out to our plane and we were kept waiting for a good half-hour where we could see other planes coming in to land every five minutes in a flurry of snow. I was convinced that we hadn't more than a fifty-fifty chance of arriving safely.

We reached Gander in Newfoundland at about three a.m. where I was able to spend two hours with Mona and Geoffrey, then General Manager of Gander Airport. It was a long time since I had seen Mona and the sight of her in their doorway, with the light flooding out from behind her on to the snow, is unforgettable.

After this short colourful interlude in Cuba I went back to price control and clothes rationing until in January 1949 I was seconded to be secretary of the first Monopolies Commission.

On New Year's Day 1949, I was given a D.B.E. It was strictly too high an honour for an under-secretary but the Bath (the appropriate honour) was not yet open to women – a point that a number of congratulatory letters made fun with since the monarch was a King. All letters are fulsome on these occasions but I couldn't help being flattered by one from Sir Herbert Williams who had been our Parliamentary Secretary in the long ago days of my Safeguarding of Industry Committees; he wrote of 'the buttons debate in the House of Commons when all the young Conservative Members were attracted by a magnet sitting under the Gallery'. But the letter I treasure most came from 'John Henry'. He was a man of wide culture and interests and of great humanity and sympathy which was laced with humour in spite of ill health. He had the rare quality in a leader of being able to make the members of his staff feel better when they left his room than when they entered it. In a charmingly informal, almost affectionate, letter that seemed to me to have the ring of sincerity, he said that my honour 'will give immense pleasure all through the Board and over a much wider field than that' and that 'you have earned everyone's deep respect and regard for your work over the last three years here – including such diverse characters as Edward Bridges, Archie Rowlands[*] (*that* will rock you) *and* J.H.W.'

I was sorry (not pleased as appeared to be expected) that my D ranked technically above Francis's K. I always hoped no one would point it out to him, though he would have been the last to mind; he always preferred me to use the 'Dame' that was mine rather than the 'Lady' that I got from him. His pleasure was added to by the fact that his cricket hero Don Bradman received a knighthood in the same list. The clever headline in the *Daily Herald* read: 'Knight of Cricket, Knight of Coal [Will Lawther of the N.U.M.], Peer of Food [Sir John Boyd Orr] and Dame of Dress [me]. Could Francis have prompted it I wonder? He had been a *Daily Herald* journalist for many years in the past.

Evelyn had received her D.B.E. the year before, having finally outstripped me in 1946 when she was made deputy secretary in the Ministry of Town and Country Planning. The fact that we two were regarded very much as a pair in the Civil Service appeared in the Press and in many of my letters: Dick Plummer's was typical of him: 'Two Dames in one house is better than any panto'; and John Maud[†] wrote that it 'restores the proper public picture of yourself and Evelyn'.

Dr Janet Vaughan, principal of Somerville College, wrote to invite me to dine in Hall on 26th February, 'when we hope to have Dame Evelyn Sharp and Professor Agnes Headlam-Morley

---

[*]Sir Archibald Rowlands.
[†]Later Baron Redcliffe-Maud.

here for a joint celebration of your distinctions'. It was an extraordinary, even hilarious, occasion from the moment when Evelyn and Agnes got up simultaneously to give the speech of thanks, and Evelyn told the assembled undergraduates that, judging by us three, 'they needn't struggle to get "firsts", a "second" would do just as well'. After dinner, there was the experience of being lionised, sitting either end of the never-before-entered Senior Common Room while Dr Vaughan brought up the dons one by one to talk to us; I found myself discussing moral philosophy as though I had never been away with a don young enough to be my daughter. In proper Varsity tradition, we were offered port. I refused but Evelyn, always ready to try anything once, accepted with unfortunate after-effects during the night. At ten precisely, we decided that both we and the dons had had enough and swept grandly out. This, however, proved not to be the end of the story. We were staying in College and since the port had given Evelyn a premonitory headache, we went in search of a gas ring where we could make tea. Finding none in the passage, we were directed to a room where we found the 'living-in' dons assembled at ease, obviously breathing sighs of relief that 'that' was over and getting down to a shoes-off gossip about us. Instead, they made a very good grace of asking us to join them, and an amusing and more relaxed party was had by all.

The Monopolies Commission to which I was seconded as secretary in January 1949 had the status of an independent statutory body. I had at first had hesitations about accepting the appointment because, as I argued to John Henry, it could well be a disadvantage to one's career to be away from Headquarters for a period of years; I suggested that I and other seconded officers should get some financial *quid pro quo* for this, and also that it should be open to the Commission to give equal pay since the staff was appointed by them – though the Act required the Secretary's appointment to be approved by the Board. I got 'no' to both suggestions and of course in the end I couldn't refuse; I was the obvious choice because I possessed what knowledge of the subject the Board of Trade had, and had been responsible for the Act in its drafting stage.

That had been a most interesting experience. We at the wartime Reconstruction Department had gone with confidence to our first meeting with Parliamentary draftsmen to explain what we wanted the Bill to say. Almost at once we were in difficulty. What precisely did we mean by 'restrictive practices'? What by 'monopoly'? As the saying goes, we all know what an elephant looks like but how to describe an elephant to someone who has never seen one? In the end the problem was brilliantly solved by the lawyers with the phrase – 'the conditions to which the act applies', leaving the long and detailed descriptions of those conditions to later sections of the Act, where their cumbersomeness did not matter.

The new Commission had to get down to work quickly because the Board of Trade began by referring not one but three cases to them. The members were all people prominent in their sphere of industry or the professions and the Chairman, Sir Archibald Carter, had previously been head of the Board of Customs and Excise. He led his team of many talents with a light rein and he left the staffing and running of the office and the preparation of documents to me.

We moved into a large and very grand private house in Upper Brook Street requisitioned for us by the Ministry of Works and I had the pleasure of giving them instructions about its decoration; I didn't have to accept Ministry-of-Works-cream.

From the first, we adopted a procedure (which I claim to have invented) under which we dealt separately with our two distinct tasks: we held informal 'Clarification' hearings to establish whether 'the conditions to which the act applies' existed and formal 'Public Interest' hearings to consider whether any such conditions 'operated or might be expected to operate against the public interest'. Normally, Counsel appeared only at the Public Interest hearings. Before the clarification stage, there was a great deal of work for the staff collecting information from the associations and firms concerned. We had an astonishingly wide power to demand disclosure; it became the practice at the beginning of enquiries for members of the Commission's staff to go to the offices of those concerned, and take away large bundles of documents, including confidential correspondence and minutes of private board meetings.

In the autumn of our first year it was decided that I should accept an invitation from the American Government to visit the United States in order to study their anti-trust law and see what aspect of it might be relevant to the Commission's work here. My visit was paid for and arranged through the Americans under the Marshall plan and classed as 'technical aid', the first such project to be approved for the U.K.

Again the Press was favourable, again I was the 'short skirt champion' but this time there was an exception: 'It's outrageous to use Marshall Aid dollars to advance the study of anti-trust action' commented the *Daily Express* on 7th October. I had already left for America when it was learned that Beaverbrook himself had given instructions for my visit to be panned, so there was no time to warn me before the *Daily Express* representative, a Mrs Webber, came aboard with the pilot as we entered New York harbour. Not that it would have made any difference to what I said. Mrs Webber was wholly ignorant of the subject, asking such questions as: 'Do you feel it is right that Marshall Aid money should be used to damage British business?'

I did not record the interview at the time but according to a note made later, my answer was: 'That is not at all what it is being used for. The monopolies legislation in England has the support of all political parties and a large section of British industry. Experience gained over here will help in the administration of that legislation.'

The result of the interview was a highly slanted article: '"We'll bust some trusts" says Lady Meynell' screamed the *Scottish Daily Express* on 10th October, and to the question – 'Do I think it wrong to use American money to try to break up British business?' 'No I don't. The Americans were delighted with the idea. They gave me the dollars immediately I asked. . . .'

There were questions in Parliament, an embarrassed Commission, and long telephone calls and cables to and fro across the Atlantic. The article was a travesty of what I had said and even at one point a direct lie: we were able to get a copy of Mrs Webber's shorthand note which confirmed my record, not the one printed in the newspaper. Francis had come with me to America on a business trip of his own, and he was present during the interview:

ABOVE LEFT: Mona, her husband Geoffrey and me at Pisa
ABOVE RIGHT: On the breakfast terrace at Waterfield Castle at Aulla
BELOW: Self launching a ship for the South Eastern Gas Board

Cutting from issue dated 6-Dec-1955

Good Evening, Madam

From a four-figure job, a top woman Civil Servant retires to life on a farm

A desk for Dame Alix

BEAUTIFUL women are bad enough for my ego. Brainy women petrify.

Reluctantly I went to interview one. An hour later, my ego intact, I left—sorry to go.

The woman who preserved my self-confidence was Dame Alix Kilroy, who has just retired as an Under-Secretary in the Board of Trade, a job that carries a four-figure salary.

She is also Lady Meynell, wife of Sir Francis Meynell, poet, publisher, typographer and advertising director.

☆

SHE married Sir Francis in 1946, the year he was knighted. For nearly 20 years she had been Miss Alix Kilroy to Whitehall and she saw no reason to change that.

There was a slight amendment in 1949 when she became Dame Alix in recognition of her services at the Board of Trade.

In retirement she will prefer to be known as Dame Alix Meynell, a delicate compromise with independence, personal achievement and the social conventions.

She proclaims that she has retired "to her private life." ... But she intends to do part-

by CAREN MEYER

time work, possibly in the industrial field, she will certainly not qualify as a lady of leisure, with or without a capital "L."

In 1925, when the Civil Service admitted women for the first time to the higher-grade examinations, she was one of three who passed.

Dame Alix, now 52, owes much of her independent outlook to her remarkable mother who sought adventure as a young girl by going to plague-ridden India as a nurse.

She married a naval man

☆

there and during his long spells at sea brought up their five children (four girls, one boy) using highly unorthodox methods.

Sleep, said Mrs. Kilroy, is a waste of time. So none of the children went to bed before 11 p.m.

All five appeared to be far too virtuous for Mrs. Kilroy. She organised annual "mobbing days" to encourage their evil instincts. "Mother thought the results rather disappointing," Dame Alix told me.

☆

WHEN seven Alix was abjured: "For heaven's sake don't accept other people's ideas. Think for yourself."

In the middle of her schooling Alix was taken by her mother on a prolonged holiday abroad. When she returned the school suggested the vacation might well be prolonged indefinitely.

Mrs. Kilroy was unperturbed; and Alix stayed at home studying. She won an Exhibition to Oxford, the first girl from her road to her school ... She graduated ... Greats, passed ... law. She ... Service.

Commission and went to America to study legislation there against private restrictive practices. She went back to the Board of Trade after three years with the Commission.

During the war Sir Francis Meynell went to the Board of Trade as adviser on consumer needs. He was no stranger to her because they had already known each other for many years. He is 12 years her senior. They now live in Bloomsbury. Sir Francis's son by his first marriage lives there, too, with his wife and two children.

If Mrs. Kilroy were still alive she would be slightly dis-

furniture and colo... even in his wife's... he who decides a... have a new frock or... who leafs throu... magazines, takes h... and buys clothes fo...

"He's got much... I know what he fee... She tries to reme... a little make-up. H... She would be quite... adorned.

His latest effort... her? A beautiful ple... ture, his retirement...

☆

During the ... Lady Meynell ... charge of ... control. ... scheme, ... In 195 ... secretary ... Commission.

Miss Kilroy's New Job—"A. K." to the hierarchy of the Board of Trade—who, in private life, is to be secretary of the Monopolies and Restrictive Practices Commission. Another distinguished ... Mrs. Joan Robinson, the economist ... and but for Miss Kilroy's appointment ... she would have had a monopoly of ... feminine influence on the Commission.

Miss Kilroy has been at the heart ... the administration of clothing coupons. Her new appointment will strengthen the belief in some quarters that clothes rationing is to be abandoned or much modified. The trade ... great respect for her, but on one ... she argued against the New ... Mrs. Kilroy's mother was a Greg ... her grandmother a Greg ... famous in Manchester in its ... free competition was ... religious belief.

Suffolk County Council Ele... Brett Division *

May 2nd 1985.
8 a.m. to 9 p.m.

VOTE ... ne Alix M ...

SDP L... Allia...

COCKFIELD, BILDESTON, BR... ...LDEN, BRETTENHAM, HITCH... with CHELSWORTH, KETTLEBA... PRESTON ST. MARY, W...

☆

Express Staff Reporter: New York, Sunday

LADY MEYNELL, 46-year-old £35-a-week civil ... from London, who is in New York to spend two we... 666 Marshall aid dollars (£236), watching how th... cans break up big business trusts, said today: "...get back to England we'll bust some... Lady Meynell and Restrictive Practices.

It is her first visit to America. ... poet and business-man husband S... Sir Francis is himself on a ... £10-a-day dollar - allowance ... business excursion.

Lady Meynell is the first Briton ... ...arshall aid grant to ... ...ne has been promi... ... Civil Service for ... idea, and for th... rade she battled ... look ... skirts. ... she said ... I get ... campaigns.

industries

is, now, we are investi... ... industries—electric ... ...yables, matches, match... ...achines, and cast iron

... there may be more, in... ...hemical base. But we didn't ... ...how how to proceed, so I ... ...ened to talk to the admini... ...ion of the Anti-Trust laws. ... rusts are not against the ... ...osecuting attorneys in a ... ...a State Government in a ... ...a copper company.

... I think it wrong to use ... ...sican money to ... to use ... ...ritish business by No. I don't ... ... of Americans were delighted ... ...s the idea. They ... delighted ... ...ie dollars immediately I asked ... ...akers in all with me in ... ...ellers' cheques.

...n't knew our Government ... ...ouldn't give money for such ... ... project, so I didn't ask it, but ... ...e is providing me with ... ...ecretaries.

Opinions? No

"Socialist monopolies? Well, ... I admit, nationalisation is the ... monopoly practised in the ... Socialist Government, but we are ... not concerned with that.

"My Anti-Monopoly Commis... ... on won't even try to make mono... olies mean and through nationalisa... tion. We will deal with trusts ... and price rings the Government ... ...recommend to us.

"And I'm just a civil servant, ... you know. We are not allowed ... opinions on subjects like ... nationalisation.

"But about shopping she said ... "I am sure £5 a week will ... not be enough though I may ... stay with friends and the time ... Sir Francis will probably have to ... give me some of his daily £10. ... "I want to bring some things— ...for instance, can ...openers and ... ...tin-openers and my ...

Slacks And Shirt

SINCE she married ... Francis in 1946, Lady ... Meynell has spent her week ... in Suffolk, feeding the ... chickens and digging in ... garden ... As a civil servant, Dame ... Kilroy—she was one of the ... first two women to enter the ... higher examinations for grade ... she has earned a reputation ... for taking pains and for her ... antagonism towards the long ... She fought against the New ... and faced hecklers with facts ... ...eetings with facts.

☆

Lady Meynell: going to the U.S. on Government business

...he known when she arrives i... Washington.

It is no pleasure trip. She ... plans to study various aspects ... of American legal and ad... ...inistrative action in coping ... with private restrictive prac... ...ices, and during her stay will ... ...ave discussions with officials ... ...e U.S. Department of ... ...Justice and the Federal Trade ... ...Commission.

☆

ME ALIX KILROY, who has ... ...een described as the brain ... ... the Government's price- ... ... campaign, was named ... ... Board of Trade yesterday ... ...secretary of the Monopolies ... ... Restrictive Practices Com- ... ...on.

private life she is Lady ... ...ll, wife of Sir Francis ... ...ll.

'ust usts' ady nell

I admit my skirt is a bit ... short," said Miss Kilroy. It was ... just eighteen inches from the ... ground.

"I do not pretend to be an ... authority on fashion, and I ... certainly am not a model of ... fashion. But I should hate ... to have to look dowdy. And ... the supply of women's clothes ... would certainly have to be ... curtailed if long skirts ... became a general rule."

She examined her hem and ...

Dollars f... LADY ME... ...tary of ... on Monopolies ... tive Practices, ... spend 666 ... dollars on a ... United States.

The amount is ... principle is impo... Lady Meynell ... see how they ... with their trusts ar...

Misapplied A...

IT would certain... good thing it th... ...ernment, instead of ... vast new monopolie... ...upted some of the old... Maybe capitalist. An... ...has something to teach ... this business.

But it is outrageous t... Marshall Aid dollars ... finance the study of a ... trust action. That study... not the slightest bearing ... Britain's crisis. It has n... connection with the purpos... that Marshall Aid ... supposed to serve.

It is bad enough that... Britain is taking the dollars ... at all. But it is far worse ... that she is taking them ... needlessly and applying ... them wrongfully.

Memories of a public life

old newspaper man that he was and with his experience of public relations at the Board of Trade during the war, he was convinced that I had said nothing that could in any way support the *Express* article.

New York was sweltering at 92°F when we disembarked and the first words spoken as we stepped ashore were not encouraging. 'Well,' said our porter setting off with our luggage along the quay, 'what are we going to do with England now?' a reference I suppose to the fact that we had a socialist Government. We were to discover that for the ordinary American socialism was no different from the dreaded communism. As I expressed it to myself, the American social scene then was like Dickens with modern plumbing: if you were poor it was your fault, and if you protested, you were 'pinko'.

I don't like great heat, even in the invigorating New York air, and I had a cyst on my eyelid which had to be operated on the next day. So (as Francis reported) I was feeling only fifteen per cent when we went to Sunday lunch with Bill Benton (later Senator Benton) in his Virginia-style pillared mansion, fifty miles from New York. I went only because he had promised to give me introductions to industrialists so that I could hear the other side of the anti-trust picture from the one I should learn from Government agencies. There must have been at least twenty people at lunch, both adults and children, all sitting at a long refectory table waited on by black servants in a very large dining-hall with floor-to-ceiling windows looking out over a wide estuary. It was like a scene from *Gone With the Wind*. But I got little pleasure or relaxation out of it because my host spent the time attacking British business for inefficiency.

This was by no means the first time I was expected to listen to attacks on British business and on Britain. Usually I felt I was seen as a rather backward student to be taught what the United States considered right which must therefore be right for the United Kingdom, but at other times I was treated as the representative of my Government – a mini-ambassador – who should be ready to deal with criticisms both of British industry and of the policies of the Labour Government.

My American visit was a gruelling two months of travelling and interviewing; seldom fewer than three interviews a day, and

Francis and I could not always be in the same city at the same time. I started with two days in Ottawa where my friend Keith Jopson was economic adviser to the High Commissioner; he saw to it that I met 'everyone who was anyone'. For a reason I can't define I felt much less foreign than in the United States and I found their attitude to monopoly to be more like ours – it was less ideologically convinced and their procedure – facts first, opinions second – was not unlike ours.

Next, to Washington – for nine days where all doors that I wanted opened were opened for me, including particularly those of the Department of Justice, the Federal Trade Commission and the various Commissions that controlled and regulated the rates and services provided by private monopolies like power, transport and the telephone: 'Never was there so much socialism . . . but they don't even know it,' said Francis who joined me for part of my time in Washington.

I was surprised to be called Alix on my second interview at the Federal Trade Commission; and also by another American custom, the introduction of family to one's place of work. I was invited to a formal dinner at the F.T.C. where wives were present hatted and grandly dressed and sporting large orchids. There was roast beef in my honour but, in place of wine, everyone was served with a glass of milk. This, I learned, was because Government offices were 'dry'. I gathered that the men were not deprived because hip-flasks were brought out in the men's washroom.

Francis and I had one interview together, in Washington. It was with the Under-Secretary of State, William Clayton. He had a mass of white hair and a Southern accent. 'Why don't you in Europe federate?' he asked. I still think my spur-of-the-moment answer, 'History is in the way', made a lot of sense.

In Chicago – two days or was it three? – I used one of Bill Benton's introductions to get industry's views, and I was invited to dinner by the 'Chaos Club', a joint gathering of some thirty economists and lawyers from the two local universities – Chicago and North-Weston. With one exception the company favoured the utmost rigour of the Sherman Act and shared the view of the representative from the Department of Justice that business, left to itself, is up to no good. However, the evening

was regarded by all as being primarily an occasion for question-
ing me on British legislation. I had given a prepared lecture on
this to the Georgetown University in Washington but the Chaos
Club was a very different audience and less well-informed on
what our legislation consisted of, though extremely ready to
criticise it. Towards the end of an extremely exhausting two and
a half hours, someone remarked that, whatever I might say,
Britain's most important economist did not agree with me.
When I asked who this might be, I found it was generally agreed
to be Sir Arnold Plant. I could only say that like other people
economists differ in their opinions and that two very prominent
economists – Mrs (later professor) Joan Robinson and Professor
G. C. Allen – were members of our Monopolies Commission. I
may even have implied that Arnold Plant was second rank to
these. I don't know; it was the end of a very very long evening.
Almost exactly the same exchange was reproduced later at a small
dinner discussion at Columbia University, New York. I only
learned later that Arnold Plant had recently been lecturing in the
United States. Someone wrote and told him that I had been heard
to denigrate him and I learned that he had complained to Sir
Frank Lee, who had just replaced John Henry as my permanent
secretary.

After Chicago, Francis and I took a week's holiday and flew
to San Francisco to stay with friends. But I took time off to see
officials in San Francisco and to have a meeting with the Vice-
President and other representatives of Standard Oil of
California. In Chicago, I had seen the Chairman of the International Harvester Company. The tale from both great firms was
very much the same: the general principle of the Sherman
Anti-trust Act was not directly attacked – to do so would have
been almost like criticising the American constitution – but both
felt that there was a tendency under it for mere size to be
attacked *per se*. Both firms also agreed that the legal cost to
industry of the whole apparatus of the Sherman Act, together
with the fair trade laws, was substantial; in addition companies
had to insure against having to pay treble damages and there
was the day-to-day use of attorneys to ensure that no offence
was committed.

After my two months in America I had learned enough to

write a thesis about the working of the Sherman anti-trust act with its demand for competition and about their fair trade laws demanding that that competition be fair – you could lampoon them, I felt, by saying that together they meant that everyone must run the race but the winner must have his head cut off. I had learned that the little man in business was seen as the object of protection quite as much as the consumer. But at the end of the day Beaverbrook had been right: the philosophy behind the American legislation (monopoly is wrong and to be condemned *per se*) and ours (it is only to be restrained if it acts against the public interest) was basically so different that their experience could have no practical bearing on the working of our young legislation.

The two years following that hectic American tour were equally hectic at the Commission: there were Public Interest hearings and report drafting for our first three enquiries, and preparations for Clarification Hearings for three further references. Our first report was signed that November (1950) and the other two in 1951. And they were fairly massive documents of from 100 to 200 closely packed and argued pages largely drafted and redrafted by the staff and argued through the Commission. We needed more staff and larger premises. I applied successfully for an extra assistant secretary on a temporary basis and we moved from Upper Brook Street to an equally grand but considerably larger requisitioned private house in Regents Park. My additional assistant secretary was a man I had worked with before and liked and a recognised high-flyer. I asked him to take over responsibility for Electric Cables (the largest of our new enquiries) but unfortunately, when he produced his draft report, I found that we had a serious disagreement. He had not considered that a form of quota called 'allocation', operated by agreed differences in delivery dates, was a restrictive practice, whereas I did. I had done a good deal of work on this enquiry in its early stages and I knew that the industry could be devious. I was convinced that a hidden restrictive practice did exist behind the term 'allocation' and insisted to him that it should be in the report as such. He clearly felt strongly that I had interfered unjustifiably with the work of a senior colleague for I learned – though not directly –

that he had mentioned it to Sir Frank Lee, our permanent secretary. He would certainly never have intended this to result in a mark against me but since Frank knew nothing of my work personally, I have reason to believe that it did.

I left the Commission in March 1952 at my own request. I had now been an under-secretary for six years and I was in the top four of my rank of equal seniority. If I was to get further promotion, it would be soon and I did not want to be away from headquarters when the opportunity came.

I had thoroughly enjoyed the job, both the independent command and the quality of the work which was more like academic research than the usual work of a civil servant because we had both the time and the duty to burrow out the truth. After I left I was invited to give a talk about the Commission's work both at the L.S.E. and to the Manchester Statistical Society. I was especially pleased as well as honoured by the second of these because of my official and family links with Manchester. I took the opportunity of these talks to explain in some detail the huge task laid on the Commission by its statute, requiring them not only to enquire in depth but to explain the reasons for its conclusions in detail; and I suggested that instead of being criticised for slowness we ought to be praised for speed in completing five reports in three-and-a-half years.

Three years' experience had suggested to me the desirability of a significant change in procedure which I could never get the Chairman to agree to, but which I believe had the sympathy of my successor. Our practice at Public Interest hearings was for the staff to prepare questions to be put to witnesses but for them to be asked only by members of the Commission. I found this galling at my rank and also inefficient. The Commission's questions constituted the only cross-examination of witnesses and were based on a close study of the facts, which necessarily were often known better to the staff than to the members; it was extremely frustrating when the point of our questions was not appreciated and they didn't get asked. I felt that the work of the Commission would benefit and be speeded up if its chief executive had a voice. It was, I think, my only serious difference with the Chairman.

I was given a really splendid parting present in the shape of a pair of Wedgwood urns inscribed round the rims with the names of the members and the words: 'Given to Dame Alix Kilroy, the first secretary of the Monopolies Commission, by its members: 31 March 1952.'

17

Last Years in the Civil Service

My full-packed years at the Monopolies Commission had been quite as busy with personal happenings at Cobbold's and Cliveden Place.

At Cobbold's we fulfilled a long-nursed ambition to be 'real' farmers by buying a small farm, called Manor Farm, in Monks Eleigh. Mr Batting, until then the tenant farmer, had readily agreed to become instead our farm manager and we built up a dairy herd of Red-Polls that we called 'Monks'. We chose Red-Polls because they had no horns and so couldn't hurt each other and were dual purpose, but this last we found to be a doubtful blessing for they were only average both for milk and beef.

I don't think we ever made more than a minimal profit, if indeed any, but it was all the greatest fun and, from the moment we took over, a visit to the farm on Sunday mornings was a 'must', to talk knowingly with Mr Batting of prospective calvings, of milk yields and butter-fat content. And we had the pleasure of providing a better quality of life for the charming Battings with their three little girls. When we gave up farming on Francis's retirement, the sale of the herd helped to start Mr Batting with his own farm in Australia. Asked for memories of our early beginnings he wrote that: 'After 14 years we had free electricity and free milk and green-sand spring water. . . . I had the latest farm machinery to use . . . and a herd of pedigree Red Polls to manage! My heart's desire.'

Mona and Geoffrey took up farming about the same time as we did but for them it was a harsh living, not a pleasant hobby. They could not afford comfortable Suffolk land and in March 1950 took possession of a farm in Cornwall that overlooked the sea but had much marginal land. I became close to Mona again as we did what we could to help with advice and with cash for domestic amenities like refrigerator and water heater that they would not afford for themselves.

Meantime, at Cliveden Place there was a wedding. Benedict was married in June 1950 to Hildamarie Hendricks and because her parents lived in the United States the reception was at No. 19 in Evelyn's big sitting-room. Benedict was only twenty and still at University but before long they moved to 16 Great James Street, home of Nonesuch in the days of its glory, that he had inherited from his mother. There we were to join them (though keeping separate households) when we left Cliveden Place in 1954 – a move that brought us close to them but broke the everyday link with Evelyn and with our Jean who had become over the years almost part of the family, a relationship underlined, as it were, when she began calling us 'A.K.' and 'F.M.'.

The other family happening in 1950 was the arrival of my brother at Salcombe in the yacht he had designed and built himself; it was half-Chinese junk and he called it 'Boleh' which means 'Can do' in Malay. It justified its name because the seven months' voyage home from the Far East which Robin has described in his book '*Boleh*',[*] was without serious incident. She carried a crew of five and Robin had to use all his fortitude to refuse a sixth, his retriever-sized grey and white mongrel 'Dopey'. He decided that 'the heat, lack of exercise and difficulty over sanitary arrangements' would have been too much for the dog; he does not appear to have considered whether they would also have been too much for the humans. After he had been back in England for some months, the friends with whom he had left Dopey had themselves to come home and Robin paid the dog's passage back, after which they were never parted until Dopey's death (nursed devotedly in extreme old age) the day before his master's own death.

When the cable arrived announcing Boleh's imminent arrival, Francis and I drove through the night and arrived at Salcombe early in the morning. It was a bright breezy day with a short choppy sea. 'One thing I am not going to do', I thought, 'is to disgrace my naval ancestors by being sick.' I asked for a drink and was given a half tumblerful of gin with a dash of angostura. I felt no more qualms.

Francis's sixtieth birthday the following year was quite as much a watershed for me as my own twenty-sixth had been. For the first

[*]Published by Hodder & Stoughton 1951.

time I saw him as vulnerable and ageing; for the first time envisaged our leaving behind the active happiness of young middle-aged life and realised that the twelve years between our ages could mean that we would both step into old age when I would be still relatively young. I don't believe that Francis had the feelings that I had about this birthday. He was full of success as Director of the Cement and Concrete Association, where his considerable business qualities could be married to his concern for the arts, encouraging the production of beautiful surfaces for concrete and beautiful buildings and gardens for the home of the Association. He was also planning the rebirth with Nonesuch of his career in publishing. I was interested, of course, but I was so full of my own work during the day – as indeed was Francis with his – that there was little time to learn much about each other's, and in the evenings and on holidays we both tended to leave our work behind us.

I was surprised and distressed to be offered the post of Comptroller of Companies for my return to the Board in March 1952 since it was known at that time as a dead-end job and not likely to be offered to someone in the running for promotion. Establishment did not insist and I was given instead I.M.6 a mainstream political department. But I returned to a very different hierarchy and assessment of my worth from the one I had left three years earlier. Overton and Wattie had both gone to other Government departments and John Henry had left the service. In their place were now, as permanent secretary, Sir Frank Lee and, as second secretary, Sir Henry Gregory. I had met Frank Lee casually as a friend of Evelyn's but he had never been a personal friend of mine and if the truth be told, I had never liked him; probably this feeling was mutual. His first official experiences of me had not been encouraging, starting with a memory of the *Daily Express* row and following with complaints from Arnold Plant and my assistant secretary at the Commission. Henry Gregory too had only come to the Board of Trade after I left to go to the Commission. He greeted me at our first official meeting with: 'I know, of course, that you have the reputation of being a difficult person to get on with . . .' I was completely flabbergasted; it was the first time to my knowledge, that I had

had other than friendly and easy relations with my bosses at the Board.

In the nine months following my return to the Board, there were two vacancies for second secretaries. One was filled by a Board of Trade man who was junior to me, the other by someone brought in from another department. Given my reputation before I went to the Commission, this proved me right in my fear that secondment could be personally damaging. Had I been at headquarters, Frank Lee would at least have known something of my work.

The chief responsibility of my new department was the administration of the Board's Distribution of Industry policy. In essentials, the policy was the one that Wattie and I had worked out together at the wartime Reconstruction Department: with the help of 'carrots' (financial assistance of various kinds including factories to let) and 'sticks' (Industrial Development Certificates – I.D.C.s) to take work to people in the development areas, to diversify their industrial base and to try to reverse the southward trend of industry, wealth and poplulation.

Amongst the staff were my old friend and former A. P. Arthur Burgess, and a new colleague. Stewart Edwards[*] who had great clarity of mind as well as capacity for detail, qualities that don't always go together. He and his wife Nica are among the valued personal friends that my civil service career has brought me.

The job was one in which I could put heart as well as head. Indeed it commanded the enthusiasm, even a sense of mission, of all the staff. We set up a publicity demonstration room at the Board of Trade with maps and details about all the development areas; we issued and distributed widely a publicity document called 'Room to Expand' – the name was suggested by Francis; and we described the types of 'carrots' offered to firms in the development areas, graded according to the relative needs and advantages of the area. We had arguments with the Ministry of Housing of which Evelyn was now permanent secretary. They wanted industry for their new towns which consequently were in competition with the development areas, and I see that I chaired a joint committee with her department which tried to iron out the

[*]Later U.K. Minister (Economic) in Bonn.

problems of priority; I think in the end we had to give I.D.C.s in all cases to new towns wherever the main enterprise was prepared to move with its employees.

We worked a good deal through the Regional Organisation left over from the war years for which I was also responsible. It had at one time been a very important body of people covering the interests of many Government departments at a local level, and responsible to the Treasury, but after the war their work was mainly for the Board of Trade and the Conservative Government that followed the Attlee Government transferred responsibility for them smartly to the Board of Trade. Some Regional Controllers resented what they felt to be demotion and I had quite a fight to keep them.

Outside Northern Ireland, which was given the largest inducement since it was the most difficult place to get industry to move to with its absence of local power and long lines of communication, our chief worries were Scotland and Merseyside. I resented the fact that we never could get firms from the Scottish Lowlands (where employment was good) to move north, so that Scotland's unemployment areas had to look to England or America for help. Our proudest achievement was to get sections of the motor car industry to move both to Scotland and to Merseyside.

During my time, we added one development area: North East Lancashire. I went there myself before making the recommendation, and was received at Burnley Town Hall by the Mayor, a small woman, wizened and bent, who had been a weaver from childhood. Her lady mayoress was also a life-long mill girl. Both appeared old but probably they were not. The pathetic thing to me was that the long arm of the tragic Thirties stretched forward into the Fifties. All those I saw were obsessed with the suffering of that time and when they pictured to me the plight of the unemployed and the dismal future they saw for Burnley, they were not really talking of NOW but of THEN.

However, all was not invariably plain sailing for me on the political front. It was when our President was Peter Thorneycroft that a major firm applied for permission to expand *in situ*. It was outside any development area and not even in a new town and I recommended that it should be refused. Word came that the

President thought it should be granted, and Henry Gregory and I met him to discuss it. I argued that the size and influence of a firm should not affect our decision and that if we were going to apply our policy only to small firms, it would be ineffective and we might almost as well scrap it. 'Are you then really advising that perhaps we should now get rid of the I.D.C. control?' asked the President. To Henry Gregory's embarrassment who thought (perhaps rightly) that I had been carried away by my sense of injustice, I answered rather bluntly: 'Yes, in those circumstances.' I ought to have played for time. I ought to have said – 'Well, President, there are of course arguments both ways: there are obvious dangers in clipping the wings of large firms since they may decide to expand abroad instead; and there is the acknowledged risk that outlying plants established in a development area on grounds of public policy will be the first to close in a depression; on the other hand, Government has to be seen to operate its policy with an even hand and the smaller firms will come to resent it when they learn that the larger ones get their way. . . . Would you like me to prepare a paper for you?'

But I didn't say that. Perhaps I thought the decision was being made only on the grounds of political expediency; perhaps I had been too long in the Monopolies Commission where it was our duty to look for the truth and there was 'world enough and time' to find it – and where political considerations were irrelevant. . . .

I was too much concerned about Francis's sixtieth birthday to worry about my fiftieth in 1953 but that year was memorable for the twin uncles' eightieth – though they maintained that 'we don't feel old at all' – and for the first of what became a series of no less than thirteen annual holidays in Italy at a converted castle owned by my friend Gordon Waterfield. On that first visit, our holiday companions were Pamela and Martin Zander but usually we were a party of six or more and our guests were as varied as at Cobbs. Gordon had inherited the castle from his parents and he lent it to his fortunate friends on the basis that they paid wages, food and a nominal rent. It stood on a rock above the village of Aulla in the foothills of the Carrara mountains. It was filled with old Florentine furniture and controlled and served by a smiling

Italian couple, 'fairy' guardians of a magic world of gracious living: Maria would have taken a prize among the first rank of French chefs and Vittorio was major domo, gardener and butler all in one: his meticulous accounts included everything from wages and the castle's own wine, pressed in the old way by human feet, to one aspirin, and the result was incredibly cheap.

Our routine was breakfast on the terrace under a ceiling of vine leaves and grapes, a picnic – rain or shine – in one of the many places that became established by tradition, and in the evening bridge or ping-pong which could be played with skill on the small library table with a net consisting of a row of books. You changed for dinner because it was served with great chic, with tall (altar) candles, gleaming silver and white napkins.

The marvels of the Castle were added to by an introduction from Gordon to Percy Lubbock who lived in a villa by the sea near Lerici and who let us use his private bathing place of smooth sun-soaked rocks in a circle of cliffs. A household name in the literary world, I found him alarmingly learned. He was a large unwieldy man who was even then having trouble with his eyes that was to end in blindness and Francis used always to spend part of the day reading to him.

On one day we explored beyond the villa to the next village, Tellaro, built down the side of the cliff with a tiny fishing harbour at the bottom and approached only by footpath. While I was taking photographs, I left my handbag with money and passport on the sea wall there and didn't discover it until we were eating ices in Lerici: back we went along the coast road in gloom until we were stopped by a builder's lorry with gesticulating workmen who made us know by signs that the bag had been found; they had even telephoned to the Lerici police to search for us. The obvious mayor of the village stepped out from a gathering of the inhabitants and led me down to the bottom of the village where, with a dramatic gesture, he threw open the door to disclose, on the dead centre of the family dining table, my handbag. I was made to open it to make sure nothing was missing and then there was a triumphal progress up the narrow path with, as it seemed, a head at every window and I smiled and bowed from side to side displaying the handbag: 'Trovata, sacca trovata' was all the Italian I could muster. I felt as if I was in a scene in a musical comedy.

In the following years, we were to visit Venice, Verona, Florence, Rome, Siena (of all Italian towns the most entrancing with its rose-red brick and narrow streets) but the castle – THE castle – was the place to which we could never return often enough. Years later Janet, our elder granddaughter (then still a child), leaving at the end of a castle holiday, would sigh and make the final comment: 'We have to leave this Heaven!'

I retired from the Civil Service at the end of November 1955 when I had been thirty years in the Board of Trade. Why just then? It was unusual to retire before you had served forty years. The reasons I gave were that I wanted more time to spend with my husband and also that I wanted to take part in the running of our farm – 'From Whitehall desk to farm forms' was a headline in *The Daily Telegraph*. Leisure to spend time at Cobbs, when the Civil Service still required its staff to work on Saturday mornings, may have become even more beguiling; but taking part in 'running' the farm with Mr Batting as farm manager and Game looking after the pigs at Cobbs could never have been more than a hobby-job for me. It cannot have weighed very heavily in so important a balance.

I cannot deny that an unstated reason for my going then was the fact that on the retirement of my boss, Henry Gregory, earlier in the year, the resulting promotion went to a man who had worked under me in the past and was very much my junior both in age and seniority. Besides the hurt to pride of being passed over, this was the final eye-opener as to my future prospects. Things might have been different if I had not gone to the Monopolies Commission or if John Henry had remained at the head of the Board of Trade; in either case I might I suppose have got that promotion but I don't believe that in any circumstances I should have wanted to serve my full term of forty years, which would have meant my continuing in full-time employment many years after Francis retired.

When Francis wrote to Evelyn to congratulate her on becoming a permanent secretary, she answered that she felt it wrong that she should have advanced so far ahead of me but 'I knew that in her marriage, Bay had the better part'. She was entirely right.

I was given a quite splendid send-off: not one but two retirement parties, one from my own department, and one from the rest of the Board with a present of a cameo brooch and a large cheque. The arrangements were masterminded by Douglas Carter the senior of my assistant secretaries who said that there had to be two parties because a hundred senior colleagues wanted to join in 'bidding you farewell' as well as 'over sixty people in I.M.6, including typists, messengers and our colleagues in the Registry'.

My own department's party was undoubtedly the more moving because I was given the impression that the affection was real and regret at my going sincere. Douglas made everyone laugh by quoting from a book he had come upon, written a hundred years ago, which said that 'even a highly gifted woman must not . . . presume upon such gifts for fear of rousing a man's jealousy of her importance', and added that in his first year in the Board of Trade 'two young ladies looking like a couple of film stars' had joined the Board of Trade Badminton Club – 'one was A.K. and the other was Dame Evelyn Sharp'.

There were any number of friendly remarks and compliments at the two parties and I also got some very charming letters of which I treasure most two from men whose first years as assistant principal had been served under me and who thanked me for the start I had given them. I have kept no copy of the speech I made but I do remember my last words and that I meant them: 'What I regret most is the fact that when I go out of this room this evening, I shall no longer be a civil servant'.

What Followed . . .

Thirty years in Whitehall; thirty years a civil servant. As it turned out, it was to be only half of my 'working' life. My brother, Robin, already retired in the early way of the fighting services, had sent me a telegram on my last day as a civil servant: 'Welcome to the unrestricted and manifold activities of retirement.'

How right he was. I found to my relief that retirement was by no means the unlimited leisure that I could picture *without* pleasure. If the truth be told I spent my retirement night lying awake tossing and turning, wondering how I should manage without my job, and facing painful regrets that I should never again be 'a person of importance'. I had watched older colleagues retire and die on their golf courses, deprived in a single day of occupation, personal importance and the company of colleagues. Now I could feel with them a little. That experience was to lead, twenty years later, to my starting a species of employment bureau for voluntary work where professional experience would be useful. I called it the Company of Professional Elders – C.O.P.E. for short. In any case I needed a job because my Civil Service pension would not be paid until I was sixty. I had written letters before I retired, enquiring about part-time paid Government employment but I couldn't expect immediate results. So I began at once on a piece of research that Francis had cleverly manufactured for me. He was just embarking on the publication of the post-war Nonesuch Bible and he said he wanted me to find out which parts of it ought to be printed as verse. I applied for a reader's ticket at the British Museum and spent absorbing hours of research there. It was the beginning of my personal involvement with the Nonesuch Press.

My retirement had been noticed in the national press and an article in *The Evening News* pleased me particularly with a half-page spread headed: 'A Desk for Dame Alix' which began: 'Beautiful women are bad enough for my ego. Brainy women petrify me. An hour later, my ego intact, I left – sorry to go.' And of course the headline hit the nail on the head. One of the things I was going to miss was that desk I had wanted as a child and possessed from my first day at the Board of Trade. I asked Francis to give me one as my retirement present. However, within a few months, the letters bore fruits, the most important and time-taking of which was a second career in the gas industry, several years on the Board of the Harlow New Town Corporation; a member of the Performing Right Tribunal and of several enquiries into restrictive practices connected with agricultural marketing. For a short period I even went back to the Monopolies Commission as a member.

I was to be thirteen years in the gas industry as a member of the South Eastern Gas Board and Chairman of the Consultative Council that looked after its consumers. It was part-time but a full experience and I gained a great respect for those who worked in it both for their efficiency and for their devotion to the public interest. When I arrived, I found my council of consumer representatives at odds with the industry and mistrustful of its officers. Coming from the Civil Service, I had a natural fellow feeling with the staff of the industry and I didn't find it difficult to wear two hats – as a Director on the Board and as Chairman of the consumers' council.

But I was also free now to take a public stance in political matters. I was glad of that a year later when the Suez crisis divided the country. I was (and I still am) profoundly shocked that my country (and Anthony Eden especially, admired champion of the pre-war League of Nations) should be justifiably branded aggressor and breaker of the Charter of the United Nations. Russian tanks were invading Budapest at the same time and an unforgettable Vicky cartoon had them claiming to be acting (like us) as international policemen. We were at Cobbs when we heard the first news and I remember weeping as I walked up and down the lawn discussing it with Francis. My distress brought Mrs Stowe out to ask who had died.

We went to the huge Sunday protest rally in Trafalgar Square and to the packed meeting in Westminster Hall the same evening, and 'Eden must go!' shouted Francis into the silence of a London theatre after the playing of 'God Save the Queen'.

I was to have opportunities to take an active part in the C.N.D. Campaign: Diana Collins (wife of the late Canon Collins) invited me to join a deputation of women to women M.P.s in December 1958; and in March 1962 I would have the honour of leading a deputation to Harold Macmillan (then Prime Minister) consisting of prominent women, including two F.R.S.s. I prepared myself with the horrific details of Hiroshima and insisted on telling Macmillan what, of course, he knew already, but he was impressed with what the others said as, one after another, they urged an end to testing in the atmosphere. He was heard to say afterwards that the opinions of knowledgeable women should not be underestimated. Perhaps we had some hand in bringing about the Test Ban Treaty.

Francis and I were both early members of C.N.D. when there seemed a possible hope that if only Britain (still then a Great Power) would give up her bomb, others would not seek to acquire it and that might somehow stop the nightmare. That chance has passed. Since you can never *un*invent the bomb it now seems to me that the distant hope must be that one day the super powers will police the world.

It was not until very much later in life that I would become involved in party politics, as a founder member of the SDP and, at the age of eighty-three, I would stand as SDP candidate (admittedly unsuccessfully) in the Suffolk County Council elections.

In 1967, after nearly twenty-two years at Cobbold's Mill, we moved to the Grey House in Lavenham. The parting from Cobbs was not a complete one because the new owners were Irene and Sherry Shelton with whom, and their children, we had built up a friendship in the intervening years. They continued to make us welcome there, after we left. In any case, we managed to leave without sorrow because we made the move together and from the first felt completely at home in the Grey House.

Both now retired, we were free to enjoy each other's company without interruption though, with his eye to my probably lonely future, Francis encouraged me to involve myself in local concerns and to continue with my part-time jobs until I relinquished them to work with him on his autobiography. Though we had married late, we were to achieve our silver wedding the year that Francis was eighty. We never got bored with each other's company and I don't think a week went by in which Francis failed to tell me he loved me. Even when I was over seventy, he would tell me after a party that I had been the most beautiful person in the room and I would glow with pleasure – a little from vanity, however unbelieving, but overwhelmingly because he still saw me that way. Though for me he was always beyond all counting the most important person in a room, I did not tell him so often enough. Wives take note. It is too late when you are widowed.

Francis died on 10th July 1975 and I found that my greatest deprivation was that I had to do without joy. But I discovered that, in time, there can be worthwhile life and happiness even in widowhood. Contrary to the rules of mathematics, in marriage 1 + 1 equals not 2 but 3; two together produce a larger whole than two people who are separate and I have also found that, since Francis's death, I have become more of a person because I have absorbed something of him – a species of immortality which is comforting though by no means enough for me.

If I had my life over again, how would I change it? Very little. When I was young enough to collect mottoes, a favourite of mine was Romain Rolland's, 'No regrets! they unman the heart we need for tomorrow.' I still like the sentiment but 'No regrets'? Of course regrets. There is the massive one involved in widowhood and there are two others: I have outlived all my dear siblings; and I have never had a child and so never the dear title 'mother'. But I am neither alone nor lonely for I have a step-son and grandchildren who are full of care for me and I for them. I am very proud of the title 'Gammer'. Benedict's first child, a son, died tragically at Cobbs after barely a year of life but I have two granddaughters: I was their Gaffer's wife before they were born and I don't think of them as 'steps'. I am rich too in nephews and nieces on both sides of the family, and Bimbi's daughter and her husband actually live near me in Lavenham.

I have been incredibly fortunate in my life. As I read the very many letters that have survived from my two mothers, my siblings and my uncles, I am humbled by the Niagara of love that launched me and followed me through life. Moreover, I have lived through an extraordinary period of history with two world wars and unprecedented public violence and suffering, the rise and fall of fascism, the Nazi death camps and the 'Darkness at Noon' of Stalin's Russia. And yet my life has been easy and happy; it is an often unrecognised truth that individuals can be happy in the most appalling public circumstances. Even at eight-four I still feel life before me. I am still learning something new if not every day or week at least every month. I still dream of influencing events. Still at moments I long to hear the swish of my skis on snow or feel the sway of the slow foxtrot danced with Francis to the music of 'Night and Day' and find myself thinking – next time I will do so-and-so, next time, next time – and can hardly accept that there will be no next time. Even now, for me, life is not long enough.

Index